Human Resources Management Planning

With the assistance of Constant H. Botter

HUMAN RESOURCES MANAGEMENT PLANNING

Guvenc G. Alpander

AMERICAN MANAGEMENT ASSOCIATIONS

Library of Congress Cataloging in Publication Data

Alpander, Guvenc G.
    Human resources management planning.

    Bibliography: p.
    Includes index.
    1. Manpower planning. I. Title.
HF5549.5.M3A44 1982   658.3'01   82–71306
ISBN 0–8144–5750–9

First Printing

To my wife, Bonnie Ann Alpander

Acknowledgments

I gratefully acknowledge the assistance of my colleague Constant H. Botter, professor and former dean of the School of Industrial Engineering at Eindhoven Technical University in the Netherlands. He substantially contributed to each chapter of this book and wrote the first draft of Chapter 6. I am also indebted to him for providing an environment extremely conducive to research at Eindhoven Technical University, where the first draft of this book was written. Without his help this book would not have materialized.

I want to thank Richard T. Brucher for editing the manuscript and making many useful suggestions, and Dean W. Stanley Devino for his administrative encouragement. I am also grateful to Caroline A. Dane, Alice T. Pellegrini, Margaret Rocheleau-Shina, and Patricia V. Thompson for typing several drafts.

Contents

CHAPTER 1

The Era of Human Resources Planning

Personnel administration has only recently emerged as a specialized field. The personnel function, however, has been necessary for as long as people have organized in groups and worked to achieve common goals. Personnel in any organization, at any time, have had to be trained, led, motivated, and remunerated. As society has changed, so have organizations: Personnel functions have improved, new ones have been added, and some have become more important than others. Personnel administration has become a major organizational function, equal to production, marketing, and finance.

Nevertheless, defining the personnel function remains difficult, because its sphere of influence differs from organization to organization. Traditionally, it has been defined by a series of functions: employee recruitment, selection, training, and development; wage, salary, and benefits administration; health and safety research; and the like. For the convenience of the organization, the functions have been grouped in one department.

As long as organizations could draw on an abundant pool of workers and could hire and fire personnel as operating conditions dictated, management could execute the basic personnel functions of recruitment, selection, training, and development with relative ease. Personnel could be regarded as costs, production factors that could be controlled according to short-term production requirements. However, changes in managerial philosophy, increasing competition for skilled personnel, the changing composition of the labor force, and increasing legal, political, social, and economic pressures are causing changes in perceptions of personnel and, therefore, the personnel function. Management is learning to regard employees as assets, resources to be protected, nurtured, and developed. Moreover, in response to changing perceptions of the organization and increasing environmental pressures, management has begun to recognize that careful personnel planning is vital to defining and developing long-range business and organizational plans.

Recent organizational history indicates that we have entered a new era: the era of human resources planning (HRP). HRP is a systematic process for setting policies governing the acquisition, use, and disposition of personnel in order to achieve organizational objectives. HRP emphasizes providing and making the best use of human resources for short- and long-term purposes: for accomplishing future organizational goals as well as for producing goods and services in the present. In its emphasis on employees as assets instead of as costs, and on long-term planning for contingencies instead of on short-term reacting to conditions, HRP seems to depart radically from traditional personnel practices. In fact, HRP has evolved naturally during the twentieth century; it builds on rather than subverts the traditional personnel functions.

The Evolution of the Personnel Function

The evolution of the personnel function in organizations is interwoven with the political, legal, economic, cultural, and technological forces of society. These ever-changing forces influence the development of various management philosophies and practices. A survey of the major movements in management philosophy and the personnel function puts in perspective the new concern for HRP. This section groups the movements under the five major headings that best represent the literature.

The Scientific Management Movement

The so-called scientific management movement developed from 1870 to 1914 as a result of growing concern for improving methods of running manufacturing organizations. During the nineteenth century, management sought, in effect, to fill existing jobs with available bodies, making little or no attempt to match employee characteristics with job conditions and requirements. Toward the end of the century, Frederick Taylor in the United States and Charles Babbage in

England, the leading proponents of the scientific movement, sought to devise new management principles based on measurement and experimentation.

Taylor and Babbage advocated what amounts to an engineering approach to management responsibilities, resulting in systematic studies of managerial techniques and procedures, job requirements, and employee characteristics. Because efficiency became the prime economic yardstick, the movement captured the enthusiasm and imaginations of managers. Managers attempted to improve production efficiency through the division of labor. Management set about to determine the best method for designing a job—chiefly by analyzing the job according to its component tasks, determining the job specifications, and then establishing the best procedures for performing the tasks and defining the employee characteristics required by the job.

Scientific management also advocated that the person with the most appropriate characteristics be selected for performing each job and that this selection be based on psychological testing. The movement idea that had perhaps the strongest impact on personnel management was that management could select the right employee for a particular job and that wage incentives would motivate the employee to do the job well.

The appearance of efficiency experts to promote increased production contributed to the movement's decline in popularity, particularly among labor unions. The job-oriented management techniques debased employees. Practices such as piece-rate wage payments, production line speedups, and rate setting created new problems in employee dissatisfaction for managers. Nevertheless, the concepts of scientific management have had lasting impact on personnel activities, even in today's organizations. Especially useful are the movement's insights into the nature of work and personnel selection and the contributions to job evaluation and wage and salary administration.

As organizations grew in size, the personnel function evolved as a separate entity. Full-time jobs were created for employment specialists, who were responsible for recruiting, selecting, testing, and placing personnel. Soon, wage and salary administration required a full-time specialist to develop job descriptions, job specifications, evaluations, and wage rates. This was the beginning of modern-day personnel departments.

The Administrative Science Movement

Taylor and the scientific management school looked at the organization from the bottom up. With its emphasis on improving job design and task performance, the orientation was primarily micro. Around 1916, however, the French industrialist Henri Fayol pioneered the administrative science movement, a management philosophy with a top–down perspective. Fayol attempted to provide fundamental principles for general management and organizational structure, particularly as these principles relate to planning, organizing, and controlling production activities. Fayol defined such concepts as unity of command, span of control, centralization of decision making, and managerial authority. He studied the overall functions of managers and the total structure of the organization. His perspective was macro.

The administrative science movement's impact on the evolution of the personnel function was in the area of execution rather than content. The emphasis was on finding better structural arrangements in performing personnel functions rather than on improving the nature of the function itself. The personnel function, segmented into several subfunctions, became centralized in organizations with the creation of small but powerful personnel departments near the top of the organizational hierarchy. Possibly for the first time, a planned approach to the personnel function (who should do what and when) emerged in larger organizations. This movement was particularly strong in France, where centralized administration has been in existence since the time of Napoleon.

The Human Relations Movement

From the late 1930s to the early 1950s, the human relations movement flourished, chiefly, at first, as a backlash to the impersonal aspects of scientific management. Human relations stressed the importance of individuals as organizational resources. It emphasized interpersonal relations, communications, and leadership as ways to improve worker and organizational productivity. Elton Mayo, Fritz Roethlisberger, and W. J. Dickson, with their classic Hawthorne Works studies, were instrumental in the creation of this movement.

The Hawthorne Works experiments revealed that sociological and psychological variables (teamwork, participation, loyalty) often influence employee output more deeply than the physical conditions of the work environment (temperature, illumination, length of work periods). Accordingly, personnel management flourished and gradually became the mechanism through which concepts from social psychology, sociology, and anthropology could be applied at the workplace. The personnel function required the management training and development subfunction. Organizations began to spend large sums of money to train their managers in human relations techniques. Line managers began to attend training programs in the management of human resources through improved communications, leadership styles, and motivational techniques.

The emergence and acceptance of participative management as a leading contributor to organizational success increased the importance of human resources among other inputs in the production of goods and services. The status of personnel departments increased, especially in the 1940s. In order to improve worker productivity, the personnel function in these years focused on the individual employee, the small work group, and the managerial practices of supervisors.

As with scientific management, the human relations approach gradually lost its appeal. It became apparent during the 1950s that neither approach, practiced independently, could solve the complex problems faced by organizations. Nevertheless, the human relations movement left its mark on organizations. Managers know that without competent people to handle them, money, machinery, and equipment cannot achieve organizational goals.

The comparative impact of the scientific management and human relations movements on major personnel functions is illustrated in Figure 1. Emphasis on employee satisfaction and on wage and salary administration were derived primarily from the scientific management movement. Management development, on the other hand, is a byproduct of the human relations movement.
Figure

The Revisionist Movement

A movement asserting that neither the general principles of scientific management nor those of human relations have universal application gained momentum during the 1950s. This revisionist movement combined concepts developed in earlier years from the behavioral sciences, economics, and engineering, and created new knowledge in the form of a science of management. Herbert Simon's research on the functioning of organizations, Chris Argyris's pioneering works on the impact of the organization on the individual,

Figure 1. Impact of scientific management and human relations movements on key personnel functions.

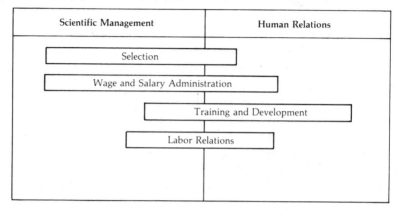

and Rensis Likert's studies of organizational climate and efficiency were founded on the dissatisfaction with concepts of previous eras, which often lacked scientific rigor and validity.

The revisionist movement became more apparent during the late 1960s in the publications of T. Burns and P. R. Lawrence, who are identified with the situational, or contingency, school of thought. They advocate that there are no universal principles of management; instead, each principle must be evaluated and applied according to the circumstances of a particular situation. This concept directly affects today's practice of personnel management.

Organizations, before adopting new programs—for instance, those based on the successful experiences of a competitor—as valid for their own situations, investigated the conditions under which the new program might be successful and whether or not these conditions existed in their organization. Concepts that were thought of as common sense were subjected to rigorous tests based on sophisticated methodologies. Leadership styles were analyzed, and employees' scores on hiring selection tests were carefully compared with their actual performance on the job to make sure the tests were valid. As a result, organizations experienced fewer disappointments from random applications of behavioral science techniques to their management of personnel. The emphasis on sophisticated research methods and empirical investigation created the need for personnel research specialists within organizations who could evaluate and interpret the results of scientific investigations and bridge the gap between the researcher and the practitioner. The appearance of scientifically trained professionals in personnel departments contributed to the acceptance and increased status of the personnel function within the organization.

In the 1960s, the term *manpower planning* entered the vocabulary of practicing managers. During the sixties, manpower planning primarily involved the forecasting of the personnel flow into the organization and the supply of appropriate personnel from outside sources. Forecasting the changes in demand for personnel generated by external factors and productivity improvements was often done outside of personnel departments. Organizational personnel requirements forecasts were made by the unit in charge of consolidating business plans and communicated to personnel departments in the form of future personnel requests. The research of this era revealed the feasibility of manpower planning and contributed to its development as an important management function. However, manpower planning was invariably separated from the other traditional personnel functions.

The Welfare Era

The current periods in the United States and in the Common Market countries can be described as the welfare or the affluent era. This era is not solely a product of the 1970s; it has been developing since the turn of the century. The concern for the general welfare of employees and of all human beings has its roots in the paternalistic management styles of the past and the present.

Increased concern for the welfare of the employee is reflected in existing legislation in the United States and especially in Western Europe. As a result of this legislation, and employee demands, indirect compensation now constitutes over 30 percent of total employee compensation in the United States. This figure is at least 45 percent in Western Europe. Such federal legislation as the Equal Employment Opportunity Act (EEOC), the Occupational Safety and Health Act (OSHA), and Affirmative Action (AA) have all contributed to the increase in employee welfare.

The increased social legislation of the welfare era has led to inflexibility in the use of human resources in the United States. This inflexibility is reflected in the difficulty of hiring, firing, and laying off employees in organizations. This situation also exists in Western Europe and Japan. Once hired, employees are not easily fired. Although organizations can control the use of financial, technological, and raw materials resources, the control of human resources has gradually decreased.

The acceptance of human resources as assets is one significant consequence of welfare-related legislation and public and union pressure. In fact, management is beginning to regard human resources as fixed assets. Hiring decisions become very important when firing becomes difficult. In other words, inflexibility necessitates the careful planning of the acquisition and utilization of human resources.

The revisionist movement, on the other hand, emphasizes the individual employee and his or her planned development in the organization. This movement necessitates rational decisions on the part of the management vis-à-vis the employees. That is, management coordinates training programs, performance evaluations, wage and salary administration, and many other personnel functions with short- and long-term objectives in mind. The pressure for manpower planning comes from within the organization. The revisionist movement also views human resources as potential bottlenecks in the organization's progress toward efficient goal attainment, since human resources are considered to be most difficult to manage.

From Manpower Planning to Human Resources Planning

The need to plan the procurement and utilization of human resources at first led to the emergence of a primarily quantitative manpower planning function, often located in a department other than the personnel department. Although the manpower planning function was gradually moved to the personnel department, its scope was still restricted to forecasting activities. At first, manpower planning was a new and often independent function in the personnel department. The integration of manpower planning with the other personnel functions did not occur until the 1970s.

As manpower planning grew in importance, it became increasingly strategic and began to dominate other personnel functions. Consequently, a change in terminology occurred. To emphasize its importance, *manpower planning* began to be called *human resources planning* (HRP), a change also reflected in the changing titles and often increased status of the personnel managers. Many large and medium-size organizations began to give their personnel managers the title of Vice President for Human Resources. In a 1979 survey, Alpander found that out of a sample of 195 major U.S. corporations, about 65 percent of the titles of the highest functional personnel executives were Vice President, Director, or Manager of Human Resources.[1]

This change in title seems to be a byproduct of changing management philosophy. Interviews with over forty executives from some of the 195 corporations that participated in the 1979 survey confirmed that the change in title expresses top management's growing concern for the planned acquisition and utilization of human resources and its recognition of the importance of human resources to achieving organizational goals.

In Europe, title changes have not occurred as rapidly as in the United States. European multinationals have kept the traditional title of personnel manager or personnel executive for the highest officer in the personnel function. This does not mean that such European multinationals as Philips, Unilever, Shell, Renault, or Volvo do not value human resources. As mentioned, in many Western European countries the flexibility with human resources is very limited. Social legislation (e.g., work councils) has greatly reduced management's authority to alter the composition and/or decrease the number of the human resources. In many Western European countries work councils are the highest decision-making bodies in organizations, and they have sizable employee representation. European companies have more reasons than American companies for systematically planning the acquisition and utilization of human resources, because their flexibility in using human resources is more limited. Executives with top functional responsibility for human resources occupy influential positions in these organizations and participate in strategic decision making.

The change in terminology from manpower to human resources planning reflects the growing importance of human resources in organizations. Traditionally, HRP has had two orientations, one specific and technical and the other general. The specific approach emphasizes the technical aspects of personnel planning, particularly the development of mathematical and statistical models for determining optimum personnel requirements. The technical approach separates the forecasting of human resources needs from human resources utilization, which emphasizes increasing the employees' abilities and motivation to produce. As late as the 1970s, almost all organizations used the specific approach, and many still do. Although the predictive (forecasting) and utilization functions may be carried out in the same department—often the personnel department—they are treated as two distinct activities.

Literature on the specific, technical HRP approach is abundant. For example, Gascoigne[2] and Lane and Andrew,[3] who espouse the specific approach, provide many useful quantitative forecasting tools to apply to human resources planning. The specific orientation is also apparent in many personnel management texts, where the forecasting aspects of HRP are introduced in one or two chapters independent of the rest of the material. Even the books by Burak and Walker[4] and Sikula,[5] which promote the general approach, treat the HRP component separately from other personnel functions.

The general approach to HRP equates HRP with personnel administration as a whole. England's Department of Employment and Productivity follows such an approach. It defines HRP as the strategy for acquiring, utilizing, improving, and preserving an enterprise's human resources. Implicit in this definition is the need to: (1) evaluate present labor resources, (2) forecast future labor needs, and (3) take measures to ensure the availability of labor resources when they are needed.

This orientation embodies the forecasting, recruitment, and utilization components in the HRP process. The general HRP approach horizontally integrates the planning and utilization activities. Significantly, the general, integrated approach takes into account both the qualitative and the quantitative components of HRP. However, as Walker[6] points out, in practice, a horizontally integrated approach to HRP is not easily achieved. Many built-in constraints make HRP a difficult activity and inhibit its acceptance as a major management function.

Vetter[7] has made one of the few serious attempts at articulating a horizontally integrated view of HRP. He defines HRP as "the process by which management determines how the organization should move from its current position to its desired manpower position." However, Vetter has in mind top management personnel only. Vetter identifies four phases in HRP:

- Developing personnel inventory forecasts.
- Establishing objectives and policies.

- Designing and implementing plans.
- Controlling and evaluating the plans.

He suggests that although each phase is an activity for a specialist, all four must be incorporated into the process if HRP is to be meaningful. For example, one cannot undertake a management development program without having quantitative information about future management needs.

The transition from manpower planning to human resources planning has four stages. First, manpower planning refers primarily to forecasting activities that often occur outside the personnel department and that are generally independent of other personnel functions. The relationship between strategic business planning (SBP) and manpower planning is one-way. Only after strategic business plans are formulated or consolidated does the appropriate unit in the organization receive relevant information concerning future business objectives and begin translating them into future human resources requirements.

Second, HRP replaces manpower planning when the activity takes place within the personnel department or under the jurisdiction of an executive who also supervises the personnel function. This is the specific approach to HRP. Third, when HRP is horizontally integrated with other personnel functions, the approach becomes general. When the approach is general, the planning function is not just an appendix to the personnel department but an integral part of the major personnel functions.

Fourth, HRP becomes complete when the horizontally integrated HRP becomes integrated vertically with SBP. This complete integration occurs when management establishes a reciprocal relationship between HRP and SBP. The outcomes of SBP directly influence HRP activities, and HRP begins to influence the outcomes of SBP and thus the direction of the organization. Figure 2 illustrates this relationship.

Examples of the complete approach to HRP (both horizontally and vertically integrated) can be found in the literature that emphasizes the demand and supply aspects of human resources. McBeath[8] provides a highly integrated model of HRP by dividing it into two stages: first, the detailed planning of personnel requirements of all types of employees during the period of the strategic business plans, and second, the planning of the human resources supply to provide

Figure 2.   Complete approach to human resources planning.

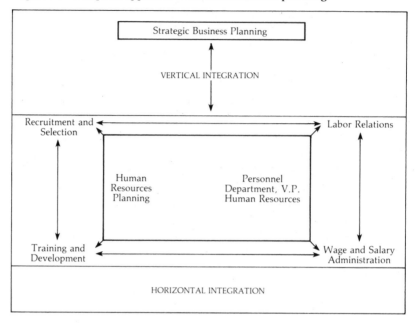

the organization with the right type of personnel at the right time. The second stage, in particular, can be problematic.

For example, the Philips Company, a large Dutch multinational, recently decided to build a new plant to exploit its competitive advantages. But because labor mobility is very low in Holland, Philips is responsible for providing employment for the same workers, at the same plant, for the next 20 to 30 years. To implement the strategic decision to build, the planners had to take into account not just the availability of qualified human resources but also ways to include changes in the manufacturing technology to match the characteristics of the labor force 20 years ahead. The production machinery and procedures the employees use today may prove inefficient as the current labor force grows older. Because it is difficult to transfer employees, and almost impossible to replace them, Philips has attempted to incorporate characteristics of tomorrow's labor force into today's production planning process.

Such thinking seems to be gaining in popularity. Whether any American enterprise consciously follows such a policy is not the issue at this time. What is important is the fact that human resources aspects have to be given greater emphasis in policy decisions.

The difficult and complicated transition from manpower planning to vertically and horizontally integrated HRP requires total organizational commitment. Our 1979 survey revealed that not many organizations are in the HRP phases: Only 15 percent of the 360 respondents indicated that their organizations had implemented an integrated HRP process. Even the general approach to HRP is rare. Our survey found that only 30 percent of the companies had achieved horizontal integration in HRP.

Our decision to present a normative model that makes possible horizontally and vertically integrated HRP stems from the need exhibited by managers and the changes in the legal, social, and economic environment of the organizations. As business environments change, strategic plans change accordingly, thus affecting a company's qualitative and quantitative needs for human resources. However, the very complexity of business organizations and the difficulties in forecasting the rate and direction of environmental change, which limit effective planning, create the need for careful planning.

Beyond the Welfare Era

The evolution of the personnel function is closely tied to the changes that have taken place over many decades in management thought and philosophy. The scientific management, administrative science, human relations, and revisionist movements have all helped shape modern personnel administration. The restrictions put on the utilization of human resources by social legislation and by the changing philosophy of work have fostered the need for planned personnel management.

The concept of manpower planning emerged as a consequence of the changes in the legal, social, and economic environments of the organizations. The term manpower planning has been gradually replaced by the term human resources planning. Inherent in this change of terminology is the integration of the forecasting of human resources requirements with other functional areas of personnel administration and with organizational objectives as specified in strategic business plans. The definition of HRP as a systematic process of acquisition, utilization, and disposition of personnel to achieve organizational objectives reflects the commitment to a completely integrated approach.

The wealth of federal legislation and related Executive Orders that characterized the seventies has altered the personnel function. Today, many contemplated amendments to existing laws and new bills are aimed at increasing the impact of current regulations on the acquisition and utilization of human resources. Some of the expected changes in the United States will be in the areas of equal employment opportunity (EEO) and affirmative action (AA). The impact of EEO and AA will be even stronger during the eighties. Changes in Social Security legislation making employee contributions almost 8 percent of their covered income by 1990 will affect compensation planning and the ratios of wages to benefits of the total compensation packages.

Similarly, open-retirement legislation will change the characteristics of the labor force and require organizations to update their retirement benefits. For instance, a 1978 survey of Sears, Roebuck and Company employees indicated that 45 percent of the employees would rather continue to work beyond age 65 than retire. This means that Sears, which employs approximately 430,000 people, will have to hire 7,000 fewer people and make 30,000 fewer promotions during this decade than during the last decade.[9] If the results of the Sears survey are any indication of what may happen in other sectors of the economy, the need for the planned acquisition and utilization of human resources will increase drastically in the 1980s.

One of the major complaints about the personnel function by line managers during the 1970s has been the failure of personnel specialists to anticipate the impact of equal rights legislation, AA, OSHA, and the regulations imposed by the Employee Retirement Income Security Act (ERISA). Many line managers have felt rather heavily the impact of such legislation because their organizations were not prepared for the changes required by law. Many managers now suggest "management by anticipation" as the best way to cope with future changes. Personnel specialists will have to develop sensing techniques to discover future problems and recommend corrective action rather than wait for their arrival.[10]

Another important development of the 1980s will be the increasing need to relate individuals to organizations. Reduced employee

turnover rates coupled with the inflexibility in human resources acquisition and utilization will necessitate more than ever that job satisfaction and employee commitment to organization become coreq-
uisite for sustained employee productivity. Another strategic consideration will be the need to find ways and methods for integrating minorities, the elderly, the handicapped, and other groups with the
bulk of the labor force and to improve their productivity.

Including motivational considerations and labor force characteristics in plant design and layout will gain in importance and create the
need for human resource input in overall business planning. Anticipating change and preparing plans to meet new challenges will be a
permanent characteristic of the personnel function. Personnel administration became professionalized in the 1970s. The 1980s are already calling for a series of new techniques and behaviors. HRP is
here to stay. Organizations without efficient and integrated HRP
processes will undoubtedly be heading toward difficult relations
with their personnel.

Summary

The evolution of the personnel function has followed closely the
changes that have occurred over many decades in management
thought and philosophy. The scientific management, administrative
science, human relations, and revisionist movements have all helped
shape the emergence of modern personnel administration. The restrictions imposed on the utilization of human resources by social
legislation and the changing philosophy of work have created the
need for a planned approach to personnel management.

The concept of manpower planning emerged as a consequence of
the changes in the legal, social and economic environments of the organization. The term manpower planning has gradually been replaced by the term human resources planning. Inherent in this
change of terminology is the integration of the forecasting of human
resources requirements with other functional areas of personnel administration and with organizational objectives as specified in strategic business plans.

Such integration is becoming imperative as human resources are
gaining more importance among other resources and are becoming
less and less flexible. Increased social legislation governing the use of

human resources has contributed to their inflexibility, as reflected in the difficulty of hiring, firing, and laying off employees. Although organizations can control the use of financial, technological, and raw material resources, the control of human resources has gradually decreased.

In light of the increased importance of human resources as fixed assets, the need for a more planned approach to the acquisition and utilization of employees has become prominent. Progressive organizations have created a comprehensive HRP function that integrates employee recruitment, selection, training, development, compensation, and evaluation with each other and with the organization's strategic business plans.

HRP, when defined as a systematic process of managing the acquisition, utilization, and disposition of personnel in order to attain the objectives of the organization, reflects a completely integrated approach.

CHAPTER 2

The Importance of Integrated
Human Resources Planning

The continued success of an organization depends on its ability to acquire and use effectively the resources it needs to produce and market its products and services. Usually this process involves some type of business planning. To compete, the organization must be able to anticipate, influence, or control the forces with which it must interact to conduct business. Strategic business planning (SBP) is one of the foundations, especially in the larger organizations, of successful business operations. SBP is a systematic procedural method that usually involves an annual planning cycle.

In the past, managers directed their planning primarily toward product markets, new materials, and technological developments. Strategic decisions about the allocation of scarce resources mostly covered product development and investments in hardware. Employees, with their individual goals and attitudes, were dealt with only on a reactive basis. That is, management allowed short-term production requirements to dictate the hiring and firing of personnel. However, the conditions of employment are changing rapidly. Legal, political, economic, and social developments have begun to limit the flexibility organizations once enjoyed in acquiring and using human resources. Rights of due process, unions, scarcities of skilled personnel, and the like prevent companies from hiring and firing at will. When organizations lose their flexibility in using resources, bottlenecks occur that slow down the planned production process. The resources must then be handled very carefully. Human resources are no exception.

The ultimate success or failure of an organization will not depend on the restrictions imposed by the economic, political, social, and technological problems, but rather on its human resources. As the vice president of a large auto-parts manufacturing company put it, the 1979 operations of his company were not restricted by their marketing, manufacturing, or technological capabilities but by their not having the right people at the right time to take advantage of the economic conditions to produce the products the market demanded.[1] This bottleneck encountered by many organizations might have been avoided if the human resources had been given their due importance among other resources in the strategic business plans.

Personnel: A Most Critical Resource

The human resource overlies all other resources and may determine an organization's eventual success or failure. All organizations have potential access to financial and other resources such as equipment, technology, and raw materials. But people make the decisions about acquiring and using these resources for production. The capability of the people who make these decisions, produce goods, and provide services immediately affects the organization's efficiency and effectiveness. An organization can operate at full efficiency only when it has the necessary personnel to convert inputs into high-quality outputs. Having the right people in the right place at the right time makes an organization competitive.

The personnel problem, however, is complex. Many organizations tend to overstore human resources in order to not be caught short of critical personnel. An organization with excess personnel impairs its performance almost as much as if it had a shortage of human resources. Spending power is reduced because of excessive human resources costs, while capital expenditure on new equipment, product development, inventories, and debtors must be curtailed because cash assets are not available.

Organizations should continuously reappraise their human resources needs against updated plans and objectives. If an organization has excess personnel, it must trim the fat to stay viable. Because it is often objectionable or difficult to lay off, fire, or reallocate excess personnel, management usually seeks other ways to reduce costs. But a typical method such as holding down wage and salary levels may further impair the success of an organization, since it has an immediate impact on the quality of employee performance. HRP attempts to match the supply of human resources with the requirements of the organization. Companies must make this match if they can lay off people only after engaging in complicated legal procedures involving unions and government, as is the case in nearly all European countries.

HRP: A Solution to Growing Human Resources Inflexibility

HRP has acquired greater importance because of the increased inflexibility of personnel. More and more companies have difficulty adjusting their human resources to meet the fluctuations of the business cycle. It is becoming difficult to hire and fire employees as conditions demand. Even in the United States, the trend is toward greater permanency in employment. In Japan and in many Western and Eastern European countries, employers do everything possible to keep employees once they have joined the organization. Not only are human resources being considered an asset, they are now being equated with any other fixed asset a company may have.

Hiring permanent employees has many ramifications: Even if one considers only their salary, and not their impact on the profitable use of other resources, the costs are high. For example, if a production worker is hired at a salary of $15,000, in 20 years at a constant annual cost of $25,000 the company will spend half a million dollars. Despite the expenditure, management often makes hiring decisions casually. Yet the same company may follow an elaborate procedure before paying $25,000 for a new machine. Decision makers request—in writing—considerable investigation into the need for the machine, its optimum specifications, and its future use. Authorization for making this type of capital expenditure is often given at a higher level than is the case for hiring a new production employee.

The written justification required for such a capital expenditure may cover the following points:

1. A financial justification showing recovery of the investment within, say, three years.
2. Methods of financing.
3. Expected level of machine use.

4. Flexibility of the machine's potential use in the future (that is, whether or not it might be used for other purposes in the future).
5. The cost of operating the machine.
6. The possibility of its creating potential industrial relations problems.
7. The obsolescence potential and write-off plans.

Business planners should give the same consideration to hiring a production employee. Employee costs increase as it becomes more and more difficult for employers to lay off personnel who exceed production requirements or whose skills are obsolete.

Clarifying the Meaning of HRP

To clarify the meaning of the term *human resources planning* as it is used in this book, we will explain the two basic types of planning: strategic and operational. Strategic planning is the process by which management evaluates and integrates into policy decisions the present status and future impact of change in its operating environment. The essential information supporting top management's strategic decisions is then communicated through the organization. Strategic decisions concern primarily the organization's problems with structuring the firm's resources in a way that creates maximum performance potential. Operational decisions, on the other hand, maximize the efficiency of the organization's day-to-day activities.

In practice, a clear division between strategic and operational planning is academic. Long-term objectives affect short-term goals and actions, and the current concerns in an organization obviously influence the firm's future direction. Distinguishing between strategic and operational HRP is as unrealistic as attempting to differentiate the future from the present. However, the long-range, strategic decisions about significant issues must be differentiated from the daily, routine activities of short-term planning.

HRP, then, is primarily part of the strategic planning process. We will not discuss the day-to-day operating issues concerning human resources, such as supervision and on-the-job training. Rather, we will concentrate on the broad and far-reaching decisions, such as overall wage structure and employee development, that influence the availability and capability of personnel in organizations.

• Human resources plans used in strategic planning must have a time frame of a year or longer. Short-term planning for hiring and using employees lies in the domain of operational planning and thus outside the scope of this book.

• Human resources plans represent long-term objectives in broad, general terms. Operational plans express specific goals and the means to achieve them. For example, HRP includes forecasting the internal supply of managers for the years to come, but not designing a recruitment program to acquire several graduating engineers within a given year.

• Human resources plans usually pertain to some relevant environment (for example, competition) and relate to long-term business plans. Operational human resources plans focus on internal issues and indicate, for instance, how departments should acquire and use personnel.

• Human resources plans state relative objectives. For example, an organization may state that its pay structure for professional and managerial personnel will reach and remain in the top 20 percent of the pay structures of all relevant organizations. This objective and the means to achieve it are set forth in a human resources plan. But because the objective can be attained in any one year, it is timeless and externally oriented. On the other hand, operational plans concerned with organizational human resources goals are specific. For example, the same company may strive to have 50 percent of its managers complete a particular executive development program for next year. The attainment of this specific goal can be measured regardless of environmental conditions and competitors' actions.

Many organizations have extensive plans for a variety of personnel actions, such as training and development, recruitment and selection. Often, however, the plans are carried out in independent and sometimes contradictory ways. The plans for personnel action become strategic when they are reciprocal or at least sequential. Since it is difficult to achieve such interrelatedness, a systematic approach to acquiring and utilizing human resources must relate to overall strategic business objectives if it is to be practicable. This book presents methods for developing interrelated, concerted personnel actions.

Figure 3.   Vertical and horizontal integration in personnel actions.

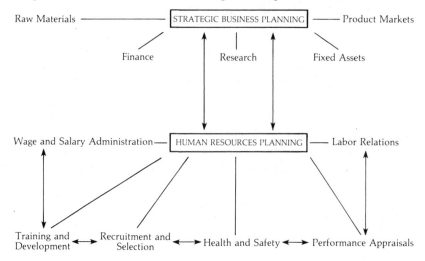

Until recently, top management had considered HRP to be an adjunct business planning function. The HRP process usually starts only after basic missions, broad business objectives, and strategic projects have been established. Seldom has management considered current and projected availability of personnel when establishing strategic business plans. In these cases, HRP becomes reactive and less effective. To be really effective, HRP should be vertically integrated with strategic business planning (SBP) and horizontally integrated with personnel activities aimed at meeting the present needs of the organization and its members. Figure 3 depicts this relationship.

Factors Influencing SBP

Human resources plans, like all strategic plans, are influenced by many factors. The more important factors include market conditions, technology, the economy, and the human resources themselves.

Market conditions. Changes in markets are often precipitated by the competitors. Organizations competing in the same market constantly watch one another and assess each other's strategies. Developments in the market directly influence SBP in terms of basic missions and objectives and methods of attaining them. Therefore, strategic business planners must continuously receive information from the market environment.

Technological change. Most organizations today face rapid technological changes in the inputs, the processes, and the outputs of production. For instance, the electronics industry experiences a phenomenal rate of change: Many products become technically obsolete before they reach production. Unpredicted events can range from a change in the manufacturing process or a change in the production equipment to a completely new product. Companies must therefore plan in broad terms that allow quick responses to urgent and unforeseen requirements.

Economic situation. Planners must watch and analyze national and international economic trends. The price of energy and raw materials, wage and salary levels, and general price levels are but a few of the economic conditions that influence SBP. General economic conditions also include changes in government regulations. Sometimes changes in taxation and in general legislation affecting an organization can be anticipated.

Financial considerations. The availability and stability of financial resources affects strategic planning. Changes in the sources of financial support must be considered. Revenue-generating internal sources as well as outside backers must be continually assessed, and strategic plans must be altered accordingly.

Human resources considerations. The feasibility of any strategic plan depends on the quantity and the potential of the people who make the plan operational. Strategic plans that ignore the potential of human resources fail. Human resources limit the boundaries of organizational growth potential more than any other factor. Before completing strategic business objectives, planners must have a satisfactory answer to the question: Do we have, or can we get, managers, technical personnel, and operative employees?

All these potential influences on SBP are interrelated and should not be considered in isolation from each other. For instance, technological and product changes affect markets and marketing methods. If a new market or product requires a different selling method, SBP must consider the issue before setting final objectives. Market research may indicate that it is not feasible to launch new products that are being developed by the R&D department until appropriate marketing methods have been prepared. Personnel as well as equipment and facilities may affect production schedules. Even if adequate facilities exist, projected production increases may fail to materialize unless planners consider such human resources issues as shifts and overtime.

A change in marketing strategy necessitated by technological developments may affect the financial situation. A company that shifts from serving only half a dozen large customers to serving many small customers must adjust its credit control procedures, adopt machine accounting, change invoicing procedures, acquire additional personnel, and retrain existing personnel to cope with the new demands. SBP that lacks such considerations will be unrealistic.

Blockages to Effective SBP

To be effective, strategic plans must be pragmatic, systematic, and comprehensive. Consequently, planners must anticipate obstacles during both the formulation and the implementation stages of SBP.

Behavioral obstacles may block planning at any level of the organization.

- Resistance to change causes unfavorable attitudes toward SBP. Planning usually means change, which may produce anxiety in individuals and/or groups.
- If the need for planning is not recognized, day-to-day actions may lead to unrecognized or undefined and time-consuming goals.
- Uncertainty about the future undermines planning. Many managers like the present, the status quo, because it is more definite than the uncertain future. Lack of planning burdens managers with many routine tasks they could delegate to others. Ironically, the demands of time often cause managers to put planning on the back burner. Managers may regard the task of SBP—gathering and analyzing information, designing and carrying out new procedures, and the like—as mere tasks to be performed rather than as important means for facilitating and improving their work.

Informational issues may block the SBP process.

- Incomplete and inaccurate information may discourage the strategic planners and discredit the planning process itself throughout the organization.
- An overload of raw, unanalyzed information may cause the planners to discard indiscriminately some of the data. To influence the organization's missions and objectives, the various functional departments—manufacturing, R&D, marketing, finance, and personnel—will inundate the planners with data specific to their departments.

Expenses pose another obstacle to SBP.

- Direct costs include salaries of the people involved, and the acquisition, storage and retrieval of planning data. Indirect costs include traveling and the time needed for writing, discussing, evaluating, and rewriting the planning reports.
- Competing demands for a company's diminishing finances can stall the SBP process. As a rule, efforts put into SBP increase when the company has abundant financial resources. When the company experiences survival problems, it generally cuts expenditures for SBP.

SBP faces roadblocks not only during its preparation but also in its implementation. Opposition to objectives and policies presents a strong barrier to strategic planning. When strategic plans are completed and the company missions, objectives, policies, and plans are specified, many individuals and/or groups may, for their own reasons, object to the goals. Strategic business plans may be attacked by internal as well as external dissidents. Sometimes the pressure to change the objectives and policies may become so intense that the strategic plans may have to be dropped. For instance, strategic plans calling for closing military installations almost invariably arouse strong resistance from the neighboring communities. Sometimes the political and public pressure to stop the implementation of such strategic plans is very effective.

- Management's failure to accept a plan creates the most important roadblock to implementation, especially if the opposition is powerful and strategically located in the organization. In such cases, SBP is not likely to progress much further than the idea-formation stage.

- Personalities of the SBP staff also play an important role during the implementation of strategic plans. Line and staff conflicts frequently occur.
- Overly sophisticated or complex strategic plans may intimidate or even mystify the average manager. If the company lacks some of the key decision-making tools—market research, management information systems, adequate budgetary control, for example—strategic plans based on advanced techniques may not work.
- Red tape or excessive bureaucracy may block implementation of strategic plans. Too much emphasis on forms may make the SBP process as unsavory to the implementors as filling out income tax returns.
- Unclear responsibility and accountability for the various parts of strategic plans may cause confusion during their implementation. If personnel are to implement a plan, they must know what is expected of them and to whom they must report. If the human element could be considered the primary culprit for the failure of SBP, it would certainly be important for its success. Strategic plans prepared without adequate input concerning human resources have increased chances of failure right from the beginning.
- The cost of implementation may prevent strategic plans from being put into practice. This often happens as a result of changing priorities due to urgent, previously unforeseen problems. During the implementation phase of SBP, organizations, in their attempts to control costs, often reduce the allotted budgets for the strategic plans. Another problem is the unplanned rise of implementation costs due to inflation.
- Inadequate feedback mechanisms or plans may cause small problems to become large, formidable barriers to implementation. Planners need feedback if they are to modify a plan to suit organizational goals. The various barriers to successful SBP make clear the importance of people, the human factor, in the formulation and implementation stages. Strategic plans prepared without adequate input from the people who must implement and abide by them have a high risk of failure, right from the start. However, the barriers themselves suggest remedies.

Figure 4.   Influencing factors, blockages, and requirements for effective strategic planning.

INFLUENCING FACTORS	BLOCKAGES	REQUIREMENTS FOR EFFECTIVENESS
Preparation Phase		

Market conditions
Technology
Economic situation
	Resistance to change
	Unfavorable organization
	Failure to recognize need
	  for planning
	Uncertainty of future
	  development
	Inadequate and inaccurate
	  information
	Overload of information
	Direct and indirect expenses
		Managerial involvement
		Consistent guidance

Implementation Phase		

Financial considerations
Human resources availability
  and potential
	Opposition to objectives
	  and policies
	Lack of acceptance by
	  management
	Personalities of SBP
	  staff
	Overly sophisticated plans
	Red tape
	Unclear responsibilities
	Cost of implementation
	Inadequate feedback mechanisms
		Allowance for change
		Potential for integration

Figure 4 summarizes the influencing factors, blockages, and requirements for effective SBP.

Requirements for Effective HRP

HRP must meet four requirements to be effective. These requirements are:

Management involvement. HRP must be drafted with the involvement of all line managers who will carry it out. However, the coordination and consolidation of HRP should take place at top levels of the organization.

Consistent guidance. The guidance provided by HRP must be persuasive and clear. HRP must provide guidance to all managers in the organization in explicit terms to allow them to acquire and utilize human resources with the knowledge that their actions are consistent with the objectives of the organization.

Allowance for change. To make HRP effective, organizations must recognize that these plans are temporal documents. HRP should be an evolving process. It must allow for adjustments to changing environmental conditions.

Potential for integration. Effective HRP is a highly integrated process. It must be integrated with the organization's strategic business plans as well as with other personnel functions, such as recruitment, development, and compensation.

Vertically Integrated HRP

Traditionally, the relationship between SBP and HRP has been sequential. Personnel departments have used SBP outputs as inputs in human resources plans. The relationship has been one-way and downward. That is, only after production requirements have been set has the personnel department been notified to proceed to recruit and train the specified personnel.

Vertical integration connotes a two-way relationship. In many cases, realistic and feasible HRP cannot be accomplished unless the SBP process takes into consideration information on current and potential human resources. For instance, planning to manufacture a product without considering whether or not the technical expertise is available may lead a company into deep financial trouble. Strategic business plans without this consideration will be unrealistic and will face many obstacles and problems during their implementation, especially when the human resources can create a bottleneck hindering organizational goal attainment. It is ineffectual to incorporate the output of strategic business plans in planning the human resources requirements and not use the subsequent data in formulating the strategic business plans. This reciprocal relationship can increase the effectiveness of planning in an organization. In fact, the regular infusion of human resources information into the SBP process, and the use of strategic business plans to further plan the acquisition and utilization of human resources in order to reach organizational goals, constitute our definition of reciprocity and vertical integration.

Unfortunately, very few companies use systematic personnel data in formulating long-range plans. The one-way, downward relationship between SBP and HRP is common. HRP is subordinate to SBP and does not begin until strategic business plans have been formulated and directives issued to the department or individuals engaged in HRP. In this sequential relationship, one event does not start until another is finished. Once broad company missions are converted into strategies and functional plans are developed, the process begins.

In a truly integrated relationship, strategic business plans are not completed until information on human resources is provided for the SBP process. Planners formulate organizational objectives only after they have considered relevant data on the quantity and potential of available human resources, both within and outside the organization.

Horizontally Integrated HRP

Horizontal integration relates personnel management functions such as training and development, wage and salary administration, and recruitment and selection to the HRP process in the organization. The integration of personnel management functions with the forecasting element of HRP allows an organization's day-to-day personnel activities to be consistent with the organization's long-range goals, policies, and product/market plans.

The activities performed within a personnel department are generally grouped under several functional headings, such as recruitment, selection, appraisal, training and development, wage and salary administration, compensation, health and safety, benefits and services, and labor relations and collective bargaining. The concept of horizontal integration ties a particular personnel function (for example, recruitment) in with projected human resources data and other personnel functions (such as wage and salary administration).

Let's use the training and development function as an example to describe horizontal integration. Obviously, we can assess the training needs of current employees by projecting their future roles in the organization. If we don't do this, the consequent training programs will be shortsighted. The programs may increase the employees' abilities to perform their current tasks, but they may fail to prepare the employees to meet the future (forecasted) human resources needs of the company.

Similarly, the appraisal and compensation functions should be used not just for rewarding good performance on current activities but also for rewarding preparation efforts to meet future human resources requirements. In practice, most companies have not horizontally integrated the various personnel actions with their human resources plans.

Because upper management has great impact on defining the direction the company will take, this level of management clearly needs horizontal integration. Being closer to the future objectives of the company, upper management observes more readily the need to meet the coming challenges and to identify future requirements. The small number of high-level managers makes horizontal integration manageable. But as one descends the organizational pyramid, employee numbers increase, making it difficult for individuals to work together in meeting future organizational requirements for human resources. At levels below top management, integration is often carried out with respect to general categories of personnel only. That is, companies may identify the future organizational requirements for, say, electrical engineers or personnel managers and may design training programs taking their future requirements into consideration.

Career plans are an attempt to accomplish horizontal integration at the individual level. Unfortunately, below the top levels of the organization, the plans are rather sketchy and often have little to do with what is actually practiced. Such inadequacies inhibit attempts to integrate HRP with other personnel functions at the lower levels in the organization. There are, of course, exceptions. Some functions, although performed at the lower levels in the organizational hierarchy, are critical to the success of future operations. People performing these functions are generally identified and their career paths more carefully designed than those of less critical personnel.

In conclusion, integration is best limited to higher management. Companies are discouraged from widening integration because of the increased uncertainties and increased number of personnel at the lower levels of the organizational hierarchy.

Is HRP Only for the Large Organization?

HRP is an involved process requiring substantial commitments of money, personnel, and time from the organization. Consequently, it appears to be beyond the reach of small organizations with limited resources. Such an assumption can be right and wrong, depending on how we define HRP. True, one seldom finds *formal* strategic business and human resources plans in smaller organizations because effective coordination can be attained rather easily without them. In small organizations, strategic decisions on human resources are taken into consideration almost continuously but in a less formal and systematic fashion than in large organizations. It is common practice for the president of a small organization and his or her few managers to meet frequently to resolve strategic human resources issues and to plan moves without necessarily developing formal plans.

Human resources are becoming increasingly critical irrespective of the size of the company. Therefore, although the material presented in this book is more applicable to larger organizations, the concepts and ideas presented are equally relevant for smaller organizations in their informal or semiformal plans to cope with strategic human resources issues.

Summary

An organization can have a competitive advantage over other organizations when it can anticipate, influence, or control the nature and impact of internal and external forces with which it must interact to conduct business. Strategic business planning is one of the major tools in conducting a successful business.

In the past, the SBP process was generally directed toward product/market, financial, technical, and environmental issues. Seldom did management consider the strategic nature of human resources. However, as organizations recognize that their ultimate success or failure depends on their human resources, they pay greater attention to the methods for acquiring and utilizing personnel. The need for HRP has grown out of management's recognition of the importance and critical nature of human input among other production factors and limiting environmental influences.

HRP for resolving problems in human resources inflexibility is a vertically and horizontally integrated process. To be effective, HRP needs to be vertically integrated with SBP. That is, strategic business plans should not be completed until information on the quantity and potential of available human resources from both inside and outside the organization has been considered. Vertical integration creates a truly reciprocal relationship between SBP and HRP.

HRP should also be integrated horizontally with such personnel functions as training and development, wage and salary administration, and recruitment and selection. By integrating these personnel functions with the forecasting element of HRP, organizations should be able to make operational personnel activities consistent with their long-range goals, policies, and product/market plans.

CHAPTER 3

Understanding Human Resources

Organizations are differentiated in terms of such elements as their products, services, location, ownership, and size. However, all organizations have goals that they strive to achieve efficiently.

At the risk of seeming simplistic, we can say that the desire to be efficient and effective defines an organization's attempts at greater productivity, which in turn equates outputs and inputs:

$$\text{Productivity} = \frac{\text{output (goods and services)}}{\text{input (material and human)}}$$

Whatever the outputs of an organization may be—its goods and/or services—it needs inputs to produce them. Of course, there are many types of inputs, both material and human.

All organizations have potential access to financial and other resources such as equipment, technology, and raw materials. But it is the people in organizations who make the decisions to acquire and make effective use of these resources of production. The capability of the people making decisions about producing goods and providing services has an immediate impact on an organization's efficiency and effectiveness. Therefore, personnel can provide a real competitive advantage for one organization over another. The human resource overlies all other resources and is a major determining factor of an organization's eventual success or failure.

Consequently, HRP is an important instrument for improving organizational performance or productivity. HRP is an activity primarily concerned with determining the human resources needs of an organization and ensuring that qualified personnel are recruited and developed to meet organizational needs.

Employee Performance

Motivation and ability to produce are unique characteristics of individuals that directly influence the level and quality of their performance. The environment of the organization, its characteristics and managerial practices, also influence employee performance. Figure 5 illustrates the basic relationships of the important factors influencing employee performance.

Employee performance is a function of a person's motivation and ability to produce as influenced by a multitude of factors. The organizational environment, which can be described in terms of its cultural, legal, political, economic, technical, and social characteristics, either directly or indirectly affects employee performance. The organizational climate, which includes such variables as managerial philosophy and policies, leadership styles, and the structural characteristics and social conditions of the work group, also influences employee performance.

Motivation: A Determinant of Performance

Much research on work and achievement motivation has been done, from which theories have been developed. Most writers have concluded that the various theories are not compatible. They simply deal with different aspects of the same phenomenon. Generally, motivation theories may be divided into two classes: process theories and content theories. Process theories determine how behavior in general is energized and sustained. Content theories are concerned with what it is within an individual or an individual's environment that energizes and sustains behavior.

Content Theories

Content or need theories identify the needs and motives within the person that energize, direct, sustain, and stop behavior. One of the most popular content theories of work motivation is Maslow's needs hierarchy theory. This theory assumes that each individual has a hierarchy of needs, and that as basic needs such as food, shelter, and security are fulfilled, the person becomes more concerned

Figure 5.   Interrelationship of three kinds of factors influencing employee performance.

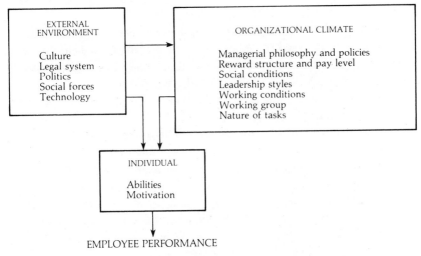

with fulfilling high-level needs such as belongingness, esteem, and self-actualization.[1]

Atkinson and McClelland state that there are three basic motives relevant to the workplace; these are the need for achievement, the need for affiliation, and the need for power. Although all people have these needs or motives, the relative strength of each motive differs from person to person. Furthermore, the particular situation in which a person is working triggers a particular motive. Atkinson and McClelland have used this theory to increase job performance by adjusting conditions so that the achievement motive is activated.[2]

Another well-publicized content theory is Herzberg's *two-factor theory*.[3] Herzberg divides motivation into "intrinsic," or job content, factors and "extrinsic," or hygienic, factors. According to this theory, the hygienic factors, such as wages and working conditions, don't actually motivate employees; they merely minimize employee dissatisfaction. On the other hand, intrinsic factors, such as full appreciation for work performed, contribute to true job satisfaction and serve as real motivators.

Process Theories

Process theories, on the other hand, refer to the ways of stimulating people to action in order to accomplish the desired goals. Process theories are generally based on the assumptions of behavior theorists such as Skinner and Pavlov, who found that behavior that does not lead to rewards tends not to be repeated.

One well-known motivation process derives from the *equity theory*. Equity theory is based on the assumption that individuals are most concerned with their situation (for example, income) in relation to a peer group, and that an employee will tend to limit his or her production to that of the peer group. This theory argues that a major determinant of job performance is the individual's perceived degree of equity or inequity in a work situation. The degree of equity is defined in terms of a ratio of an employee's effort on the job to pay or other rewards as compared with a similar ratio of a "relevant" employee in the work situation.[4]

The most widely used process approach to motivation is the *expectancy theory*. This theory has proved very useful for explaining motivation, and it is compatible with the need or content theories. There are two essential assumptions in expectancy theory.

1. People act to achieve goals or ends. Crucial to whether they act or not is whether they *believe* their action will lead to achieving the goals they seek.
2. In the process of choosing actions to reach ends or goals, people can (and do) establish preferences between actions, based on the likely outcomes of the actions.

According to Nadler and Lawler, a person's level of motivation is a function of the person's expectancy that a desired outcome will follow a particular behavior (for example, that hard work will lead to a raise in salary) and the valence or the subjective value of the outcome (how strongly the person wants the raise). The valence is strong or weak depending on whether the employee wants the raise more or less than other outcomes, such as an easier job.[5]

The expectancy model is expressed as follows:

$$M = f(I_a + I_b + E_1 E_2 V)$$

where M = motivation

I_a = intrinsic value and satisfaction employee gets while performing task

I_b = intrinsic value and satisfaction employee gets after successfully achieving goal

E_1 = employee's expectancy level that effort will lead to successful task performance

E_2 = employee's expectancy level that task performance will lead to reward

V = value of reward

Varying any one of the independent variables will change the employee's motivation. For instance, motivation will increase if a reward system is closely tied with successful task performance, as in the case of a good merit system. A reward that has great value to the employee will also increase motivation. Applying the expectancy theory becomes complex, however, when a change affects more than one variable at the same time. For instance, job enrichment will increase the intrinsic value of task performance, but if the new job is too complex, the employee's expectancy of successful task performance may decrease.

Money as a Motivator

Traditionally, theorists have considered wages to be the most important motivator of employee behavior. Opsahl and Dunnette offer several explanations of why money, in the form of wages, bonuses, and other incentive plans, motivates employees to higher performance. For example, money can be used as a generalized conditional reinforcer as in behavior modification; that is, money can be used as a reward after satisfactory performance.[6] Steers and Porter argue that money reduces anxiety. The absence of money creates anxiety, and people have a tendency to act in order to reduce anxiety.

Money, according to Herzberg, can also be seen as a hygiene factor. That is, money can eliminate a source of dissatisfaction but in itself cannot increase employee satisfaction. Finally, money helps people reach other goals. Money acquires value for an employee to the degree that it can help the person fulfill desires and needs outside the workplace. Accordingly, money can be an instrumental reward for someone wanting a new house or a long vacation but not for an employee seeking relief from a routine, boring, or dead-end job.

The use of money as a motivator has universal appeal, and money may be used in countless ways to satisfy our various needs. For example, it can be used to attract and select potentially high performing employees.

Job Satisfaction

Theorists have offered and tested many contradictory proposals concerning the relationship between job satisfaction and employee performance. One school of thought argues that there is no relationship between job satisfaction and performance. However, most practitioners believe that job satisfaction causes employee performance. Job satisfaction reflects the attractiveness of the job, and employees put greater effort into the performance of attractive duties than into the performance of unattractive or unsavory ones. Another group of researchers argues that performance causes satisfaction. Differential performance determines the level of rewards and, in turn, accounts for the employee's expression of job satisfaction.

The most widely accepted conclusion and managerial implication of the relationship between job satisfaction and job performance is that job dissatisfaction often leads to absenteeism and employee turnover, thereby reducing the level of organizational performance. Traditional methods for solving the problem of job dissatisfaction and low performance—hiring additional workers and increasing wages—can compound the problem.

An organization with employee performance problems may be able to maintain total employee performance levels for a short time by increasing the number of employees. However, this results in a greater number of personnel doing the basic work. Management must then subdivide the tasks to accommodate the increased number of workers. The excessively segmented work assignments often have a negative impact on employee job satisfaction. Job fragmentation leads to job dissatisfaction, which increases absenteeism, tardiness, and employee turnover. As Figure 6 indicates, job fragmentation lowers employee performance levels.

Job dissatisfaction also puts financial constraints on an organization. In an attempt to motivate employees, management increases wages, but for the wrong reasons and without drawing any of the benefits that usually characterize high-pay situations.

Another side effect of job fragmentation and subsequent job dissatisfaction is the reduction of employee initiative and willingness to do creative work or to assume responsibility. Solving operative problems then requires increased intervention by personnel at higher levels in the organization. Managers become trouble-shooters rather than planners. The cumulative effect could be a large reduction in overall performance.

Figure 6.   Impact of job fragmentation on job satisfaction and employee performance.

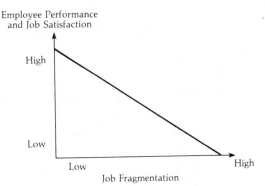

Organizations may compensate for the lower performance levels of their workers by increasing the use of other resources, such as using greater mechanization in the production of the desired level of output. In the short term, this does not increase performance because the effectiveness of other resources depends on their use by the existing personnel.

Revitalizing a company that has run down is not an easy task. A change to higher performance must take place gradually because of intense resistance from the majority of employees. This change must be introduced from top levels of the organization, and it often requires replacing managers. Under normal circumstances, achieving a minimal turnover requires at least two years. Figure 7 shows the interrelatedness of motivation theories.

Ability: A Determinant of Performance

By *ability*, we mean an employee's current capacity to perform in a given job. Ability involves a wide variety of factors, ranging from individual characteristics, such as intellectual and manual skills, to personality traits. These factors reflect the education, skill, and experience requirements found in job specifications. Ability is a somewhat stable element of job performance that enables employees to behave in some prescribed manner, whereas motivation is the effort and desire that influence how vigorously individuals will use their capabilities on the job.

Figure 7.   Interrelatedness of motivation theories.

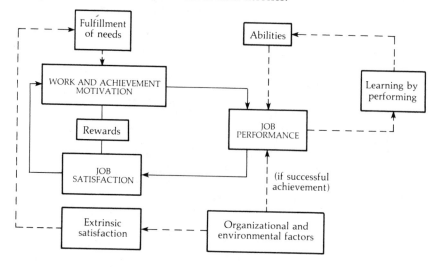

An employee's ability to perform a given activity often depends on the degree to which the person possesses the knowledge, skill, and know-how pertinent to a given task and often acquired through experience. Managers try to act on the three basic dimensions of ability. First, they want to determine accurately the level of ability required for a given job; second, they want to appraise the ability of an employee performing the job; and third, they want to take corrective action when an employee becomes deficient in a particular job requirement.

Personnel managers and other specialists such as industrial engineers define, through job analysis, the basic ability requirements of jobs. The specialists then convert these requirements into job specifications that describe the minimum employee characteristics needed for the job. Most organizations today have formal job specifications. Once an organization determines its job specifications, it tends to keep them as long as the nature of the job remains the same. For this reason, job specifications remain stable and can be expressed as education, skill, and experience requirements.

Managers must recognize that job specifications do change. The person performing the job and the person's supervisor are the natural individuals to detect the need to change the ability requirements of a job. A job title and the basic nature of the job may remain unaltered, while the methods for performing the job may change drastically. A good example is the introduction of automated data processing systems into organizations. Computer-based processing and decision-making techniques are continuously modifying the skill requirements of many jobs. A major reason for employees' resistance to change is fear of not being able to meet the requirements of the new methods and techniques in performing their existing jobs.

Managers and organizations must anticipate and follow the changing trends in the ability requirements of jobs. An employee might once have met job specifications, but in the face of technological changes in job methods and procedures, the employee may no longer possess the necessary ability to perform the job adequately today. It is the managers' responsibility to accurately define job specifications and to monitor changes in them.

Managers must also appraise employee performance. Unlike the first dimension, establishing job specifications without considering the employee performing the job, this second dimension concerns the person/job matching process. Specifically, a manager must determine whether or not an individual has the necessary ability to perform the job.

Managers also try to detect differences in abilities among individuals performing the same job. These comparisons identify employees who are high, average, or low in terms of a particular characteristic. Managers can influence organizational performance by differentiating employees who may excel or who may be deficient in a given characteristic of the overall ability to perform in a job.

The third dimension of ability obliges managers to take action after employees are identified as excellent or deficient in a particular characteristic of ability. When an employee becomes deficient at performing his or her job, the most common action is to train the employee. Other actions include transferring the employee to a different job or terminating the employee. Unfortunately, some managers may choose to ignore the situation. They may tolerate low performance by an employee and try to carry the person along for an indefinite time. This abdication of managerial responsibility, however, does injustice to the person and to the organization.

When employees excel in their jobs, their performance levels may be strengthened if managers take action for further training or promotion.

Figure 8.   Effect of the organizational and external environment on employee performance.

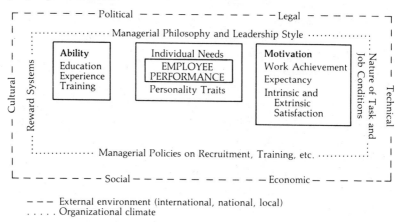

– – – External environment (international, national, local)
. . . . . Organizational climate

A General Performance Model

The two preceding sections defined motivation and ability as two major variables affecting employee performance as influenced by the organizational environment. This section presents à behavioral framework combining ability, motivation, environment, and organizational variables that explain the causes of employee performance or the lack of it. Figure 8 depicts the levels of environmental factors that affect employee performance.

Employee performance is influenced directly by the individual's ability and motivation to produce. These two variables are in turn influenced by several intervening variables grouped under the broad headings of organizational environment and organizational climate. In the current literature on organizational behavior, there is considerable controversy as to the classification of these variables according to the degree of their impact on employee performance. The controversy is even greater about the linkage between ability, motivation, and performance. The following discussion synthesizes our understanding of the existing research on this topic, shaped by our experiences in the field.

Environmental Variables

As Figure 8 shows, our model of employee performance is set within the primary environmental variables. Since our analysis is micro and focuses on the individual manager's efforts for high employee performance, we mention the environmental variables only briefly to present a complete model.

Organizations do not operate in a vacuum. They perform within their environments. Some organizations, because of the nature and scope of their activities, are influenced by fewer environmental variables than other organizations. For instance, strategic policy formulation in a corner drugstore may be influenced by fewer, and certainly different, environmental factors than that of Mobil Oil Corporation, with operations in more than 110 countries.

Organizations and individuals feel the impact of the local, regional, and international environment through a series of social, political, legal, economic, and technological forces. In the short run, one element may dominate the others. In the long run, however, the combined impact of most of the elements often overshadows the short-run impact of any single element.

The external environment plays a continuous and persistent role in the short- and long-term changes that take place in an organization. For instance, in times of economic hardship, organizations may alter their reward systems, restricting promotions, bonuses, and other organizational rewards.

The impact of the broader environment may not be as direct as are the actions of the middle managers and supervisors. On the other hand, irrespective of an organization's size, the top management of an organization must always be sensitive to the organization's environment. Figure 9 illustrates the degree of the direct impact of the environmental forces on the managerial behavior of executives in different hierarchical levels in an organization.

If we segment an organization into four levels and call these levels, from top to bottom, institutional, strategic, administrative, and operational, we see that the directness and the immediacy of the environment's impact on the behavior of managers in each of these levels decreases from top to bottom.

At the institutional level is the owner, the president, or, as in large organizations, a select group of top executives functioning as a governing board. This level of management spends proportionately more time dealing with the external environment than do other managers in the organization. Often, the changes in the succeeding levels take place after the institutional and strategic levels have adjusted their behavior to the demands of the environment.

Figure 9.   Environmental impact on different levels of an organization.

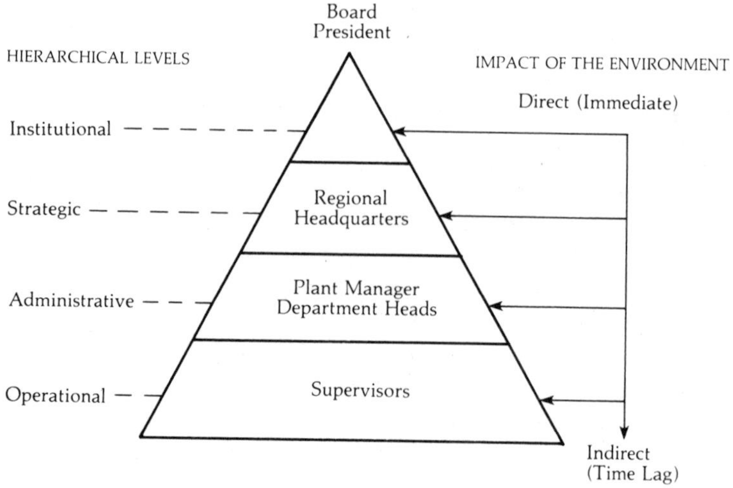

Organizational Variables

Employee performance is carried out within the confines of an organization. The organizational variables that most influence the performance of individuals and the organizational climate are (1) the nature of the task the employee is asked to perform, (2) the reward system, (3) the philosophy of management, and (4) the organizational policies concerning recruitment, retention, training, and other personnel matters.

Nature of the task. The nature of the task includes such dimensions as the breadth and diversity of the activities performed, the range of the responsibilities involved, the amount of formal authority associated with task accomplishment, the pace of activities, the scope of the supervisory and technological constraints under which the activities must be carried out, and the skills and knowledge required to perform the task. These characteristics directly influence employee performance.

The nature of the task an employee performs is the most important factor of the employee's work environment. By modifying important task dimensions to match employee characteristics and aspirations, managers can add elements to tasks that augment the intrinsic satisfaction a person receives in performing his or her job.

Reward systems. An effective compensation structure is the backbone of the management's efforts for increased employee performance. Without an effective reward system, management has difficulty creating and maintaining a supportive climate wherein employees become motivated to achieve the desired level of performance. If employees perceive the reward system as inequitable, notwithstanding the organization's good supervisory practices and personnel policies, the employees will not produce to their maximum capacity and will be only marginally committed to the organization. In general, employees desire a positive relationship between what they contribute to the organization through their jobs and what they receive from the organization in pay and other rewards.

Performance and rewards should be closely aligned, and this relationship should be clearly understood and accepted at all levels. Salary increases often fail to motivate because employees see them as something to which they are entitled rather than as something they must earn. If an increase does not occur on schedule, it causes disappointment and bad feelings. If the delay is prolonged, the employee may look elsewhere for work or complain not just about money but about petty annoyances that might otherwise have been ignored.

- If the increase is smaller than expected, the employee may feel deceived.
- If the increase is equal to what is expected, the employee will simply see the organization as having purchased his or her continued membership at a fair price. The employee will be reassured that the system is fair, but this kind of reassurance only satisfies, it does not motivate.
- If the increase exceeds expectations, the employee may increase productivity or may feel that this is compensation for work already accomplished.

The adequacy of a reward system can be measured by its contribution to attracting, retaining, and motivating employees. Properly designed reward systems seek to influence two basic decisions employees make: To become affiliated and/or stay with an organization, and to cooperate with and support the organization's efforts to achieve its goals.

Managerial philosophy and leadership. Managerial philosophy concerning the utilization of human resources and subsequent leadership styles seems to influence directly the performance environment in which superiors and subordinates interact. The broad umbrella of managerial philosophy includes such elements as centralization or decentralization of authority, the overall attitude of management toward labor, and employee involvement with decision making.

Basically, management philosophy refers to many precedents, customs, traditions, and informal procedures that establish the organizational climate. The atmosphere in an organization can encourage or discourage formality in interpersonal relations, creation and use of status symbols, lateral and diagonal communications, participative management, and many more interdepartmental procedures.

Some organizations exhibit more effective management philosophy than others. Effectiveness of managerial philosophy and leadership depends on the nature of the task at hand and the characteristics of the employees. In some organizations the climate may be informal, permissive, and participative, while in others it may be formal, strict, and stipulative. It is not necessarily true that the informal environment will be more effective than the formal one. Depending on the circumstances, an authoritarian management philosophy could be more effective than its participative counterpart.

The important point to remember is that superior/subordinate interaction within the organization is influenced by the organizational climate, and this climate differs in organizations depending on the nature of the goals, the demands of the tasks, and the characteristics of the employees. Supervisors and middle managers must recognize the overall organizational climate and follow its subtleties and the gradual changes that take place continuously as the organization attempts to adjust its internal characteristics to meet the new challenges of the environment.

Other organizational policies. Overall organizational policies with respect to recruitment, selection, training, development, career planning, job security, promotion, transfers, and conditions of employment comprise the fourth category of organizational variables. The impact of these variables on individual performance can be positive or negative. The influence of these variables will be discussed in later chapters.

Individual Variables

Ability and motivation to produce are the two major elements in our performance model (Figure 8). Assuming that the means to produce are available, a job will be performed according to a person's ability. If employees lack experience and/or knowledge, their job performance can be increased through training, coaching, and guidance. In certain cases an employee can be transferred to another job, or the job tasks can be adjusted to match an employee's current ability level.

Motivation can affect performance. Skilled, motivated employees will obtain both extrinsic and intrinsic rewards from performing their jobs satisfactorily. Extrinsic, or organizational, rewards include salary increases, promotions, and increased status. Intrinsic, or personal, rewards include the feeling of accomplishment and satisfaction experienced while performing and after successfully completing a task, the challenge of a difficult task, and the fulfillment of working without close supervision. From management's point of view, intrinsic and extrinsic rewards are valuable because they help employees attain individual goals. The meaning of the rewards, of course, can vary from individual to individual.

Role Clarity and Effective Human Resources Utilization

Research in organizational behavior shows that an organization can use human resources effectively if its members see their needs and aspirations as compatible with the demands of the organization.[7] In part, individuals' professional objectives derive from or reflect their personal needs. Consequently, employees see their organizational roles as means by which they can satisfy both their professional and personal aspirations. Job satisfaction becomes particularly important when a person can choose among several organizations when seeking employment.

Management must learn to recognize and act on the relationship between the organization's goals and the employees' personal needs and professional objectives. The more individuals see the activities they perform in the organization as relevant to their personal objectives, the greater the individuals' volunteerism becomes. Volunteerism is related to job interest, satisfaction, and other, similar variables associated with the performance of human resources.

Not surprisingly, role clarity becomes important. Organizational goals and individual objectives are often defined operationally, on the job, by the person who fulfills the role in the organization. Each role is determined by the person's activities, which are defined, in turn, by such mechanisms as job descriptions, rules and regulations, peer groups, and superiors. In day-to-day activities, problems arise when roles are unclear.

A quick review of the literature indicates that role clarity is an important variable for management to consider when it examines job interest, satisfaction, and other, similar variables. Previous studies define role clarity as the extent to which the required role information is communicated and understood by members of the organization at various levels and in various positions.[8]

The emphasis of this type of research has been on the individual's perception of a role. Role clarity is the degree of congruency between superior/subordinate perception of the subordinate's role. By having subordinates specify what the important aspects of their jobs are and by obtaining the same information about these jobs from immediate superiors, managers can determine the amount and nature of role ambiguity.

Role clarity is the agreement between a superior and a subordinate on what effective performance is. If they agree, the subordinate's work effort can be organizationally and individually satisfying. If they disagree, it is unlikely that effective performance (at least as defined by the immediate supervisor) will result. If a person has an inappropriate definition of success due to perceptual discrepancies in the definition of success at various hierarchical levels, much of his or her efforts might be wasted.

As the gap between organizational roles and individual objectives increases, management must expend greater effort to achieve effective utilization of human resources. The magnitude of these gaps may reflect the nature of the management policies, programs, and procedures used to elicit the participation of human resources.

Organizations may prevent the formation or widening of such gaps by reviewing the demands of the organization and the needs, aspirations, and objectives of their personnel. In this way organizations can free financial resources that would otherwise be used to hire additional employees to compensate for the low productivity levels of unmotivated employees.

The important implication of this chapter is that an organization can increase its productivity and at the same time help its members satisfy their needs by integrating the planning and utilization of human resources with strategic business plans and by allowing its members to personalize the plans. This fusion of employee goals and company objectives can lead to satisfactory results for both sides.

Organizational goal achievement depends on the commitments of individuals to the organization. *Socialization* and *personalization* are powerful processes affecting employee commitment to an organization. Socialization is the degree to which an individual accepts the goals of an organization and strives to attain them. From the socialization process point of view, commitment to organizations is affected by several factors.

The nature of organizational goals is obviously one of the most important variables in this process. Organizational and departmental goals are affected by the organization's infrastructure, technology, and formal organizational structure. The goals of the organization are expressed in terms of the authorized roles of individual members. The authorized role of the individual is a combination of the formal job description and existing rules and regulations within which the formal role is to be performed. Important role senders such as an influential colleague and the employee's immediate supervisor complete the definition of the role the individual is expected to perform.

Figure 10 shows the process of socialization. This process can be

Figure 10.   Process of socialization in organizations.

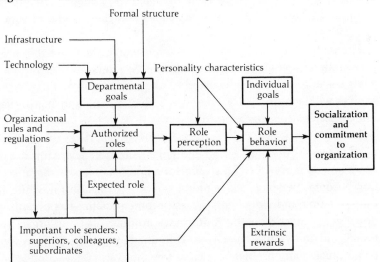

greatly facilitated by the nature of the organizational setting, if the objectives of the individuals are taken into consideration, and when the formal role is allowed to be altered to a certain degree. Through effective socialization, personal commitment to an organization is increased.

Personalization is the process through which organizational goals are modified by an individual. Employee performance is related to the degree of participation an employee is allowed in setting formal goals and plans. The tremendous amount of literature on participative management testifies to the importance of the personalization process. Individual participation in goal setting is not functional if it takes place at levels not relevant to the employee. Exchange of ideas on formal and individual role expectations should take place between the employee and the immediate superior. The concept of management by objectives (MBO) is a good example. Meaningful participation in goal setting is another example well illustrated by Likert's linking pin approach.[9]

Under Likert's linking pin concept, supervisors are involved in the departmental goal setting process. The department manager acts as a linking pin at the division level by conveying his or her subordinates' ideas to a higher management level and transmitting the decisions made at this level to the levels below. In this sense each manager is an active member of at least two groups: first, a department member, and second, a member of a higher management group composed of other department managers and their common superior.

The integrated HRP model helps management facilitate this personalization process at the strategic goal setting level. Organizational goals set in terms of the availability and aspirations of human resources will be more realistic and less difficult to attain than goals set unilaterally by top management.

Through vertically and horizontally integrated HRP, the continuous processes of socialization and personalization in organizations can be made more efficient, satisfactory, and feasible. The organization becomes personalized as individual objectives affect it, while at the same time individual employees become socialized as organizational goals affect them. Both processes produce fusion of organizational and individual objectives. Left unattended, these processes could cause many problems, such as low motivation, low productivity, and labor unrest.

Summary

Employees' performance is directly influenced by their motivation and ability to produce. Theories explaining motivation to produce can be categorized as content and process theories. Content theories are concerned with *what* motivates an individual. They attempt to identify the needs and motives within the person that energize, direct, sustain, and stop behavior. Maslow, Herzberg, Atkinson, and McClelland have provided the most popular explanations of need-oriented behavior as applied to work situations.

Process theories deal with *how* behavior is energized and sustained. They refer to the ways of stimulating people to accomplish the desired goals. Equity and expectancy theories have been used extensively to understand how a person behaves in organizational settings. Equity theory maintains that individuals will attempt to change the conditions if they perceive that they have been treated unfairly when compared with a relevant peer in the same job. The basic tenet of the expectancy theory is that people, in order to be motivated to produce, must see that their efforts result in successful task accomplishment and that successful performance results in desired rewards.

Job satisfaction is an important aspect of motivation to produce. There are many contradictory proposals concerning the relationship between job satisfaction and employee performance. The most widely accepted conclusion is that job dissatisfaction often leads to absenteeism and employee turnover, thereby reducing organizational performance.

The second major determinant of employee performance is ability. The ability to perform a given activity often depends on the degree to which an individual possesses the necessary knowledge, skill, and know-how that are pertinent to a given task and that are usually acquired through experience.

Employee performance is also affected by both environmental and organizational variables. Economic, social, political, and legal conditions shape the external environment of an organization. Important organizational variables include the nature of the task the employee is asked to perform, the reward system, the philosophy of management, and policies on recruitment, selection, training, and other personnel issues.

Another important consideration in employee performance is role clarity. Congruency between superior/subordinate perception of the subordinate's role positively influences job performance and job satisfaction.

In brief, at least three factors influence employee performance. The individual must be motivated, must possess the necessary abilities and traits, and must have fairly clear role perceptions.

CHAPTER 4

The Legal Framework of Human Resources Planning

An organization's hiring and employment policies and procedures must conform to the laws and accepted norms of society. The complete legal framework within which organizations operate in the United States is beyond the scope of this book. This chapter presents a synopsis of the legal developments specifically affecting the management of personnel and gives special attention to the issues organizations must consider in planning the selection and utilization of their human resources.

Civil rights legislation, combined with the willingness of individuals to demand rectification of past and present unfair employment practices, has made recruitment, selection, promotion, and discharge the most important issues in personnel administration. In order for organizations to be within the law, human resources plans are almost essential. These plans must conform to Civil Rights Acts, to Equal Pay and Minimum Wage Acts, to the Occupational Safety and Health Act, and to various Executive Orders and the requirements of different enforcement agencies. The entire field of personnel administration, including recruitment, selection, placement, compensation, development, promotion, transfer, and performance appraisal, is affected by legislative and executive action and by legal interpretations of the courts. Furthermore, additional legal constraints arise from contractual obligations resulting from collective bargaining.

To facilitate discussion, we will arrange into three groups the federal laws and Executive Orders that directly affect major personnel management practices. The first group deals with civil liberties,

Figure 11.   Laws and Executive Orders that affect three major areas of personnel policy.

1. Recruitment, selection, placement, training, development, promotion, transfer, wages and salary administration, and discharge of employees	
Wages and Benefits	**Equal Rights and Employment**
Walsh-Healy Act (1936)	Civil Rights Act (1866, 1871, 1964)
Davis-Bacon Act (1931)	Equal Employment Opportunity Act (1972)
Fair Labor Standards Act (1938)	Age Discrimination in Employment Act (1967)
Equal Pay Act (1963)	Executive Orders 11246, 11375, 11478
Employee Reitrement Income Security Act (1957)	
Social Security Act (1935)	

2. Collective bargaining, contract administration, and grievances	3. Physical conditions and job hazards
Wagner Act (1935)	Occupational Safety and Health Act (1970)
Norris-La Guardia Act (1932)	
Taft-Hartley Act (1947)	
Landrum-Griffin Act (1959)	
Executive Orders 10988, 11491	

equal employment, equal pay, and other issues influencing organizational policies on recruitment, selection, remuneration, promotion, transfer, and discharge. The second group covers the broad spectrum of labor-management relations. The third group covers the Safety and Occupational Health Act. Figure 11 shows which laws and Executive Orders affect several major areas of personnel policy.

The laws listed in Figure 11 should not be considered in isolation but as parts of the legal system, making a synergistic whole within the guidelines of the U.S. Constitution. These laws and Executive Orders are not the only ones human resources planners must consider, and their impact is not limited to policy areas. This review is a necessary simplification from a nonjurist perspective.

Equal Rights/Employment

Employers in profit or nonprofit organizations must abide by many antidiscrimination laws and Executive Orders pertaining to equal employment opportunity. A review of all the laws and orders is beyond the scope of this chapter. Nevertheless, executives coordinating an organization's human resources acquisition and utilization plans and activities must recognize the major legal requirements.

Provisions for equal rights in employment are based solidly on the U.S. Constitution. Specifically, the right to "due process" guaranteed in the Fifth Amendment provides the basis for individual protection against certain actions of the federal government. The Fifth Amendment has established that "no person shall . . . be deprived of life, liberty or property, without due process of law." However, the broad nature of due process is not easily applied to specific employment issues. Because of this lack of specificity, the courts prefer to refer to existing statutory law in cases relating to charges of discrimination in employment.

Another constitutional safeguard for equal rights in employment is the Thirteenth Amendment, which became effective in 1865. The primary purpose of the Thirteenth Amendment was to guarantee that "neither slavery nor involuntary servitude . . . shall exist within the United States." Consequently, this amendment has been limited to racial discrimination. However, jurists and social reformers have attempted to use the Thirteenth Amendment to attack other forms of discrimination as well.

A third constitutional safeguard is the Fourteenth Amendment, which provides "equal protection" for all under the law. This constitutional guarantee requires that all individuals similarly situated be treated equally, both in their rights and in their liabilities. The applicability of the Fourteenth Amendment to employment practices depends on the type of discrimination under investigation. For instance, in the case of *Ethridge* v. *Rhodes* (U.S. District Court, Ohio, 1967), two blacks, unsuccessful at becoming members of the Electrical Workers and Operating Engineers Union, which at the time was providing the labor supply for a state-financed university building project, charged discrimination. The court determined the Fourteenth Amendment to be applicable.

Based on these constitutional rights, specific laws providing equal employment opportunity for all have been enacted. The most relevant of these laws are the Civil Rights Acts of 1866, 1871, and 1964, the Equal Employment Opportunity Act of 1972, the Age Discrimination in Employment Act of 1967, and Executive Orders 11246, 11375, and 11478. Existing watchdog agencies such as the Equal Employment Opportunity Commission and the Office of Federal Compliance, along with the courts' current position on alleged discrimination, make it important to observe not only the letter but also the spirit of these laws.

The Civil Rights Acts of 1866 and 1871

Sections 1981 and 1983 of the Civil Rights Acts of 1866 and 1871 are often used as vehicles for suits against state and local government discrimination in employment. The pertinent sections of these acts are as follows:

The 1866 Act

All persons within the jurisdiction of the United States shall have the same right . . . equal benefit of all laws . . . and shall be subjected to like punishment . . . taxes. . . .

In *Palmer* v. NCR (U.S. District Court, Ohio, 1972), this section was used successfully in a case charging sex discrimination.

The 1871 Act

Every person . . . who subjects, or causes to be subjected, any citizens of the United States . . . to the deprivation of any rights, . . . secured by the Constitution and Laws, shall be liable to the party injured in an action at law, suit in equity, or other proper proceeding for redress.

This often-used section is now becoming less widely applied in suits alleging discrimination in employment. In a 1976 decision (*Washington* v. *Davis*), the Supreme Court ruled that standards applicable to this section of the Civil Rights Act were not applicable to suits for alleged discrimination on constitutional grounds.

The Civil Rights Act of 1964

The Civil Rights Act of 1964 has several sections, each dealing with a particular type of discrimination. Title VII is of particular relevance to employment practices. The Title VII Section of the act makes it unlawful for an employer to discriminate in employment, to fail to hire, to refuse to hire, or to discharge employees on the basis of race, color, religion, sex, or national origin. Prior to 1972, Title VII was aimed mainly at private employment agencies, employers, and labor unions with 25 or more employees or members. In 1972, the Civil Rights Act of 1964 was amended to include both private and public employers and labor unions with 15 or more employees or members. Relevant provisions and amendments to this act are covered in greater detail in the next section, on the Equal Employment Opportunity Act.

The Equal Employment Opportunity Act of 1972

According to the Equal Employment Opportunity Act, employers are prohibited not only from discriminating in employment on the basis of race, color, religion, sex, or national origin, but also from limiting, segregating, or classifying employees or applicants in any way that would tend to deprive them of employment opportunities when the basis of such classification is race, color, religion, sex, or national origin.

Title VII of the Civil Rights Act of 1964 further prohibits unions and joint labor-management committees controlling apprenticeship, training, retraining, or on-the-job training programs from discriminating against individuals because of their race, color, religion, sex, or national origin in admission to, or employment in, such programs. An employee or applicant who charges discrimination or who testifies or assists in a Title VII investigation, hearing, or proceeding is also protected from discrimination by the employer. Employers are prohibited from advertising job opportunities with specifications to race, color, religion, sex, or national origin unless such a characteristic is a bona fide occupational qualification.

The Civil Rights Act of 1964 and the Equal Employment Opportunity Act place the major legal constraints on human resources plans. However, when establishing nondiscriminatory personnel policies, managers must consider other laws and regulations as well. We discuss them next.

The Age Discrimination in Employment Act of 1967

This act prohibits employers of 25 or more employees from discriminating against persons between 40 and 65 years of age unless the employer can demonstrate that age is a bona fide occupational qualification for the job in question.

Executive Orders 11246, 11375, 11478

The executive branch of the federal government is entitled to issue Executive Orders against discrimination in employment by federal agencies and government contractors and subcontractors. Executive Order 11246, signed by President Lyndon Johnson in 1965, prohibits discrimination on the basis of race, color, religion, or national origin. Executive Order 11375, signed by President Johnson in 1967, added sex-based discrimination to the list. In 1969, President Richard Nixon issued Executive Order 11478, stipulating that hiring, promotions, and other employment practices in the federal government be based on merit and fitness and that discrimination on the basis of race, color, religion, sex, or national origin be prohibited. Typically, these Executive Orders require federal agencies to establish and maintain equal employment opportunity programs in many aspects of human resources utilization, including, but not limited to, recruitment, selection, training and development, transfer, demotion, layoff or termination, and compensation.

One consequence of the increasing interaction between private enterprise and government is that more and more nongovernment agencies are being required to prepare *affirmative action plans*. Such government regulation of employment practices has forced organizations closer to developing comprehensive and integrated human resources plans.

Preparing the affirmative action plans seems to cause organizations to upgrade their overall HRP process. For example, a government contractor cannot present required information on its number of women managers and project such employment figures for the next five years without considering other types of personnel activities. Therefore, the company invariably finds itself engaged in broader aspects of HRP.

Enforcement of the Laws and Executive Orders on Equal Rights/Employment
Various agencies enforce antidiscrimination laws and Executive Orders. Cases involving age discrimination and government contractors are under the jurisdiction of the Department of Labor. The personnel policies of all federal agencies are reviewed by the Civil Service Commission. Government contractors are also reviewed by the federal agency under whose jurisdiction they operate. The Civil Rights Division of the Justice Department can charge an employer with discrimination. State Fair Employment Practices Commissions act as watchdogs within their respective states and can sue employers for violating state antidiscrimination laws.

Two of the most active federal enforcement agencies need to be singled out. They are the Equal Employment Opportunity Commission and the Office of Federal Contract Compliance.

The Equal Employment Opportunity Commission
Compliance with Title VII of the Civil Rights Act of 1964, its subsequent amendments, and the Equal Employment Opportunity Act

is monitored by the Equal Employment Opportunity Commission (EEOC), created in 1966. During its first six years of operation the commission investigated more than 80,000 charges of discrimination, of which 17,000 involved discrimination on the basis of sex.[1]

At first, procedural restrictions created enforcement problems, but in 1972 Congress strengthened the powers of the EEOC and substantially raised its budget. Today it has five commissioners appointed by the president and confirmed by the Senate for five-year terms. Its jurisdiction extends to all businesses except the very small employers who do not engage in interstate commerce. Since 1972, the number of complaints processed by the EEOC has increased to approximately 70,000 cases annually.[2]

In addition to investigating charges of discrimination, the EEOC is also empowered to collect annually statistical information on the number of women, blacks, Hispanics, Orientals, and American Indians employed by organizations with 100 or more employees. After analyzing the data, the EEOC may direct the employers to improve their employment practices to increase the percentage of employee members of the legally accepted minority groups in different job categories.

The EEOC procedures generally begin with an employee or a job applicant claiming discrimination as defined by the law. The complaint is first referred to a state or local Fair Employment Practices Commission. Investigation by the EEOC begins after 60 days, whether or not the state or the local agency has taken any action. Investigators from the EEOC collect data from interviews, company policies, past practices, and the like to determine whether or not the charge is justified. If the EEOC finds no evidence of the alleged discrimination, the investigation stops. If investigation yields evidence of discrimination, the EEOC attempts to reach an informal agreement between the parties. If agreement is reached, the employer follows the steps specified in an affirmative action program.

If voluntary agreement cannot be reached, the EEOC can sue the employer on behalf of the complainant. If the defendant is a private employer, the case is taken to a federal district court; if the employer is a public agency, the case is referred to the Department of Justice.

The Office of Federal Contract Compliance
Each year the federal government spends billions of dollars on goods and services, maintenance and production. Most of these ac-

tivities are contracted to private employers. Approximately a third of the U.S. labor force is engaged all or part of the time in an activity contracted by the government. Federal law, including the Executive Orders, requires that these contractors provide equal employment opportunity. Today, organizations not engaged in filling government contracts or subcontracts but receiving government subsidies—such as police and health departments, schools and universities—also fall under the jurisdiction of the OFCC.

The OFCC has jurisdiction over all organizations engaged in a government-financed activity, either directly on a contractual basis or indirectly as a subcontractor or as a recipient of subsidies. The jurisdiction of the EEOC is broader and covers all equal employment legislation. The OFCC oversees that contract procedures are followed. Each contractor or subcontractor is required to develop an affirmative action plan to ensure equal employment. Periodically, the employer files a report with the government department with which it normally does its business. This report provides statistical information on the composition of the labor force on a job-by-job basis. If the overseeing government department establishes that there is an insufficient number of minority members in a given job category, it requires the employer to develop and implement a plan that will eliminate the imbalance. This plan will also specify goals and timetables to achieve the goals. The OFCC coordinates the overseeing activities of the various government departments.

The Courts' Position on Alleged Discrimination

In the 1960s discrimination cases were argued on the basis that a qualified minority applicant sought a job and that a less qualified nonminority person was hired. The courts generally demanded proof of discrimination. Because proof of this type was difficult to obtain, the courts are now looking into company employment practices. For instance, if an employer is located in a community whose population is 20 percent black and Puerto Rican, and only 4 percent of the company's employees are members of these two minority groups, the courts may inquire into the company's employment practices and may order it to take the necessary steps to remedy the inequality in employment. More recent court decisions go beyond the concern for equality in employment at the lower levels in organizations and focus on bringing a proportional representation of minority groups and women into professional and managerial positions.[3]

Undeniably, the equal employment legislation, along with the two primary enforcement agencies, the EEOC and the OFCC, have transformed personnel policies in the United States. In order to implement voluntary or court-imposed time-bound equal employment objectives, organizations need some sort of human resources plans. Affirmative action plans developed in companies having no previous human resources plans often serve as a first step toward establishing comprehensive human resources plans. A candid statement by an executive of a medium-size manufacturing company illustrates this point well:

> The single most important factor influencing the development of comprehensive long range manpower plans has been our compliance with equal employment legislation and the requirements of affirmative action programs. At first, we assigned a personnel officer to collect the necessary information and set minimum employment goals and advise the line departments of the procedures they should follow in hiring. Soon we saw the difficulty of setting employment goals without considering movement of existing personnel within the organization. We also found out that in forecasting internal supply of manpower and the organizational requirements of human resources it was almost impossible to set attainable objectives, acceptable by the government, to remedy the disproportionate employment of minorities in our organization. Although we had been contemplating for sometime to seriously engage in HRP, an EEOC investigation provided the needed impetus.

What this executive, and possibly many others, recognize is that a planned approach is necessary to remedy discrimination in employment. As affirmative action becomes increasingly influential in setting personnel policies, organizations begin to feel the need for comprehensive human resources plans that are integrated with their long-term business objectives.

Affirmative Action

Organizations involved with government contracts or receiving government subsidies are under considerable scrutiny by the enforcement agencies. For instance, Executive Order 11246 states that government contractors are not only prohibited from discriminating but also:

> The contractor will take affirmative action to ensure that applicants are employed and that employees are treated during employment without regard to their race, color, religion, sex or national origin. Such action shall include but not be limited to the following: employment, upgrading, demotion or transfer, recruitment or recruitment advertising, lay-off or termination, rates of pay or other forms of compensation and selection for training including apprenticeship.

Affirmative action describes both a general philosophy and a series of specific activities pertinent to organizational employment practices. Since the enactment of the 1964 Civil Rights Act, managerial philosophies in relation to equal employment seem to be polarized around first conforming to the law and affirmative action, next initiating steps to identify and analyze problem areas, and, finally, developing plans to ensure equal employment opportunity.

Some employers, although conforming to the law, feel that reverse discrimination in favor of minorities and women is just as unfair as discrimination against them. Managers in these organizations follow specific requirements of the law against discrimination, but they do not feel that it is their responsibility to go out of their way, for example, to the point of lowering their standards in employment, in order to redress past injustices. However, a great majority of major employers, and especially government contractors, view affirmative action as part of their social responsibility. These employers actively recruit minority or women applicants and try to eliminate traditional barriers to advancement.

As an employment policy, affirmative action is active, not passive or reactive. The organization in this sense follows a proactive process of self-evaluation and attempts to provide equal employment opportunity by voluntarily initiating steps rather than waiting to be audited by a compliance agency before taking such action.

Affirmative Action Steps

Although the government does not prescribe ways to develop affirmative action plans, we can outline certain steps that organizations, seeking to provide equal employment opportunity, generally follow.

1. *Creation of the proper managerial philosophy and attitude.* The first step in an affirmative action program is the development of a conducive organizational climate in the spirit of the Civil Rights Act. Managers involved with employment policies and practices must accept the basic premise of the affirmative action. Where necessary, development programs to change the behavior and if possible the attitude of key executives should be instituted. Programs on executive awareness of discrimination issues are generally introduced as part of specific training and development topics such as employee interviewing and selection, performance evaluation and promotion, and wage and salary administration. In these training sessions, environmental factors requiring changes in behavior and attitude can be discussed, as well as the legal, economic, and social factors of major personnel policies that need redirection.

2. *Equal employment audit.* Once management decides to embark on an affirmative action program, it must clearly understand the current employment situation. Statistical data must be gathered on the number of women and minority workers in the major occupational categories. These categories should include, but not be limited to, the nine job categories the EEOC requires organizations to file periodically. These job categories are: officials and managers; professionals; technicians; sales workers; office and clerical workers; craftsmen; operatives; and laborers and service workers. A more detailed breakdown within each of these job categories may be necessary for HRP purposes. Beyond determining the number of women and minority workers, organizations must also review their recruitment, selection, training and development, promotion, transfer, layoff, discharge, and compensation policies for possible built-in practices and procedures inconsistent with affirmative action law and philosophy.

3. *Equal employment planning.* The audit of the employment system reveals current and potential deficiencies. The next step is to plan for remedial action. First, management must determine the amount of underutilization of women and members of minority groups in different job categories. Underutilization occurs if the percentage of women or minority group members in any job category is lower than their percentage in the relevant job market.

The important issue, of course, is the meaning of *relevant labor market.* The determination of the relevant labor market depends on many factors and critical issues. The following are the basic ones:

- Local figures on the percentage of minority group members and women in the population and the labor force.
- The availability of minorities and women with the required skills.
- The traditional geographic area from which the organization draws most of its labor force in different job categories.
- Opportunities for training.
- Extent of unemployment in various groups.

Having determined the relevant labor market, management can compare the percentages of women and minority workers in each job category with their percentages in the general population. For example, community distance usually defines the geographic boundaries of the relevant labor market for low-grade job categories such as unskilled and service workers. If women make up 35 percent of a community's labor force but only 4 percent of a local firm's unskilled employees, the firm is probably underutilizing women. Where disproportions exist, management can establish goals and timetables for correcting them.

The law requires government contractors to establish goals and timetables for reducing underutilization. Other employers, especially those audited by the EEOC, are encouraged to take affirmative action steps. The goals developed must be consistent with the organization's labor flow and expected human resources requirements. This phase of the affirmative action program is closely tied to the labor supply.

4. *Eliminating discriminatory barriers to entry and promotion.* The equal employment audit might have revealed barriers for entry or for promotions that are not job related. For instance, a company may require graduation from a specific college for promotion eligibility. Another organization may send its recruiters only to certain select educational institutions and hire only the graduates of such institutions. Since these barriers are not job-related, they are considered to be discriminatory if through such practices certain groups are adversely affected. In this sense the Supreme Court has interpreted Title VII of the Civil Rights Act of 1964 to mean

that all employers [must] remove all artificial, arbitrary and unnecessary barriers to employment when the barriers operate invidiously to discriminate on the basis of racial or other impermissible grounds. . . .

The Act prohibits not only overt discrimination but also practices that are fair in form, but discriminatory in operation. The touchstone is business necessity. If an employment practice operates to exclude Negroes and cannot be shown to be related to job performance, the practice is prohibited.

In practical terms, this means that an organization must be able to demonstrate that personnel policies and procedures that have discriminatory effects relate to the jobs and predict actual job performance. The EEOC advises employers to carefully check their employment practices. Some organizations feel that they have conducted a serious goal setting process and made "good faith" efforts to achieve goals, but that negative external factors—such as "unavailability of 'qualified' candidates"—are responsible for lack of significant improvement. EEOC experience indicates that it is far more likely that negative internal factors are responsible—that is, that there are continuing discriminatory barriers in the employment system. Therefore, to achieve long-range goals and intermediate yearly targets, management must first identify where such barriers may be operating. Then it must take steps to eliminate the barriers and equalize opportunities for those suffering the effects of past discrimination.

For example, an analysis may reveal underutilization of certain groups in certain jobs. Unless management reviews the entire employment process, it will have difficulty pinpointing the cause of underutilization. How much is due to inadequate recruiting efforts? How much to the failure of applicants to survive various standards and steps in the organization's selection and promotion process? How valid is each of these standards in predicting which candidates can perform particular jobs successfully?

Testing and the Law

The Civil Rights Act of 1964 prohibits discrimination in employment on the basis of race, religion, or sex. The Tower Amendment to the act states that

it shall not be unlawful employment practice for an employer . . . to give and act upon the results of any professionally developed ability test provided that such test, its administration of, or action upon the results is not designed, intended, or used to discriminate because of race, color, religion, sex or national origin.

In *Griggs* v. *Duke Power Company*, a landmark case, the Supreme Court dealt with the meanings of "professionally developed" tests and test validation for "general" versus "particular job" use. The Court examined the appropriateness of using the Wunderlic Personnel Test and the Bennett Mechanical Aptitude Test in employee selection and a high school diploma as a condition of employment. Willie S. Griggs of North Carolina filed suit in 1967 alleging discrimination against the Duke Power Company. The key issue was whether the aforementioned requirements were substantially related to a candidate's ability to learn or to perform the particular job in question. The District Court in North Carolina ruled in favor of the company, stating:

Nowhere does the Act require that employers may utilize only those tests which accurately measure the ability and skills required of a particular job or jobs.

Griggs appealed the decision to the U.S. Supreme Court. The Supreme Court, in an 8-to-0 decision, ruled against the company, stating that

while the Act did not preclude the use of tests, they cannot play a substantial part in the selection process unless the employer can demonstrate that they provide a reasonable measure of job performance.

This Supreme Court decision set the tone for government regulation concerning employment testing. The courts now apply the following general guidelines in suits charging discrimination:

1. When tests or other criteria used by an employer eliminate more minorities and women than others, and when the applicant has established a reasonable case for charging discrimination, the employer must demonstrate that the tests and other criteria used in the selection process were job related.
2. Irrespective of the intent, if the criteria used result in discrimination, the selection process is considered unlawful.

The EEOC cautions organizations on the seriousness of test validation. Its guidelines express preference for statistically based validity studies performed by trained industrial psychologists. The preferred method is the criterion-related approach. Basically, organizations should develop measures that indicate how well an employee is performing on the job. A test is given to the applicants and then the statistical relationship between test results and criterion scores is determined. The tests have predictive or concurrent validity if the statistical comparisons indicate that there is a significant relationship between test scores and successful job performance, that is, that those who scored high on the test are substantially better performers on the job than are those who scored low.

In certain cases the EEOC also accepts content validity, that is, the results of tests that directly measure skills that are required for adequate job performance. For instance, a typing test is accepted for its content validity when used in hiring a typist, without further predictive validity studies. However, the EEOC does not accept aptitude, intelligence, personality, or interest tests as demonstrations of content validity.

Human resources planners, in developing policies for recruitment and selection, must consider how tests are viewed by the courts and insist on strict validation studies before they are used by personnel specialists or others in the organization. A strategic decision in this respect is whether to use a selection criterion with questionable predictive validity even if it only partially influences the final employment decision. We recommend that such a criterion, or any test with questionable predictive validity, not be used.

Interviewing and the Law

Often employers gather personal background information from their job applicants through application forms and/or interviews. Questions pertaining to areas defined in the Civil Rights Act of 1867 as the basis for discrimination are illegal. In other words, applicants may not be asked to furnish information on their religion, race, national origin, age, or sex. Even requiring information on educational background, for selection purposes, may be considered illegal if it cannot be proven to be job-related. In *Griggs* v. *Duke Power Company*, the Supreme Court declared illegal a high school education requirement that excluded a high proportion of the members of a minority group from employment.

Employers cannot ask job candidates about such personal matters as arrest records and salary histories unless the information can be demonstrated to be related to the job or its performance. The burden for supplying the proof is on the employer. Furthermore, employers cannot use information on arrest records and the like if the information tends to discriminate automatically against minority workers—as it would, say, in a community in which blacks make up 30 percent of the labor force but blacks with arrest records proportionately outnumber whites with arrest records.

To conclude, human resources planners should keep the following general point in mind as they evaluate their recruitment and selection procedures: Tests and information-gathering questions that may cause the organization's employment practices to be perceived as discriminatory on the basis of race, color, religion, sex, or national origin are probably illegal and should not be used.

Laws Affecting Wages and Benefits

Administering wage and benefits programs is an important element in the HRP process. Often an organization's compensation package is its chief means of attracting and keeping quality employees. Organizational strategies on compensation vary widely. Some organizations attempt to keep starting wages for certain job categories at the minimum-wage level while offering above-market wages in other job categories. Other organizations attempt to minimize costs by maintaining compensation packages below the relevant market average for all job categories. Another organization might offer wages well above the minimum legal requirements but violate the law in another aspect of the total compensation package. Compensation packages must be established within a legal framework. This section provides a synopsis of the laws affecting wages and benefits that planners must consider when they design an organization's compensation strategy.

The Davis-Bacon Act

The Davis-Bacon Act (1931), the oldest of the federal wage laws, affects contractors engaged in federal public works construction projects worth more than $2,000. Basically, this act requires that employees in federally constructed public works projects be paid at least at the prevailing wage rate and benefits in the area and that overtime compensation will be 1½ times this rate. The prevailing wage rates and employee benefits are determined by the Department of Labor.

The Walsh-Healy Act

The provisions of the Walsh-Healy Act (1936), which is commonly referred to as the Public Contracts Act, are the same as the Davis-Bacon Act. However, the coverage of this law extends to all employees of firms that hold contracts from the federal government for providing supplies, equipment, and materials costing $10,000 or more.

The Fair Labor Standards Act

The Fair Labor Standards Act (FLSA), passed in 1938, covers workers in almost all types of organizations engaged in the production of goods and services for interstate and overseas trade. It includes those organizations not directly engaged in interstate or foreign trade but providing essential assistance in the production of such goods and services. Except for the so-called Mom and Pop stores, nonchain drugstores, and funeral homes, this law covers almost all employers. The FLSA, through its various amendments, covers minimum wage rates, child labor restrictions, and equal rights for all employees.

Wage and hour provisions. The minimum wage is set by the law and is periodically amended. Wage and salary administrators should consult the Wage and Hour Division of the U.S. Labor Department to obtain the latest provisions of this law and particularly the minimum wage rates.

The FLSA calls for overtime rates at 1½ times the existing rate for hours worked in excess of 40 hours per week. The difference between this and the Walsh-Healy Act is in the method of computing overtime hours. Overtime is computed for every hour over 8 hours during any day. The FLSA computes overtime per week.

The basic wage used to compute the overtime rate must include bonuses and all incentive pay that the individual received during the normal working week. For instance, the basic rate for a job may be $4.00 per hour. The employee has worked, say, 50 hours in a particular week and has also received a bonus of $50. Now, the wage rate for the 10 hours of overtime must be computed, not on the basis of

1½ times $4.00 per hour, but on the basis of 1½ times $5.25 per hour ($160 regular pay plus $50 bonus, divided by 10 hours). Because the bonus is included, then, the real wage for this overtime is $7.875 per hour. The total earnings for this employee for 50 hours will be:

Regular time	40 × $4.00	=	$160.00
Bonus		=	50.00
Overtime	10 × $7.875	=	78.75
			$288.75

The FLSA does not cover all jobs. "Exempt" jobs include executive, administrative, and professional (other than sales) positions. Most nonsupervisory, white- and blue-collar workers are "nonexempt" and are covered by this law.

Child labor provisions. The FLSA prohibits minors between 16 and 18 years of age from working in hazardous occupations. Jobs considered hazardous are in mining, logging, meat packing, and some areas of manufacturing. Children under 16 may not be employed in any work involving any form of interstate commerce unless they are employed by their parent(s) or guardian or by an employer in a nonhazardous field who has been issued a temporary permit by the Labor Department.

Equal-pay provision. The Equal Pay Act of 1963 is one of the most significant amendments to the FLSA. The Equal Pay Act states that

> no employer shall discriminate between employees on the basis of sex by paying wages to employees less than the rate at which he pays wages to employees of the opposite sex for equal work on jobs which require equal skill, effort, and responsibility, and similar working conditions.

The Equal Pay Act has helped significantly to achieve parity between wages paid to men and women in the same occupations working under similar conditions. On the average, women still earn less than men with comparable education. Many claim that the earnings gap is due to continued discrimination, while others attribute this gap to women's lack of seniority.

Income security. Unemployment compensation, disability payments, and retirement income are regulated by the Social Security Act.

When first enacted in 1935, the Social Security Act provided retirement benefits and unemployment insurance. Today the Social Security Act provides pensions, disability insurance, and health insurance for individuals 65 years of age or older, and survivor's insurance for widows, widowers, and dependent children. Social Security provides the Old Age, Survivor's, and Disability Insurance; Medicare provides the hospital insurance. The programs are financed jointly by the employer and the employee through payroll deductions, called FICA taxes (FICA refers to the Federal Insurance Contributions Act).

Workers' Compensation Laws typically require employers to pay indemnities, based on a percentage of the employees' wages, to employees who are disabled by occupational injuries or ailments. The maximum durations of such indemnity payments are specific to each state. Workers' Compensation Laws may be compulsory or elective, depending on the state. Under the elective system, employers have the option of accepting or rejecting the law. In general, most employers elect to be covered by the law. If an employer is not covered by the law, employees disabled as a result of an occupational injury or illness may have to sue the employer for damages. Today the vast majority of states have compulsory Workers' Compensation Laws. The U.S. Department of Labor periodically publishes the coverage and the nature of State Workers' Compensation Laws.

Unemployment compensation is financed by the employers alone but is paid to the unemployed individual by the state. The amount of taxes an employer pays depends on its experience rate. The experience rate is determined by the employer's labor turnover rate. A high turnover rate resulting in unemployment benefits increases the firm's experience rate and raises its rate of taxation. This presents another very significant reason for having a planned approach to human resources management. Employee turnover is expensive in terms of the recruitment, selection, and training costs of the new employee, and also in terms of its contribution to unemployment compensation tax rates.

Workers' Compensation costs are paid entirely by the employers. Employers generally purchase insurance, though some large companies establish their own special funds for Workers' Compensation. Some states require employers to contribute to mandatory state funds. Regardless of the method of payment, employers should strive to minimize their indemnity payments by reducing work-related injuries or ailments. Again human resources planning can help organizations to ensure the safety of existing and future jobs.

Human resources planners can supply data useful for the SBP process by comparing differences among states concerning Workers' Compensation Laws. Such data often help management decide where to locate new plants.

The Employee Retirement Income Security Act

Another law affecting wages and benefits is the 1974 Employee Retirement Income Security Act (ERISA). Although no laws require any employer to establish pension plans, ERISA provides certain controls and standards regulating those pensions that are established. Basically, ERISA ensures that when an employee retires, there will be money available for his or her pension. Studies cited during the ERISA debates in Congress indicated that under the then-existing arrangements, a third to a half of all workers covered by private pension plans would probably never receive any pension at all.[4]

The following list outlines the major regulatory provisions found in ERISA:

1. The soundness of the actuarial assumption used in the funding and investing of the plan must be certified at least every three years by the actuary.
2. Pension plans must adopt one of the three vesting alternatives. *Vesting* is the legal term referring to the amount of time after which an employer's contributions to a pension plan and the employee's earnings become the property of the employee. The possibilities are:
   a. One hundred percent of all contributions and earnings after 10 years of service.
   b. Twenty-five percent after 5 years of service, 50 percent after 10 years, and 100 percent after 15 years.
   c. Fifty percent vesting when employee's age plus 5 years of service equals at least 45, and 10 percent for each year thereafter, reaching 100 percent 5 years later.
3. Employers with existing pension plans are given up to 40 years from the passage of ERISA, depending on circumstances, to fund all past-service liabilities covered under the plan (that is, liabilities for pensions not yet paid for and now required by ERISA but incurred before ERISA was passed).
4. All plans covered by the law must pay a premium to the Pen-

sion Benefit Guarantee Corporation established by ERISA to insure against failure or bankruptcy.

5. Employees who are not covered by a pension plan (and, according to a later law, even those who are) can establish their own individual retirement accounts (IRAs); they can deduct from federal income tax contributions up to $1,500 or 15 percent of their income, whichever is less.

6. Persons administering the plans must abide by established standards of conduct and accountability.

ERISA provides standards for establishing and managing pension plans and insuring them against bankruptcy. Human resources planners must be aware of the major provisions of this law when they evaluate alternative pension plans developed by specialists to suit the organization's overall strategy in human resources acquisition and utilization.

Laws Regulating Labor-Management Relations

Comprehensive laws regulating labor-management relations, and particularly the collective bargaining process, have a relatively long history in the United States. Primarily, their coverage includes, but is not limited to, the representation campaign of the union, unfair labor practices, jurisdiction, the bargaining unit, contract negotiations, and contract administration.

In unionized organizations the employment contract plays a very important role in the acquisition and utilization of human resources. Depending on the nature of the contract, organizations may lose flexibility in acquiring, developing, utilizing, and replacing their personnel. Management and the union determine the content and administration of the contract in each organization. However, federal laws regulate the collective bargaining process itself.

Four major laws and one Executive Order govern labor-management relations. These are:

1. *The Norris-LaGuardia Act (1932).* This law recognized employees' right to join a union or to organize a new union of their own choosing. It outlaws yellow-dog contracts—that is, employment contracts in which workers agree not to join a union while employed

by the company—and restricts the use of court injunctions to halt work stoppages.

2. *The Wagner Act (1935)*. This law, also called the National Labor Relations Act, is the major federal law protecting unionized workers. The Wagner Act established the National Labor Relations Board and empowered it to intervene in cases of alleged unfair labor practices and to assist in the orderly process of a union's gaining recognition by the employer. The act also defines unfair labor practices, including the following:

- Interfering with or restraining an employee's right to organize.
- Interfering with or restraining any labor union.
- Discriminating against anyone for engaging in union activities.
- Discriminating against anyone for testifying against the employer for unfair labor practices.
- Refusing to engage in collective bargaining with the legally established employee organization.

3. *The Taft Hartley Act (1947)*. This act, commonly referred to as the Labor Management Relations Act (LMRA), is to the employer what the Norris-LaGuardia Act is to the union. It attempts to prevent or correct unfair labor practices by the union. Specified unfair labor practices are:

- Coercing a worker to join, or restraining a worker from joining, a union.
- Pressuring an employer to discriminate against an employee on the basis of nonmembership in the union.
- Refusing to bargain collectively with the employer.
- Engaging in jurisdictional strikes and secondary boycotts.
- Forcing employees to pay exorbitant union fees.
- Practicing featherbedding (that is, making an employer pay for services not rendered).

The LMRA also gives the president of the United States the right to interfere with long strikes in industries affecting the national economy and security, and it requires the unions to file financial records.

4. *The Landrum-Griffin Act (1959)*. This law was enacted to curb certain additional unfair labor practices by management and improper union practices. It is commonly referred to as the Labor-Management Reporting and Disclosure Act. The major unlawful practices listed in this act are:

- Labor-management collusion (sweetheart contracts).
- Infiltration of unions by gangsters.
- Undemocratic internal union procedures.
- Misuse of union funds.
- Use of union spies by management.
- Picketing an employer whose employees have no desire to join a union or to organize a new one.

The law also guarantees union members freedom of speech and assembly, the right to sue the union, the right to secret ballot elections, and the right to nominate and vote for candidates of their own choosing for any union office.

5. *The Kennedy Executive Order 10988 (1962).* The Wagner Act (1935) guaranteed collective bargaining rights to employees in the private sector. Executive Order 10988 did the same thing for federal employees and encouraged states to pass laws granting unionization and collective bargaining rights to public employees.

These laws and Executive Orders set the framework within which the collective bargaining process in the public and private sectors takes place. They govern the rules and procedures for selecting the bargaining unit and settling disputes over jurisdiction and representation. Contract negotiations as well as contract administration must also be carried out in conformity with the existing laws.

Health and Safety

A rapid increase in industrial accidents in the 1960s and the discovery that many materials and processes used in manufacturing are detrimental to workers' health led to the comprehensive Occupational Safety and Health Act in 1970 (OSHA). This act requires employers to provide workers with safe and healthy working environments. The standards for these environments are established by the National Institute for Occupational Safety and Health. They are continuously being revised and expanded. When the standards were first issued, one month after the law took effect, they were listed in a 248-page book. The Occupational Safety and Health Commission administers the act.

OSHA inspectors, on their own initiative or in response to employee complaints, inspect employer premises. If the inspection establishes that the employer has violated a particular standard established by the law, the employer is issued a citation. Penalties carry fines of up to $1,000 for each violation. Willful and repeated violations can lead to penalties of $10,000 and jail terms, for the responsible officer, of up to six months. Furthermore, if an employer fails to correct a cited violation, the commission can impose a penalty of $1,000 per day until the violation is rectified.

The physical environment of work improved in the 1970s. Evidence suggests that the passage of OSHA has reduced the number of work-related injuries and ailments and has positively influenced management's acceptance of the need for human resources planning.[5] Many progressive organizations are concerned not only with the physical well-being of workers but also with their psychological states. As such, they focus on turnover and worker apathy problems, which negatively influence the productivity rates.

Summary

Federal and state laws regulating the acquisition and use of human resources have significant impacts on HRP. Human resources have become less and less flexible as an input in the production of goods and services. Employers face increasing legal limitations in hiring, using, transferring, and laying off employees. Human resources plans must take these legal restrictions into consideration, and strategic business plans should reflect their implications. What an organization may or may not do with its human resources eventually will affect its long-range business objectives, especially if those objectives were based on the assumption that labor would always be readily available.

The laws and Executive Orders affecting personnel policies are put into three groups. The first category of laws deals with civil liberties, equal employment, and equal pay. They primarily affect organizational policies concerning recruitment, selection, placement, training, development, promotion, transfer, compensation, and discharge issues.

According to these laws, employers are prohibited from discriminating on the basis of race, color, religion, sex, national origin, or age. The antidiscrimination laws and Executive Orders are enforced by a multitude of federal agencies primarily housed in the Justice and Labor Departments. The Equal Employment Opportunity Commission and the Office of Federal Contract Compliance are the two most important enforcement agencies. They monitor over 60 percent of all discrimination cases and provide guidelines to employers for affirmative action.

The second category of laws covers the broad spectrum of labor-management relations and the collective bargaining process: selection of the bargaining unit, resolution of disputes over jurisdiction and representation, contract negotiation, and grievance handling. The most important laws are the Wagner Act, the Norris-LaGuardia Act, the Taft-Hartley Act, and the Landrum-Griffin Act.

The Occupational Safety and Health Act represents the third category and focuses on the physical environment of the workplace. Safety departments and inspectors, primarily through accident prevention programs, are contributing to the development of comprehensive human resources plans.

CHAPTER 5

Forecasting: The Key to Successful Human Resources Planning

Forecasting is probably the most important activity in the planning process. It is the essence of rational decision making in organizations. Rational decisions are based on assessments of past trends, evaluations of the present situation, and projections of future events.

Forecasting is a systematic process by which planners estimate changes in the organization's immediate and extended environments. Forecasting and planning complement one another because forecasts identify the best available expectations while plans establish future goals and objectives. Management's choice of the planning horizon—that is, whether its plans will be short-, medium-, or long-term—depends mainly on the consequences of the decisions to be made and on the organization's flexibility in adapting to unforeseen developments. Short-term planning requires more detailed forecasts than does long-term planning.

Matching Human Resources Requirements and Potential Human Resources Availability

Matching human resources with planned organizational activities for the present and the future is one of the main problems faced by an organization. Human resources have a certain degree of inflexibility, both in terms of their development and their utilization. It takes several months to recruit, select, place, and train the average employee; in the case of higher-echelon management personnel in large organizations, the process may take years. Decisions on personnel recruitment and development are strategic and produce long-lasting effects. Therefore, management must forecast the demand and supply of human resources as part of the organization's business and functional planning processes. Long-term business requirements, promotion policies, and recruitment (supply) possibilities have to be matched so that human resources requirements and availability estimates (from both internal and external sources) correspond sufficiently.

Establishing long-term human resources requirements is closely related to SBP. Strategic business plans should provide a minimum base of information on which viable human resources plans can be built. However, in many organizations, planners forecast long-term human resources requirements without referring to strategic business plans. On the other hand, management often establishes strategic business plans without explicitly considering labor availability even though current and potentially available human resources affect the viability of strategic business plans. When human resources becomes inflexible, management must coordinate strategic business and human resources plans. Figure 12 illustrates the desired reciprocal relationship.

Forecasts provide the best estimations of future needs and events. Planning, however, establishes goals and objectives and determines the means to reach the objectives. HRP attempts to determine the human resources requirements and availability needed to attain the stated objectives.

Forecasting as Part of the Decision-Making Process

Forecasting in HRP can best be understood if it is viewed as an integral part of the decisions made in anticipation of future problems. The first phase in decision making, therefore, is *problem identification.* Problems are always subjective in the sense that they are bound to persons in specific roles. Business problems are subjectively experienced by individuals in their respective organizational roles. Thus the forecasts on which human resources plans are built vary according to the problems individuals experience in their managerial roles.

According to John Dewey, the American educator and philosopher, people start solving a problem with the problem identification

Figure 12.   Reciprocal relationship of strategic business and human resources plans.

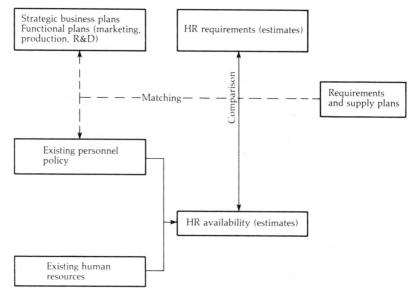

phase by intuitively generating vague solutions. Hypotheses can
then be built to solve the existing and expected problems.

   To test the hypotheses, managers begin the next phase, *descriptive
search,* by gathering relevant data from the internal and external environments of the organization. The analysis of internal data pertinent to determining future human resources requirements often
begins with an evaluation of the current organizational structure and
a determination of the capabilities and weaknesses of existing personnel. This is known as a human resources audit. The primary
sources of data from the organization's external environment are
trends in gross national product, unemployment rates, and various
industrial production indices.

   The next phase in the rational decision-making process is the
causal search, in which causal relationships are explored between the
important variables identified by the descriptive search. Planners
now review the causal relationships and build relevant models, using
many types of forecasting techniques.

   In the *predictive phase,* planners use the models built in the preceding phase to develop and test policies. With the models, the planners

Figure 13.   Integrated view of forecasting within rational decision-making process.

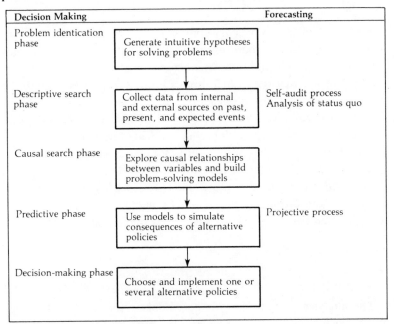

Decision Making		Forecasting
Problem identication phase	Generate intuitive hypotheses for solving problems	
Descriptive search phase	Collect data from internal and external sources on past, present, and expected events	Self-audit process Analysis of status quo
Causal search phase	Explore causal relationships between variables and build problem-solving models	
Predictive phase	Use models to simulate consequences of alternative policies	Projective process
Decision-making phase	Choose and implement one or several alternative policies	

can simulate future bottlenecks and project the consequences of applying various policies to expected problems. Eventually, one or more of the alternative policies are selected. This is the *decision-making phase*, in which the finalized plans and activities are put into effect. As Figure 13 illustrates, forecasting and problem solving are integrated processes.

Planners must use forecasts with caution, however, because the forecasts can become self-fulfilling prophecies if they are incorporated directly into plans. For example, if the planners forecast that in the next ten years all the managers in an organization will have marketing backgrounds and then incorporate this forecast into their human resources plans, it is likely that all of their managers will indeed have a marketing background by the end of the decade. Chances are, the personnel department will hire only managers with backgrounds in marketing. Because forecasts are not meant to be prophetic, planners should guard against their forecasts' becoming self-fulfilling prophecies.

An Overview of Forecasting Techniques

Forecasting has two primary components. It begins with an inventory of the existing human resources in the organization. This component is often referred to as the analysis of status quo. It is hardly possible to forecast the availability of human resources if there are inadequate data on the quality and quantity of current human resources. Although forecasting is future-oriented, no acceptable forecasts can be made unless one has an adequate knowledge of present and past trends. We base our forecasts on what we know.

The second component is the projection of the present supply and demand estimates into the future. This process involves determining both the organization's requirements for and the probable availability of human resources during the period being planned.

Analysis of Status Quo

The analysis of status quo is commonly referred to as the self-audit process, self-study, or inventory of human resources. Many techniques provide organizations with a clear, accurate description of their existing human resources. A recent survey of 195 major U.S. corporations regarding their use of forecasting techniques identified several methods of analyzing the status quo. The most commonly used methods are "Audit of Key Positions," "Manning Tables," "Skills Inventories," and "Job Analysis."[1]

Audit of Key Positions
The audit of key positions is simply a convenient way of summarizing the kind of data needed for planning key positions and for having the right managers on the right job at the right time. It entails a review of management's performance and of the effectiveness of managerial tools. The audit takes environmental factors into account to detect potential managerial obsolescence. It also includes information about each manager's age, education, years of service in the company, promotability, and possible replacements. Planners use audits primarily for career planning, placement, and transfer of executives.

Manning Tables

Manning Tables are summary staffing schedules that indicate the number of employees in each job title and category. They are used primarily by industrial engineers to establish optimum employment size in conjunction with data from job analysis and time studies. Notations may be used to further classify employees in each category. The notes may provide information about the employee's sex, age, marital status, handicaps, and other personal characteristics, as well as the training time it takes new employees to learn specific skills required for the jobs. In summary, Manning Tables provide a complete record of how workers are distributed among the jobs.[2]

Skills Inventories

Skills inventories, a specialized version of the Manning Tables, are an essential component of HRP. They provide information on the type and number of skills the organization's human resources provide at that time. Because of the large number of employee characteristics that could be recorded in these inventories, planners should include only those characteristics that are pertinent to the future requirements of the organization.[3]

Job Analysis

Job analysis is a process by which planners gather and summarize, in job descriptions, information on all the jobs in the organization. Interviews, observations, questionnaires, supervisory conferences, checklists, manuals, time-study reports, and organizational charts provide the information. Job descriptions include job identification information such as the job title, the location of the job, and its position in the organizational hierarchy.[4] Following the brief identification information is a detailed but concise description of what the employee does and how and why he or she does it. Such descriptions usually cover the nature of the assigned work, specific tasks, areas of responsibility, degree of authority, and working conditions. Finally, a statement is attached to the job description that outlines the mental and physical skills required to perform each job. These statements are referred to as job specifications.[5]

These techniques help the planners to gather necessary information on existing jobs and key managerial personnel. This information enables the planners to determine the current status of human resources and is used as the basis for projection into the future.

Projective Techniques

In addition to having an accurate picture of the current status of their human resources, organizations need to project their human resources requirements and the availability of personnel into the future. Both supply and demand estimates of human resources can be obtained through the use of a multitude of techniques, most of which require sophisticated statistical analyses. The following discussion reviews the commonly used projective techniques. Complete descriptions of these techniques are given in standard textbooks on business forecasting. Our emphasis here is on how and for what purposes these techniques are used.

It is possible to categorize projective techniques as either subjective or quantitative. Subjective techniques use a direct approach in projecting human resources requirements and are based on judgment surveys. Quantitative techniques, on the other hand, are based on a statistical analysis of past trends. These techniques often make use of intervening variables, which mathematically relate human resources requirements to projected output over the planning period.

Subjective Judgments

Determining precisely what information is needed and deciding which elements will be forecasted are significant first steps in the forecasting exercise. Forecasting generally begins with a review and listing of the relevant environmental factors, such as inflation rates and competition; major critical issues, such as changes in technology and energy sources; and internal developments, such as decentralization of operations, that may shape the future of the organization. These descriptions, if well elaborated, lead to the development of one or more "long-term scenarios." In the written scenarios, planners discuss political, legal, social, and demographic issues. Planners use the scenarios to project human resources needs. The projections are formulated in conditional terms: If this is the case, then we can expect this.

Well-formulated judgments provide the basis for the projections or forecasts. All other techniques merely help the planners to systematically analyze the data. Because forecasting is an interpretive process, judgments by experts are essential. Useful forecasting inputs are often supplied by capable managers who have had much experience in the organization. Experienced line executives and personnel managers seem to be the best source of expertise. The chief executive officers also should be tapped for their opinions and assumptions about the future. Often specialists from outside the organization can provide information not available from internal sources concerning strategic issues and important policies.

The *judgment survey* is the most common method for gathering facts and opinions from the experts. Many types of judgment surveys can be used to gather information from the experts, including: personal interviews, polls, panels and juries, mail surveys and questionnaires, and the Delphi technique.

Polls and personal interviews. Since people have their own distinct interests and opinions, surveying several people can provide planners with a more balanced view of the issue under consideration. In polls, the individuals or groups concerned are interviewed separately, and the average outcome of the individual opinions is taken as the best estimate of a future event. Personal interviews are especially appropriate for soliciting confidential information.

Panels and juries. A more sophisticated approach to surveying the opinions of managers and specialists, as described by Thomas E. Milne, is the "jury of executive opinion method."[6] It involves bringing several line managers (such as marketing, production, R&D, and finance managers) together on a regular basis and asking them to discuss and estimate future events and trends. Panels and juries give managers a forum for discussing their ideas and opinions, and allow the ideas to be pooled and evaluated. Thus panels and juries can be more valuable than impersonal surveys. However, panel discussions run the risk of degenerating into mere consensus as participants seek agreement and copy the panel leaders. To avoid such problems, coordinators brief the panelists on the purpose of the panel and the significance of the issues. Productive interaction among panelists can generate high-quality statements and opinions, unlike the stereotypical responses that interviews and polls often elicit.

Mail surveys and questionnaires. Surveys are documents with detailed questions and instructions that can be completed by the individuals whose opinions are being sought. To ensure the reliability and validity of the survey results, the forecasters must pretest the questionnaires—the surveying instruments—before administering them. Although pretesting takes time and costs money, the main problem with questionnaires is the low rate of response from busy executives. Often the respondents are not interested in the subject, and unless they are required by top management to respond, they will not return the surveys.

The Delphi technique. Personal interviewing, polls, panels, and juries all have the potential for eliciting insincere, parrotlike responses. The Delphi procedure may eliminate this disadvantage because it combines the benefits of participant anonymity and discussion, and thus prevents untimely consensus.

In the Delphi process 10 to 20 persons who are especially knowledgeable about the subject are polled. These experts give their opinions about future developments by completing a questionnaire; this is done in *several interactive sessions* coordinated by a specialist who is in charge of the forecasting process. Only the coordinator knows who is participating, and the experts never meet during the questionnaire process. The aim of a Delphi exercise is to reach expert group consensus concerning the estimates of future events through a succession of interactive rounds. In each round, experts are asked to provide forecasts (estimates) by individually completing a questionnaire. The coordinator pools and tabulates the experts' estimates, and then communicates the results to the experts. The experts are asked to provide explanations for any of their responses that differ widely from the median calculated by the coordinator.

Before the next round starts, the coordinator informs the experts of the quartile forecast levels of their last estimates. The quartiles are the 25th, 50th, and 75th percentile values of the estimates. Presumably, the range of the experts' estimates of future events will diminish as the process goes on. The median of the experts' estimates represents the most valid consensus values. The rounds are repeated until the median, the 25th, and the 75th percentile values stabilize, leading to a satisfactory consensus. This stabilization usually occurs within three to five rounds. Sometimes the process culminates in a face-to-face discussion of the issues by the experts.

General Macro Indicators

A widely used quantitative projective technique is the analysis of general macro indicators. Frequently, large organizations use macro forecasts of future events and translate them into long-term forecasts that are relevant to their own organizations. Macro forecasts are based on projections of international, national, and regional conditions and developments in specific industries. Multinational companies, for instance, are especially interested in general economic and social indicators for the United States, the countries of the Organization of Economic Cooperation and Development (OECD), and the Common Market countries as a basis for making their own projections. The strategic business plans of an organization are dominated by general economic forecasts, while the short-term plans are usually based on forecasts that utilize time-series analysis. As the time horizon of the plans extends further into the future, the use of general indicators as the basis for company forecasts increases.

One of the general economic conditions that businesses are most interested in is the change in the rate of growth of the gross national product. This condition is also used as an indicator for the business cycle. Business cycles consist of periods of expansion followed by periods of economic decline. Unfortunately, even when using the most sophisticated analyses by government experts, planners have difficulty predicting the likelihood of changes in economic activities for more than the next six months. This presents a problem for medium-term plans. However, since long-term plans require only estimates of gross tendencies rather than precise forecasts, the impact of incorrect forecasts is attenuated. This is true as long as the predicted general tendencies are accurate.

Numerous general indicators are readily available to an organization. In choosing among them, forecasters must consider the indicators that appear most consistent and most relevant to the organization's activities. The commonly used general indicators include gross national product, unemployment rates, index of industrial production, import/export balances, start of construction of new buildings, corporate earnings, industrial inventories, and the inflation rate. These data are generally published by different departments of the federal government, by banks, and by a few business periodicals. The information is available at minimal or no cost to the organization.

General indicators may be classified as leading, coincident, or lagging when compared with the organizational activity that is being forecasted. Leading indicators move ahead of the organizational activities being forecasted, while lagging indicators move behind the

Figure 14.   Relationship of general leading indicator (*I*) to specific organizational activity (*A*).

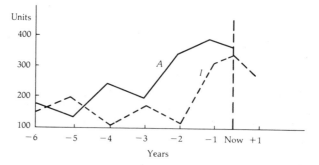

forecasted variables. Coincident indicators move at the same rate as the forecasted variables.

Many business forecasts are based on leading indicators. For example, manufacturers of concrete or furniture may be most interested in the start of the construction of new houses as a leading indicator. Figure 14 illustrates the relationship between a general leading indicator (*I*) and a specific business activity (*A*). In this illustration, the lead time of indicator *I* with regard to activity *A* is one year. That is, an increase or decrease in the leading indicator is reflected proportionately in the business activity a year later.

Finding an adequate leading indicator with a consistent lead time over the variable that the organization is attempting to forecast is often a matter of trial and error. The relationship between the two variables should be realistic and statistically sound. If no reliable indicator can be found, a forecaster may try to create a *leading index*. This is a composite made up of a number of single indicators, each of which has limited reliability. A composite leading index takes into consideration several indicators, usually by mathematically averaging them. A good example is the Dow Jones index of 30 industrial stocks in the New York Stock Exchange.

The mathematical relationship between a leading indicator and the variable the organization wants to forecast can be examined by means of correlation and regression analyses. *Correlation analysis* measures the degree of the association between the variables. Variables may have a negative relationship, a positive relationship, or no relationship. *Regression analysis* attempts to determine the nature of the relationship between two or more variables. The purpose of re-

Figure 15.   Scatter diagram of leading indicator (I) and business activity (A) from Figure 14.

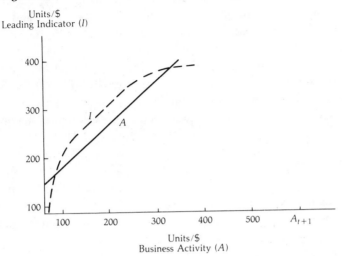

Units/$
Business Activity (A)

gression analysis is to forecast the dependency of one variable on an independent variable (for example, the leading indicator). Regression analysis is generally based on historical data derived from time-series analysis. Figure 15 illustrates a regression relationship. The data in this scatter diagram are taken from Figure 14.

A scatter diagram gives the forecasters a preliminary visual impression of the relationship between the variables. On the basis of this impression, the analyst can make several assumptions about the relationship and select a time span to be employed in the forecast. For instance, if data for the past six years (from Figure 14) are plotted in a scatter diagram, a straight line results (see Figure 15). However, if the data from five and six years ago are eliminated because they are not relevant today, the relationship between the two variables changes and is represented by a parabola. In this example, the relationship between the leading indicator and the business activity, as represented by a straight line, is positive and continuous. A parabolic relationship indicates that at first the business activity does not move as fast as the leading indicator. Later, though, the leading indicator slows down and starts to decline, while the business activity continues to increase. Answering questions about relationships between variables calls for insight into the specific area and an elementary model or theory explaining the observations.

Time-Series Analysis

Time-series analysis is the second basic quantitative method for projecting future resource requirements. Time-series and other mathematical projection techniques are based on the assumption that the past pattern or structure of behavior and the relevant underlying forces will not change drastically in the near future. But rapid and unexpected changes in the immediate environment of an organization (competitors, product substitutes, business cycles, etc.) and the ways that a firm responds to these changes can render the projections of past patterns into the future unreliable. Therefore, projections obtained from the time-series analyses should never be used as a substitute for judgment. Instead, the projections should supplement judgment. Time-series analysis always involves an interplay of judgment and quantitative analysis.

Time-series analysis in organizations is generally used for statistical time analysis of quantitative historical data, such as sales, production capacity, added value, turnover, productivity, and R&D cost. The analysis consists of observing past patterns in these data and on the basis of past trends making projections for the future. The forecaster, by evaluating past patterns, is seeking to achieve a kind of predictability.

In order to effectively evaluate and utilize past patterns, a forecaster must be able to distinguish among the five basic analytical components of the time-series analysis.

- The *trend* is a pattern of long-term movement showing either the decline or growth rate of the set of data.
- The *seasonal component* is caused by regular weekly, monthly, or yearly influences such as paying habits, temperatures, harvests, and buying patterns.
- The *cyclical component* is distinguished from the seasonal component by its periodic irregularity and by its relatively low frequency (trade cycles, for example).
- The *random component* is completely erratic and cannot be tied to any known influence.
- The *incidental component* is an irregularity caused by a sudden price or tax change, a promotional activity, a strike, or an accident. This component may be attributed to a specific factor and may or may not happen again for many years.

Figure 16.   Five basic components of a time-series analysis.

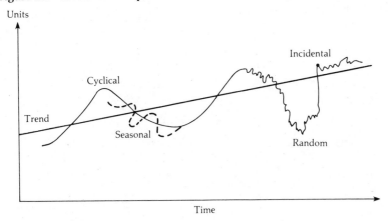

Figure 16 illustrates these components.

For forecasts that extend two or more years into the future, planners generally use time-series analysis to eliminate incidental irregularities and random fluctuations and to smooth out seasonal patterns. In short-term forecasting (for use in production and inventory control), planners try to interpret the random fluctuations, critical incidental irregularities, and seasonal variations that show up in the time-series analysis.

Time-Series Trend Analysis

Since human resources planning, as treated in this book, primarily concerns the organization's long-term human resources needs, human resources planners should understand trend analysis. The key to trend analysis is the shape of the historical data after cyclical, seasonal, random, and irregular variations have been considered and eliminated. Forecasters are interested in projecting past data into the future. They accomplish this by fitting a curve to the historical data and mathematically projecting this curve into the desired future time period. The two most relevant techniques in trend analysis are linear and nonlinear curve fitting.

Linear curve fitting. The simplest curve to fit to a series of historical observations is the straight line, as shown in Figure 16. This line may be drawn freehand on the graph. The straight line does not connect the data points, but it does reflect the trend they suggest. However,

Figure 17.   Least-squares regression line: minimized deviations of observations from straight trend line.

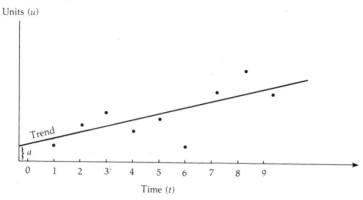

greater objectivity can be achieved if a statistical procedure is used to produce the line. The best-known statistical procedure for fitting a straight line to the data is the least-squares regression line: It minimizes the sums of the squares of the deviations of the points from that line. Figure 17 illustrates a least-squares regression line.

The equation for the simplest linear regression line (or estimate) is:

$$u = a + bt$$

where t is the time period, b is the slope of the function, and a is a constant that represents the value of u when $t = 0$ (see Figure 17). The least-squares method is a relatively simple technique described in all statistics textbooks.

Nonlinear curve fitting. It is often very tricky and inaccurate to depict long-term trends as straight lines. In reality, strategic problems require a nonlinear approach. For example, even when linear growth may be expected for a certain product during a period of time, saturation of the market for this product can bend the time series toward a saturation level. This would curve the line at the saturation point. This saturation level may even be followed by a period of decline, as illustrated by the model of the product life cycle shown in Figure 18. A similar rationale can also be used in projecting the future human resources requirements of a manufacturing company. The number of employees required to produce a product is usually tied to the number of units produced. However, projecting the linear relation-

Figure 18. Product life cycle model.

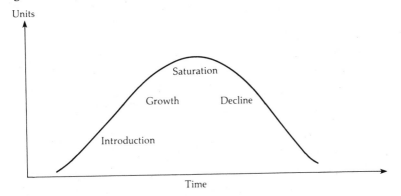

ship of the past into the future to determine human resources re-quirements without taking into consideration the impact of manu-facturing technology would be quite naive. Often, increased batch size leads to mass production and to economies of scale. Automation and other labor-saving devices may become economically profitable after the number of units produced reaches a certain level. There-fore, the linear relationship of past trends may not hold true in the future. As the number of units produced increases, the company may actually experience a reduction in its labor force.

In practice, only a small number of curves are used with any fre-quency to fit historical time-series data. Once forecasters have de-termined the best type of curve for the historical data, they can project the trend into the future. Valid extrapolation is possible only if the underlying factors that produced the historical shape continue to dominate.

For all practical purposes, the most common curves used in fore-casting economic, demographic, social, and technological develop-ments are:

Straight line	$U = a + bt$
Parabola	$U = a + bt + ct^2$
Simple exponential curve	$nU = a + bt$
Logistic curve	$U = \dfrac{S}{1 + ae^{-bt}}$

In these expressions, U stands for the units per time period t, n represents an exponential power, and S stands for the saturation

Figure 19.   Logistic or biological curve.

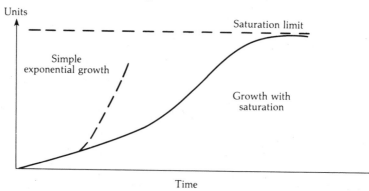

Units

Saturation limit

Simple
exponential growth

Growth with
saturation

Time

limit. The letters *a, b, c,* and *e* are constants (*e* is the natural base).

The shape of the logistic or biological curve is sketched in Figure 19. This trend mode is based on the assumption that social growth patterns are S-shaped. During a product's introduction period, its growth is exponential. Exponential growth assumes a constant relative growth pattern during specific time periods, although growth trends will never reach the extremes. Following the introduction period, growth trends tend to decline in a linear curve, finally becoming asymptotic to zero. Because of its shape, this curve is called an S curve. Examples of this type of growth pattern are readily available in the saturation phenomena of markets for products and services.

Model Building and Computer Simulation

Frequently, planners must combine several forecasting methods and techniques into models in order to obtain practical forecasting results. A logical forecasting sequence begins when forecasters solicit expert opinions concerning certain future conditions and analyze the general leading indicators. These activities are followed by detailed time-series analyses and model building.

A *model* is a mathematical representation of a real-world situation. By changing and manipulating the variables and parameters of the model, forecasters can discover the potential consequences of the changes. When a computer is used to alter the variables in a model, the process is called *computer simulation.*

Due to the increased capabilities and performance/price ratios of computers in the 1970s, model building and simulation methods have gained the attention of forecasters and planners. The computer era is making flexible simulations possible.

Developing an adequate and effective model for use in forecasting is a laborious job, but computers can facilitate the process. In computer simulation, many variations of a model may be produced. This leads to the construction of models that are more realistic than was once possible. However, the experience and intuition of the seasoned manager should never be replaced by such mathematical models. Managerial insights may be intelligently utilized in determining the different variables of the model and their basic modes of interaction, as approximated in the real world.

The major advantage of simulation by computer is the simultaneous consideration and manipulation of several variables. Computer simulation helps human resources forecasters match long-term human resources availability with future human resources requirements. Simulation enables management to project the effects of alternative policies regarding human resources flows within the organization (entries, promotions, transfers, and exits), using the almost unlimited possibilities provided by the manipulation of the variables in the model. Data on available personnel and on the human resources required for the planned period can be fed into the computer. The determinants of the long-term supply (given the existing personnel policies) and demand (given the strategic business plans) for human resources can be modified to produce the best fit. The alternatives can then be presented to management for its approval.

Selection of the Forecasting Method

Selection of the proper forecasting method depends on the goal and the time horizon of the planned activity, the availability of the sources and data, the time and cost limits set by management, and the importance of the decisions to be made on the basis of the forecast. This selection is also a matter of judgment and experience. Forecasts require subjective judgments, especially in the beginning of the forecasting process. Therefore, forecasts will always be debatable. For this reason, the managers who implement the plans should participate in the forecasting process from the beginning, by seeking facts and offering opinions. Forecasts should not be made by specialists isolated from managerial problems and decision-making processes.

Managers should understand the particular forecasting techniques used to produce data for their planning processes. The data resulting from the forecast must be reasonable and believable to the manager who will be making the plans. The quality of a forecast comes from using *several* techniques in combination with common sense, and not from a sophisticated use of just *one* technique.

Summary

Forecasting may be the most important part of HRP. It is the first step in the development of workable human resources plans. Forecasting is a systematic process designed to obtain the best available expectations in relation to the future availability and need for human resources.

Forecasting can best be understood within the HRP concept if it is viewed as part of the decision-making process. Therefore, the starting point in forecasting is problem identification. Following problem identification is the descriptive search. The data are then analyzed to establish causal and predictive relations between major variables. Finally, a decision is made concerning the organization's future human resources needs. This decision is incorporated into the human resources plan.

The selection of the appropriate forecasting method depends on the goals of the forecast, its time horizon, the availability of data, and time and cost limitations. In general, it is best to combine several methods rather than to use just one sophisticated technique.

Forecasts have two components. The first, analysis of status quo, is aimed at obtaining information on the current status of human resources. The second component involves the determination of future human resources requirements as well as the availability of these human resources during the planning period.

During the first phase of forecast development, an inventory of human resources is obtained, and the strengths and weaknesses of the organization's human resources are evaluated. Thus there is a quantitative and a qualitative element included in this phase. The quantitative element is the easier of the two to obtain, since it deals with lists of employees. It involves the determination of the current number of employees by department and functional specialization through the use of key position audits and Manning Tables. The qualitative element entails an evaluation of the overall strengths and weaknesses of the human resources. Although such qualitative information is available in the organization, it is highly decentralized. Therefore, it must be aggregated in a meaningful fashion in order to be useful. This is done through skills inventories and job analyses.

During the second phase of forecast development, future human resources requirements are projected. The most common projective techniques used in forecasting human resources demand and availability include subjective judgments by experts, interpretation of general macro indicators, time-series analysis, and model building.

CHAPTER 6

Considerations in Forecasting the Demand for Human Resources

Employers have to hire workers, establish working conditions, pay wages, and train and develop employees to meet changing human resources requirements. Changes in an organization's demand for human resources result from consumer behavior changes, product and service developments, and technological innovations. Employees change jobs for both professional and personal reasons, and the reasons may be, but are not always, related to wages. Changes in human resources requirements and job changes (or human resources mobility) influence both short- and long-term forecasts of human resources requirements.

An organization's requirement for labor is affected by structural, cyclical, and allocative changes in its environment. Structural changes may be caused by technological innovations and new product and service developments. Such innovations often require new job skills and can affect employees' competence on the job and their attitudes toward their work. Cyclical changes in, say, consumer spending affect unemployment and underemployment rates. Finally, changes in institutional images, product demand, and government wage and labor policies affect not only the allocation of labor to various occupations, industries, and regions but also the level of wages, locus of work, and leisure. Mobility of human resources is to be viewed in terms of employee attachment to industry, occupation, and region. Changes in employee attachment often depend on employees' knowledge of the labor market conditions, employer policies toward hiring and laying off personnel, and legal restrictions. Human resources mobility is also affected by protective agencies such as labor unions.

Forecasting human resources requirements is not just a matter of meeting projected production demands. It is a complicated process involving such complex factors as labor mobility, structural, cyclical, and allocative changes in an organization's environment. These considerations in forecasting the demand for human resources certainly make forecasting a key element of the HRP process.

Revenues, Productivity, and the Demand for Human Resources

The demand for human resources is a derived demand. It depends on the demand for the products or services that human resources produce. If the demand for a product or service increases, the demand for human resources usually increases. The demand for labor (D) is a function of an organization's marginal productivity. Marginal productivity (Pm) is the additional output (ΔO) that one additional unit of labor (ΔL) will produce when added to the current level of labor. Thus

$$Pm = \frac{\Delta O}{\Delta L}$$

However, demand for labor does not depend solely on the marginal productivity and the demand for the product. There will be low or no demand for labor, no matter how high the marginal productivity is, unless the product or service being produced has a positive marginal revenue. In other words, the additional product or service (ΔO) must be sold at a profit. The positive marginal revenue (Rm) justifies the additional labor. Similarly, even if the product or device has a high demand and produces a high revenue, there is no demand for additional labor if the marginal productivity is very low. Demand for labor is a question of cost and benefits.

The marginal revenue of the output is the additional revenue (ΔR) that the added output (ΔO) brings to the organization. In nonprofit organizations, revenue equals the value of the service delivered by that organization. So

$$Rm = \frac{\Delta R}{\Delta O}$$

The demand for labor (D) is a function of Pm and Rm:

$$D = f(Pm, Rm) = f\left(\frac{\Delta O}{\Delta L}, \frac{\Delta R}{\Delta O}\right)$$

To forecast the human resources requirements of an organization, one must consider how the demands for the products or services produced change and how these changes affect the actual number and type of personnel employed. For all practical purposes, the change in the demand for the product or service should be converted into changes in the number of human resources required to produce the desired amount of output. This conversion process can be accomplished with the use of the appropriate predictor(s), a factor to which the variable that has to be predicted is related. For instance, the relevant factor for predicting the future demand for faculty at a university may be the number of expected students. If projections on the number of students are available, all the university officials have to do is relate the number of students to the number of instructors. For a supermarket, the dollar volume of sales may be the relevant factor on which forecasts of human resources requirements can be based. The appropriate business predictor for a steel company could be tons of steel.

Selection of an Appropriate Predictor

A critical step in forecasting is the selection of an appropriate predictor. The business factors forecasters use in converting output projections into human resources projections must relate to the primary nature of the business. If future output projections are made in terms of volume, the business factor used in the conversion process should be the projected volume of the output. On the other hand, if business forecasts are made in terms of gross sales, the dollar value of the sales should be used as an indicator in projecting future human resources needs. In the university example, it would be irrelevant to use the research budget of the university to predict the future needs for instructors.

Projections for an entire organization's human resources requirements can be misleading, especially if the organization is large and there are significant differences between its units or divisions. In such cases, human resources requirements are forecasted in terms specific to the divisions. In multiproduct organizations business plans are prepared at the division and/or plant level and consolidated at corporate headquarters. The need for divisional forecasting is not so apparent in small organizations with little or no product and market diversification.

Translating Strategic Plans into Human Resources Requirements

An organization's future human resources requirements depend strictly on its planned activities. SBP, which anticipates changes in market conditions, the economy, competition, and finances, is the corporate instrument for setting organizational objectives.

The problem now is to translate these long-range business plans into relatively specific human resources requirements. This can be done by translating planned activities into tasks that have to be accomplished and combining these tasks into functions that correspond to employees' skills, experience, and educational levels. In small organizations it is possible to consider all tasks directly, but in larger organizations a more structured investigation is necessary.

In large organizations, work-study techniques can be used to determine the relationships between projected output and human resources requirements. However, these techniques suit short-term operational forecasts only. Generally, short-term forecasts are made at the plant or operating-unit level and are good for less than one year. Estimating medium- and long-term human resources requirements usually requires aggregate or global data on output projections. In practice, forecasters generally use more than one predictor.

Commonly Used Predictors in Industry

As mentioned in Chapter 5, several indicators and methods can be used to forecast future developments and events. The selection of the appropriate method and indicators for forecasting human resources requirements depends on the time horizon of the plans and the nature of the available data. Most of the forecasts are based on projecting past patterns, revealed through time-series analysis, into the future.

In general, future human resources requirements are derived from

Table 1. Bases used in forecasting human resources requirements in industrial organizations.

Functional Departments	Human Resources Requirements Determined by:
Manufacturing	Value added + productivity per plant or capacity group
Research	Total sales
Product or service development	Sales per business unit and competitive position
Sales	Sales per business unit and competitive position
Market research	Competitive position
Technical after-sales service	Total sales + product characteristics
Purchasing	Type and amount of materials purchased
Accounting	Value added and degree of automation
Personnel	Total personnel available

the forecasted demand for the products or services offered to the market. In manufacturing, the value added—a product's selling price minus the costs of the materials and supplies needed to produce the item—is one of the most common indicators used in forecasting human resources requirements. Table 1 summarizes the different indicators commonly used in forecasting the human resources requirements of the various units of an industrial organization.

To forecast human resources requirements in manufacturing, often the total value added for the enterprise is divided according to each plant or even in terms of capacity groups within the specific plant. On the other hand, in forecasting future requirements for research personnel, total sales turnover of the company is used as a predictor. In sales and product development, human resources requirements are forecasted according to planned sales turnover in separate business units or divisions of the company.

In conclusion, selecting an appropriate predictor is probably one of the most difficult tasks in converting business activities into human resources requirements. Table 1 illustrates the most common predictors used in determining human resources requirements in different departments of industrial organizations. In manufacturing, for instance, value added and productivity per plant or capacity group are the most widely used predictors of human resources requirements as a result of changes in the firm's output.

Establishing Relationships Between Predictors and Human Resources Requirements

Selecting the appropriate predictor or indicator is only the first step in forecasting human resources requirements. The second step is determining the operational relationships between the predictor and the personnel requirements. Just how does the factor used as a predictor affect labor requirements? Are changes in the predictor and personnel requirements proportional? If so, in what ratios? Determining the operational relationships between predictors and human resources requirements can be difficult, but it is one of the most critical stages in the forecasting process.

As long as forecasters understand that the relationship between a predictor (independent variable X) and the human resources requirements (dependent variable Y) is not one-to-one, they can introduce limits and conditions that appropriately qualify the relationship to give it validity. For example, product volume may be the key predictor upon which the strategic business plans for a cement plant are built. However, it may take almost as many workers to operate a modern plant at half capacity as at full capacity. From a technological and economic point of view, a 20 percent drop in the production of cement will not have a significant effect on the number of employees needed to manufacture the cement. But a 40 percent drop in output may lead to a 10 percent cutback of workers in the manufacturing department, while a 60 percent drop may require the total shutdown of the plant (see Figure 20). Forecasters must consider the proportional relationships between the predictor and labor requirements when they select the key variables on which they base their forecasts. The more the forecasters know about the variables—and how they affect one another—the greater the accuracy they can achieve in their forecasts.

Misunderstanding or misusing predictors is not the only cause of poor forecasting. Too frequently, forecasters fail to anticipate the effects of new technologies in the manufacturing process. Changes in technology will nearly always affect the predictor/resource requirement relationship. If the strategic business planners predict technological changes, but don't tell the human resources planners, the forecasts of human resources requirements are not likely to be accu-

Figure 20.   Relationship between used capacity and human resources requirements.

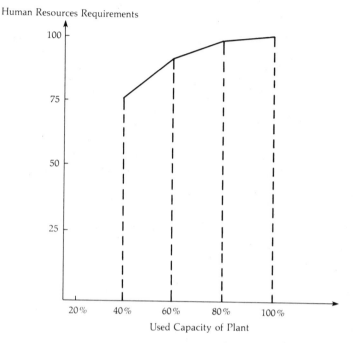

rate. If human resources planners are not in close touch with strategic business planners and new developments, they will not be able to include the impact of the expected changes in technology on the relationship between the predictor and the human resources variable. This is another reason why HRP and SBP should be integrated. In an integrated approach, such technological changes can be taken into consideration. Also, when HRP and SBP are integrated, the human resources planners are better able to observe the future direction of technological change.

Productivity Ratios

Output per employee is defined as labor productivity. Future human resources requirements are not affected only by the output, by the process used to convert the inputs into outputs, or by minimum labor requirements. Forecasters must also consider the rate of change of productivity. For instance, the productivity of the same category of labor used to produce the same product may have increased, decreased, or stayed the same over the previous years. Changes in productivity ratios may indicate changes in the combination of inputs, which, in turn, may have been caused by improvements in inputs and processes.

To effectively forecast long-term human resources requirements, planners need the productivity ratios for the previous five or more years. As a rule of thumb, one needs to use data from at least as many years in the recent past as the number of years in the forecast period. That is, if an organization wants to forecast its needs for human resources eight years from now, it will need productivity figures for the past eight years.

Productivity can be measured in terms of time standards and/or labor inputs:

$$\text{Productivity} = \frac{\text{output}}{\text{standards}} \quad \text{and/or} \quad \frac{\text{output}}{\text{labor input}}$$

Highly routine and repetitive tasks generally lend themselves to engineered work standards. Work studies can reveal standard times per unit of output. Matching the actual production time to the standard provides a measure of existing production efficiency. For example, if engineered standards are set to define a "standard of normal" amount of output per punch press operator, the productivity of an individual punch press operator could be based on the estimated number of parts punched (meeting quality requirements) over a specified time. Obviously, though, engineered work standards are not easy to apply to many jobs. Engineered work standards are not appropriate for complex and nonroutine work, even if the output can be measured in a tangible way. The productivity of punch press operators in the organization could also be defined as the number of parts actually punched per year, divided by the number of operators. This is a common way to define productivity.

The important element in establishing productivity trends is to be as specific as possible with respect to human resources categories and labor market conditions. If possible, productivity trends must be established for all critical human resources categories in the organization. If an organization is forecasting its demand for human resources in terms of labor grades, productivity ratios must be determined separately for all critical labor grades. On the other hand, if

the forecast is for the total number of employees, a productivity figure for the entire organization would be sufficient.

An Illustration: Forecasting Human Resources Requirements in ABC Company

The ABC Company is a very profitable, well-managed, and rapidly growing producer of concrete products. The company started in
1973 in one town, producing and selling originally conceived and developed concrete products used in the building and agricultural
markets. In 1979, to reduce physical distribution costs, the company
built its second plant 200 miles north of its original location. At the
end of 1980, the company employed 54 persons at its two sites.
Table 2 gives relevant data on the company's operation over a five-
year period.

The data reveal that ABC's purchases as a percentage of the production costs remained constant over the five-year period at about 39
percent. The value added for ABC was around 61 percent over the
same period. Wages and salaries averaged about 29 percent of the
production costs.

Table 3 shows the total number of employees subdivided into

Table 2. Data on ABC Company over last five years.

	1976	1977	1978	1979	1980
			(In thousands)		
Production	$1,180	$1,590	$2,080	$2,470	$3,360
Purchases	480	650	760	880	1,290
Added values	700	940	1,310	1,590	2,070
Wages and salaries	340	520	610	670	990

Table 3. Number of employees at ABC Company over last five years.

	1976	1977	1978	1979	1980
Production workers	19	25	27	30	37
Technical staff	3	4	5	5	7
Supervisory personnel	3	4	5	6	10
Total	25	33	37	41	54

Table 4. Value added per manufacturing worker.

	1976	1977	1978	1979	1980
Value added per worker	$36,800	$37,600	$48,500	$51,300	$55,900

three groups, for the same period. From our analysis of the data in Tables 2 and 3 we may conclude that the value added per production worker over the last five years increased continuously, as shown in Table 4. For instance, in 1976, when there were 19 production workers and the overall value added was $700,000, on the average a production worker's contribution to the overall value added was $36,800 ($700,000 ÷ 19 = $36,800).

On the basis of the results of the foregoing years, the commercial and technical capabilities of the firm, and the expected market possibilities, management forecasted a yearly production growth of 30 percent for the coming years. Management now wanted to forecast its human resources requirements for different categories according to their strategic business plan.

Management based its forecast on the number of required manufacturing employees on the planned production growth of 30 percent and on two critical factors from the past five years: the 61 percent value-added figure and the increased value added per manufacturing worker. Figure 21 shows management's projection. A freehand line connecting the past data shows the realized value added per manufacturing worker in ABC Company. Forecasted value added for the planned years is shown by the broken freehand line. The projected value added per production employee for the years 1981 to 1983 is $62,000, $67,000, and $72,000, respectively. The results of the approximated calculations and forecasts for the years 1981, 1982, and 1983 are shown in Table 5. The number of production workers required for 1981, 1982, and 1983 is calculated by dividing the projected total value added by the per employee value added. For instance, in 1981 the ABC company expects to have 43 employees ($2,670,000 ÷ $62,000 = 43).

The expansion of the production line required new machines that had to be built by the technical personnel. This required about a 50 percent increase in their numbers for the coming years. The projection of the increase in the number of technical personnel to manufacture and maintain the new machines and equipment used in

Figure 21. Realized and predicted values added per manufacturing worker.

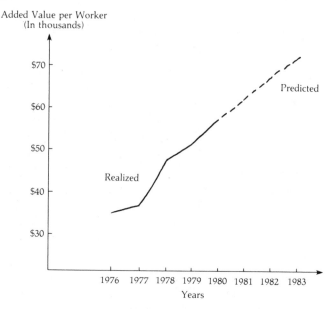

production was based on actual production figures. That is, if a machine requires two employees to build and maintain it, then two machines will require four employees. Management subjectively estimated that the marketing group as well as the accounting department and supervisory personnel needed to be strengthened. A 70 percent increase in supervisory, accounting, and marketing personnel was estimated over the next three years.

Table 5. Realized (1980) and forecasted human resources requirements in ABC Company at the end of 1980.

	1980	1981	1982	1983
Production ($000)	3,360	4,370	5,680	7,380
Value added ($000)	2,070	2,670	3,460	4,500
Value added per production worker ($000)	56.9	62	67	72
Required production workers	37	43	52	63
Technical staff	7	9	10	11
Supervisors, marketing, accounting	10	13	15	17
Total human resources required	54	65	77	91

Forecasting Human Resources Requirements Subjectively

In organizations or specific situations where it is difficult to quantify future output estimates, subjective forecasting methods will yield better results than attempts to quantify data for use with objective forecasting techniques. This is especially true in service organizations where production functions cannot be quantified for projection into the future. In such cases a subjective approach directly forecasting future organizational human resources requirements is more practical and will also yield better results than attempting to quantify production estimates and converting them into projected human resources requirements. Of the many subjective forecasting methods available, the Delphi technique provides forecasters with the best way to synthesize what experts think are the likely future developments in an industry. The Delphi method of querying experts to achieve consensus and other subjective methods are discussed in Chapter 5.

A 1974 study by the U.S. Civil Service Commission illustrates the validity of the Delphi concept in forecasting executive personnel needs.[1] The service wanted to determine whether opening a new training center—one possible decision—would increase the demand for executive personnel in two years. At the same time, the service needed to forecast the likelihood of a cut in its budget—another possibility. The service followed a three-stage process to forecast the executive personnel requirements:

1. Dividing the forecast problem into its relevant factors.
2. Gathering and quantifying the subjective preferences and probability judgments of experts.
3. Converting the quantified opinions and factual data into a schematic depicting the predictions.

The actual forecasting problem was split into two elements: the probability of a budget cut and the probability of a new training center. Using the Delphi technique, a coordinator from the Civil Service personnel department questioned 16 knowledgeable individuals in the service on the two possibilities. (Only the training center problem will be discussed here.)

Suppose 10 of the 16 people questioned expected that the new training center would be established. This can be interpreted to give a probability of 0.625, or 10 out of 16, that a new training center would be built. On this basis, the coordinator began to develop human resources plans. This included recruitment, selection, orientation, training, and remuneration of the personnel for the new training center. Had the probability of the expected outcome been greater—say, 0.8—the service would have developed more detailed human resources plans. In the actual case, only very broad plans were prepared for staffing the training center in the first year. Plans were included for training certain key personnel who would be transferred to the new training center from other parts of the organization. Other activities involved preparing organization charts, analyzing functions, grouping positions, and developing plans for recruiting top-level personnel for the new training center.

The following year a new expected outcome would be obtained, and depending on the estimated probability of the establishment of the new training center, human resources plans concerning the staffing of the new office would either be altered or canceled. Human resources plans would be prepared with more specificity and with a greater reach if the probability for the creation of the training center has increased. The opposite would be true if the probability has decreased.

Strategic Decisions to Reduce Employment

Well-managed organizations, when they forecast their personnel needs, consider how to adjust employment levels when their demand for human resources drops. Most organizations, when faced with small cutbacks, rely on normal attrition due to turnover and retirements to reduce employment. But when larger cutbacks in personnel are necessary, management must make certain policy decisions about different methods of reducing employment. Such decisions are strategic and require advance planning. They are certainly an important element of HRP. An important factor in determining the size of the reduction in human resources is the organization's choice between laying off employees and reducing their working hours. An organization's ability or willingness to produce for stock is also important in determining the size of employment reduction. Another factor is the degree of labor force mobility between different business units within the same company. A very important factor is the pressure from unions to minimize employment cuts.

Once management decides to reduce the number of employees, it must decide who should be terminated or laid off. Most organizations tend to lay off marginal performers first. However, if the organization is unionized and there are many employees of long standing, the policy of dismissing marginal performers has many flaws. As a result, most organizations use some form of seniority-based layoffs. In order to do so, however, the organization must first decide how to determine seniority. Certainly, the method used to determine seniority will affect which employee(s) will be dismissed. The most common methods of counting years of service are in terms of job, department, and company-wide employment. Which system best suits a particular organization depends on circumstances unique to that organization. In many cases the method is determined through negotiations with the union. Nevertheless, management can arrive at a solution acceptable to all or most parties involved if it follows well-established criteria.

Criteria in Choosing Among Alternative Seniority Systems

In choosing criteria to evaluate alternative seniority systems, most organizations consider (1) the degree to which the system helps the organization retain its most valuable personnel and minimize personnel moves as a result of extensive bumping, and (2) how easily the system can be administered when the situation returns to normal. We will look at each of these criteria individually.

Retaining valuable personnel. Organizations with or without a seniority system are interested in retaining their most valuable employees. Too narrow a seniority system (job seniority) may be costly to the company. Assume that there is a temporary slack period in the company's need for skilled electricians. A job-related seniority system would require laying off electricians. If these electricians accept employment elsewhere, the company may have to undertake expensive recruitment and training programs for new electricians when business picks up. It is therefore in the interests of the organization to select a seniority system that enables it to keep its more valuable personnel.

Bumping. Putting any seniority system into effect creates a series of undesirable personnel movements. A good employee may be bumped from his or her job by a senior employee from another department who was bumped by a person of even higher seniority. In large companies personnel cutbacks may generate thousands of job shifts, causing nightmares for personnel administrators as well as line managers.

Return to normal production. When an organization starts to bring its production capacity back to pre-layoff levels, it begins to recall employees. The order in which employees are recalled may affect the speed with which normal production is reattained. Obviously, the company is interested in recalling first its most valuable employees. Therefore, it is to the advantage of the company to have a policy enabling such a practice. This could be the recall of individuals according to job needs and not according to the generally accepted premise of last one out, first one recalled.

Summary

An important consideration in forecasting an organization's future human resources requirements is the linkage between its human input and the expected changes in its output. An organization's demand for labor is affected by structural, cyclical, and allocative changes in its environment. A major problem in HRP is converting forecasted changes in the level of output or services into changes in the organization's human resources requirements. An important consideration in making the linkage between changes in output and changes in human resources requirements is the selection of an appropriate predictor. A predictor is a factor that relates changes in output or service to changes in human resources requirements. Another important consideration is labor productivity.

CHAPTER 7

Forecasting the Attrition of Human Resources

In this chapter we will discuss how human resources data can be analyzed to provide human resources availability estimates to the planners during the SBP process. Forecasting the availability of human resources can be difficult, and even impossible, unless relevant human resources data inventories exist. Building practical human resources data inventories and information systems is discussed in Chapters 8 and 9. Human resources data inventories provide an organization with meaningful information on the current status of its human resources. This information is useful in the early stages of the SBP process. However, as strategic business plans take shape, planners need refined estimates of the availability of human resources. Refined forecasts of internal human resources supply show what the current organizational workforce will look like in the years covered by the plans. To be of use in the SBP process, the forecasts must be specific to the personnel categories that the organization uses to classify its human resources.

Forecasts of the internal supply of human resources are crucial in the integrated planning process, that is, when human resources inputs are used in determining business objectives. Integration cannot occur unless forecasters provide meaningful information at appropriate planning levels. The process of forecasting the internal supply of human resources starts when the planners request information on the availability of certain types of personnel. The human resources availability forecast should be worded simply and transmitted immediately to the planners. That is, if the planners need only general information on the various functions of employees, the forecasters should not include in their reports irrelevant personal data on all the employees. Details, where generalizations would do, will hinder rather than facilitate the planners' work.

Many techniques are available for forecasting what the internal supply of human personnel will be in two, five, or more years. The key to such forecasts is predicting the turnover rate. The turnover rates include employees who will leave the organization for any reason: voluntary retirement, forced retirement, medical or disability retirement, death, resignation, or leave without pay (where the employee is expected to return in the future). In predicting the turnover rate, forecasters must also consider the consequences of promotions and transfers within the organization.

Much of the earlier work on turnover rates was economic in nature. It considered the crude wastage rate by dividing the average number of employees for a given time period by the number of employees who left during that period. The percentage was then projected, by various statistical techniques, into the future period for which plans were being made.

Initially, the forecasters used trend analysis techniques to calculate three- to five-year averages of separations in broad categories of jobs. The mean number of separations for the three- to five-year period was then projected for the coming year. However, unless the organization is very stable, this type of historical forecast is not adequate because the crude wastage rate is not particularly revealing. It can be useful for analyzing turnover for specific areas, such as job categories, departments, age, sex, and reasons for leaving, but not for calculating the average turnover rate.

Various sophisticated methods of statistical analysis and mathematical models offer ways of overcoming the questionable validity of the historical approach. In this section, however, we will concentrate on the collection and storage of data that can be used in turnover analysis. The type of information and how it is collected and stored are more important than the quantitative techniques used in projecting the information into the future. The reasoning here is simple. Analyzing the variables that influence turnover and meaningfully categorizing the turnover data are of primary importance. Methods and procedures in analyzing the turnover rate take precedence over statistical techniques and mathematical models of forecasting.

Factors Influencing Turnover Rates

Most analyses of employee turnover focus first on motivational factors specific to the individual and on the organizational environment, and then project the impact of these factors on the number of resignations, retirements, and the like. A number of important generalizations about employee turnover rates have been documented.[1] Traditionally, employee turnover rates decrease as the length of service increases, decrease as the skill requirements on jobs increase, are higher among women than men, are higher among married women than single women, and differ widely among organizations.

Because the predictability of the generalizations has been documented, it provides a useful basis for forecasting turnover rates. For example, a company now hiring more women than before should anticipate a higher turnover rate in the coming years. But knowing the general characteristics of turnover rates helps planners only in limited ways. The generalizations do not lend themselves to specific analysis, nor do they account for the uniqueness of an organization or its operating circumstances. Over the years, many causal variables influencing turnover rates—more specific than those just mentioned—have been identified. Examples of such specific variables follow. Unfortunately, empirical evidence of their impact on employee turnover is only fragmentary.

Organizational Factors[2]

- Perceived roadblocks in personal and professional growth within the present organization.
- Perceived limits on personal and professional growth within the present organization.
- Dissatisfaction with the location of the organization (for personal or family reasons).
- Lack of job security.

Job Factors[3]

- Uninteresting nature of the job.
- Dissatisfaction with pay.
- Dissatisfaction with policies concerning salary increases, promotions, career development transfers, and other related personnel matters.

- Dissatisfaction with conditions surrounding the job.
- Dissatisfaction with supervisors, peers, and/or subordinates.
- Lack of autonomy in performing the job.

Competitive Factors[4]

- Better-paying offer.
- New job perceived to be more satisfactory in some aspects (other than pay) when compared to present job.

Personal Factors[5]

- Reasons for working no longer exist (retirement from full-time employment).
- Working no longer attractive when opportunity costs are considered.

Organizational and job factors are generally treated under the concept of job satisfaction, and the evidence indicates a direct relationship between job dissatisfaction and turnover. But forecasters who use causal factors to predict employee turnover encounter several problems. The first problem is the sheer number of factors that could contribute to an individual's decision to leave the organization. The factors—almost any combination of those listed—could be so numerous that they resist meaningful analysis. Furthermore, reasons for leaving an organization could be different depending on the length of time an individual has been in the organization. Tavistock Institute, which carried out lengthy research on the various career phases and turnover patterns, identified three career phases during which causes for turnover could be difficult: the period of induction crisis, the period of differential transit, and the period of settled connection.[6] These phases act as intervening variables, making a difficult analysis even more difficult. Pay, for example, may contribute to turnover if the individual is in one career phase, but it may have no impact if the employee is in another phase.

A second important problem in using causal factors to predict turnover is related to the method of data collection. In most cases, causal factors have been identified by some type of exit interview in which the organization attempts to discover the person's reasons for leaving at that time. But information gathered at exit interviews may not be valid because employees generally do not give their real reasons for leaving. Employees have few incentives for being candid or honest because they are terminating their relations with the organization. Moreover, they may hide the real reasons if they are concerned about future references. Using causal variables in forecasting turnover is at best difficult. It requires people with behavioral science skills. In short, the large number of causal factors and the variety of the special conditions on which the causality depends, plus the unreliability of the data collected from the exit interviews, prevent many organizations from undertaking meaningful turnover analysis.

Categorizing Turnover Data

If planners can meaningfully categorize statistical information on turnover, they can reduce their dependence on causal factors in determining turnover rates. This does not mean that organizations should not try to isolate and define causal factors. Determining causality aids forecasting; more important, it provides the only way to reduce the turnover that inhibits organizational performance. However, since in this section our interest is in forecasting turnover efficiently and reliably, we will concentrate on the use of statistical turnover data without elaborating too much on the factors contributing to turnover (causality). We contend that by properly recording and categorizing turnover data, an organization can increase the accuracy of its predictions.

Turnover data should be recorded in at least these categories: the employee's department, age, sex, marital status, position title, and length of service with the organization. The analysis is based on the assumption that depending on these characteristics, the choices made by individuals to resign or to retire will exhibit a probabilistic frequency pattern. The validity of this assumption is greater in large organizations than in small and medium-size ones. Once forecasters have collected information on employee turnover rates per category for at least three years, they can predict the turnover rate with reasonable accuracy.

Forecasting Employee Turnover

As mentioned earlier, turnover is caused primarily by resignation, retirement, death, disability retirement, and unpaid leave. Of these categories, resignations and retirement account for more than 97

Figure 22.   Steps in forecasting turnover rates.

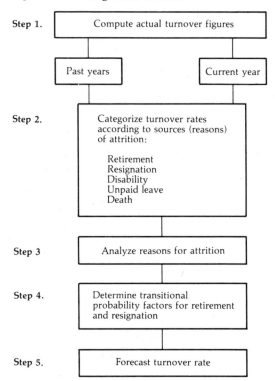

percent of the turnover in nonmilitary organizations.[7] We will concentrate on these two categories in our explanation of how to compute actual and probable attrition in an organization. Figure 22 indicates the steps to be followed in forecasting employee turnover.

Step One: Computing Actual Turnover Figures

The first step in forecasting turnover is to compute current and past turnover figures with the desired degree of specificity. For instance, one can compute turnover figures for all managers, all employees, all engineers, white-collar versus blue-collar employees, all manufacturing employees, mechanical engineers, electrical engineers, and the like.

Specificity of the information should be meaningful to the users of the information. It depends, then, on the organization's purpose in predicting its internal labor supply. The total number of personnel in an organization could be divided into several segments according to groups of pay grades (the broadest categorization), job families, sub-job families, and job titles (the most specific categorization). Categorization is discussed in detail in Chapter 8.

Many large organizations use broad categorizations of their personnel for strategic planning purposes. It is quite common to find employees classified in 20 groups of pay grades. Under such a system, turnover rates can be computed for each pay grade. On the other hand, more refined forecasts can be made in terms of job families.

Depending on its size and product or service, an organization can have over a thousand positions. Employees can then be grouped according to their position titles: clerk/typists, industrial engineers, market researchers, account executives, and so on. Accordingly, turnover rates can be calculated for the given year(s) for each of these specific categories.

Step Two: Computing Turnover According to Sources of Attrition

Breaking down the turnover in terms of the sources of or reasons for attrition is the next step. As already mentioned, resignations and retirements account for over 97 percent of all attritions in nonmilitary organizations. Of course, there are exceptions, especially in high-risk civilian organizations such as police and fire departments. In such organizations a higher percentage of attrition is due to death or disability retirement. Another source of attrition is unpaid leave of absence, but it makes up only an insignificant percentage of the total turnover figure.

Figure 23 illustrates how turnover can be divided according to its sources of attrition. In this example, employees are classified according to pay grades or broad groups of job families. Total attrition for each grade is obtained by adding up resignations, retirements, deaths, disability retirements, and other sources. The process is repeated for each category. Forecasters should prepare tables for each available year to develop a historical data source to be used in predicting employee turnover rates.

Step Three: Analyzing Each Source of Attrition

Resignations. Knowing the percentage of attrition due to resignations in a given job category is important. However, for predicting turnover, planners need a detailed analysis of each attrition source. Introducing certain intervening variables—age, marital status, length

Figure 23.   Classification of turnover data according to sources of attrition.

Pay Grade Category	Resignations		Retirement		Death/Disability Retirement		Other		Total Attrition	
	N	(%)	N	(%)	N	(%)	N	(%)	N	(%)
1										(100)
2										(100)
3										(100)
4										(100)
19										(100)
20										(100)
Total										(100)

of service—increases the predictive value of the turnover analysis. Consider age, for example. Young employees resign from their jobs more often than do older employees. An organization using a meaningful classification of its employees by age groups can get a clear picture of the frequency of resignations in different jobs by various age groups. An analysis of the historical data on certain job categories may reveal that a large number of the employees who resign are under 26, while few who are over 41 do so.

Marital status can also affect the forecasting of resignations. Historically, married employees have been more stable than single employees. Similarly, by classifying employees who have resigned from positions in a given job category according to their marital status, one can determine whether the generalization about stability holds true for a particular organization. If there is a significant difference, this factor should be introduced in forecasting turnover in given categories of employment.

Length of service also enters into the resignation picture. It has been said in industry that the longer an employee stays in an organization, the less likely it is that that employee will resign. Some organizations have found that employees who resign can be grouped into three categories according to the length of their service. An employee's period of orientation, which covers the first two years of service, can be characterized as the indoctrination crisis. While undergoing the initial socialization process, the employee is not sure about the organization. At the same time, the employee's attempt to personalize the immediate environment is slow to bear fruit. The employee's commitment to the organization is not fully nurtured.

Thus the employee's continued reassessment of the situation contributes to the decision to leave or to remain in the organization.

The middle period starts after the individual has become established in the organization and is exploring alternative organizations for faster career advancement or career change. The employee's move to another organization can be vertical, diagonal, or lateral. The move is vertical if the individual advances in his or her line of work, but in another organization. An engineer becoming a supervisor or a clerk becoming a secretary are typical examples of vertical moves. Diagonal movement involves a career change to a better job and improved conditions with another organization. Lateral movement, on the other hand, involves either a career or just a job change into another organization but with no perceived improvement of the conditions or job expectations. Lateral changes may be precipitated by family pressure, health, and the like, as well as by career moves. Of course, some job and career changes can be downward. However, it is difficult to operationalize such moves because individuals rarely will admit that their new positions are inferior to their old ones. At best, they will rationalize the move, seeing it as lateral rather than downward.

The last period usually starts five to ten years before the employee reaches retirement age. Here the person considers one last move before ending a working career. As with moves in the middle period, the final move can be vertical, diagonal, or lateral.

Clearly, the mobility rate among all employees is much higher in the first period, the indoctrination period, than in the second and third periods. Similarly, the turnover rate is higher in the second period than in the third period. In the stable periods between these distinct phases—say, after employees have settled into their jobs but before they contemplate a change—the resignations associated with length of service are comparatively low. An analysis of the resignation patterns in terms of length of service can provide an organization with a reasonably accurate picture of its future. An organization's strategic business plans may require that in five years about 40 percent of all the engineers employed will be in their first career period. This organization should expect a much higher attrition rate among its engineers than it is facing today. Therefore, the company should be prepared to either recruit more engineers or make the employment conditions more attractive than they are today to maintain the existing level of employee turnover.

Retirement. Attrition caused by retirement can be analyzed in the same way as attrition due to resignation. However, the analysis is simpler. There will be no need to categorize attritions caused by retirement according to age groups, marital status, or length of service because of the relatively small numbers involved. Generally, it is sufficient to record the decisions of the individuals who have reached their first year of retirement eligibility, second year, third year, and so on.

To establish a base of historical data, planners should record, for each year, the number of employees eligible for retirement, according to their year of eligibility. The actual number of persons retiring in each eligibility category should also be recorded. To define a trend that has predictive value, planners should accumulate retirement data for at least the past three years.

Recent federal and state legislation in the United States has eliminated compulsory retirement. However, for all practical purposes, organizations can determine the likelihood of employees staying on the job after becoming eligible for retirement. One or two individuals will always continue working beyond the upper limit the organization has informally established.

Death and disability retirement. A very small proportion of the attrition could be due to deaths and disability retirement. Actual figures should be collected for several years and classified in terms of job categories. Direct projections of this attrition, based on historical data, can be made. These data are also readily available in an organization's safety records, which are required by law.

Step Four: Determining Transitional Probability Factors

Computing transitional probability factors for the two most important types of attrition—resignations and retirement—is the next step in forecasting human resources turnover. The transitional probability factor is the modifier of the traditional trend analysis used in projecting attrition rates for different categories of the workforce. A transitional probability factor is a linear regression modifier that primarily influences movement from one time period to another. It is relatively easy to calculate the transitional probability figure: Divide the number of resignations in a given employee category in a given year by the total number of employees in that category at the beginning of the year.

To illustrate the computation of a transitional probability factor, we will follow the procedure that a major U.S. bank uses to forecast resignations. In this case, the bank wants to project the number of employees in labor grade 10 who will retire in 1982. Employee age, length of service, and, to a lesser extent, marital status can be important intervening variables in the forecasting process. In this example, we use age and length of service to compute the transitional probability factor of attrition by resignation. Though the case is hypothetical, the figures for the personnel in labor grade 10 are real. Table 6 presents the bank's resignation figures for 1977 through 1981.

Age. From the data presented in Table 6, we can establish that during the five-year period an average of 219 employees per year in labor grade 10 resigned. Of these individuals, 17.5 percent were under 21 and 19.2 percent were between 21 and 25 years of age. The results of these computations are shown in the "Five-Year Mean" column in Table 6.

The next step in establishing a weighted transitional probability factor is to superimpose on Table 6 the actual number of employees, categorized by age groups, that the bank had in this labor grade. Table 7 shows this superimposition. It shows, for example, that there were 3,000 employees in labor grade 10 at the beginning of 1981; by the end of the year, 200 people had resigned. Thirty of these employees resigning in 1981 were under 21 years of age. Table 7 presents similar information for each age group over the five-year period. The last column in Table 7 lists the specific transitional probability factor to be used in projecting probable resignations for the forecast period (in this case 1982).

The transitional probability factor is obtained by dividing total number of resignations for the five-year period, as classified by age categories, by the total number of employees for the same period in that age category. To illustrate:

$$.15 \begin{pmatrix} \text{transitional} \\ \text{probability} \\ \text{factor} \end{pmatrix} = \frac{192 \text{ (total employees under 21} \\ \text{during 1977–1981 who resigned)}}{1,310 \text{ (total employees under 21 during 1977–1981)}}$$

We will illustrate the forecasting process with a concrete example. Suppose that at the beginning of 1982 the bank has 3,200 employees, distributed as shown in Table 8. By multiplying the actual number of employees in each age category by its corresponding transitional probability factor, we can forecast attritions caused by resignations during that period.

Table 6. Distribution of employees in labor grade 10 who resigned in 1981, 1980, 1979, 1978, and 1977 according to age group.

Age Category	1981 N	1981 (%)	1980 N	1980 (%)	1979 N	1979 (%)	1978 N	1978 (%)	1977 N	1977 (%)	Five-Year Mean N	Five-Year Mean (%)
< 21	30	(15)	40	(18.2)	39	(16.6)	40	(17.8)	43	(20)	38.4	(17.5)
21–25	35	(17.5)	43	(20)	47	(20)	45	(20)	40	(18.6)	42	(19.2)
26–30	30	(15)	40	(18.2)	42	(17.9)	40	(17.8)	38	(17.7)	38	(17.3)
31–40	45	(22.5)	38	(17.3)	42	(17.9)	38	(16.9)	40	(18.6)	40.6	(18.6)
41–50	20	(10)	23	(10.5)	26	(11.1)	24	(10.7)	23	(10.7)	23.2	(10.6)
51–60	25	(12.5)	26	(11.8)	30	(12.8)	27	(12)	23	(10.7)	26.2	(12.0)
> 60	15	(7.5)	10	(4.5)	9	(3.8)	11	(4.9)	8	(3.7)	10.6	(4.9)
Total	200	(100)	220	(100)	235	(100)	225	(100)	215	(100)	219	(100)

Table 7. Distribution of total number of employees in labor grade 10 and resignations, according to age group.

Age	Category	1981	1980	1979	1978	1977	Five-Year Total	Transitional Probability Factor for Resignations in Different Age Groups
21	A	240	270	280	260	260	1,310	.15
	B	30	40	39	40	43	192	
21–25	A	450	455	500	490	455	2,350	.09
	B	35	43	47	45	40	210	
26–30	A	300	310	355	350	305	1,620	.12
	B	30	40	42	40	38	190	
31–40	A	760	745	775	770	730	3,780	.05
	B	45	38	42	38	40	203	
41–50	A	740	755	780	770	750	3,795	.03
	B	20	23	26	24	23	116	
51–60	A	300	350	360	350	310	1,670	.08
	B	25	26	30	27	23	131	
61+	A	210	215	210	225	190	1,050	.05
	B	15	10	9	11	8	53	
Total	A	3,000	3,100	3,260	3,215	3,000	15,575	
Total	B	200	220	235	225	215	1,095	

A = total number of employees.   B = number of resignations.

Table 8. Age distribution of total number of employees in labor grade 10 at beginning of 1982.

Age Group	Number of Employees
<21	250
21–25	500
26–30	310
31–40	750
41–50	800
51–60	350
61+	240
Total	3,200

As in predicting retirements, many organizations using transitional probability factors in forecasting resignations work with a single number. They take the cumulative average of the number of employees at the beginning of each year in a given category of labor and the number of resignations in each year, without being specific about the age distribution of the employees. Applying the single transitional probability factor, we predict that 224 employees will resign in 1982.

To calculate the single transitional probability factor, add up the number of employees who resigned during the five-year period and then divide this figure by the sum of the numbers of employees at the beginning of each year. To calculate the probable number of resignations in 1982, multiply the total number of employees in all age groups at the beginning of 1982 (see Table 8) by the single transitional probability factor. In our example, the calculations are as follows:

Year	Number of Resignations	Number of Employees
1981	200	3,000
1980	220	3,100
1979	235	3,260
1978	225	3,215
1977	215	3,000
	1,095	15,575

$$\text{Single transitional probability factor} = \frac{1,095}{15,575} = 0.07$$

Number of probable resignations in 1982 = 3,200 × 0.07 = 224

We would achieve a more accurate forecast of the internal supply of labor for a given job category if we used the transitional probability factors for each of the different age groups. Calculated on the basis of the probability factors for each age group, the probable resignations in 1982 are: $(250 \times .15) + (500 \times .09) + (310 \times .12) + (750 \times .05) + (800 \times .03) + (350 \times .08) + (240 \times .05) = 221$. The difference of 3 between the two estimates may not seem significant at first. But given the costs of replacing employees, that overestimate could lead to overbudgeting for salaries in that job category and possibly tight budgeting elsewhere in the organization as a consequence.

We can also compute the attrition due to resignations by averaging the number of resignations over the past five years and using this figure as the projection for the following year. Based on this method, the probable number of resignations would be: $200 + 220 + 235 + 225 + 215 = 219$.

Of the three methods for predicting attrition, this third method is the least accurate. Using separate transitional probability factors achieves the best accuracy. By developing cumulative figures in the age distribution of employees and resignations, organizations will be able to compute transitional probability factors for accurate forecasts of the human resource flows in the organization.

Length of service. Age is not the only intervening variable forecasters should consider in computing transitional probability factors and predicting resignations. Research on turnover has also demonstrated a relationship between the number of years an employee has been in the organization and the probability of that employee's resignation at any given period. As pointed out earlier, this relationship is not linear. The probability of resignation is high during the early stages of an employee's career, at mid-career, and finally ten years or so before retirement.

Employees could be categorized according to significant length of service periods. Table 9 gives the distribution of employees in labor grade 10 of the bank we have been discussing according to the employees' length of service during the past five years.

On the average, over the five-year period, one out of ten employees who had been with the bank for under six years resigned. The specific resignation transitional probability factor for this group of employee is .10. On the other hand, the likelihood that employees in the group with 6 to 15 years of service will resign is only .04, or less

Table 9. Distribution of employees who resigned, according to length of service.

Years of Service		1980	1979	1978	1977	1976	Total	Probability Factor for Resignations A ÷ B
<6	A	90	112	115	113	105	535	.10
Early in career	B	1,020	1,065	1,109	1,078	1,027	5,299	
6–15	A	51	52	58	57	54	272	.04
	B	1,265	1,298	1,350	1,352	1,277	6,542	
16–20	A	14	16	17	16	11	74	.08
Mid-career	B	170	190	196	191	165	912	
21–25	A	18	16	19	17	14	84	.07
	B	230	228	265	260	224	1,207	
26–30	A	10	11	13	12	15	61	.10
Late in career	B	105	118	129	130	107	589	
31–35	A	5	3	2	3	6	19	.05
	B	70	66	75	72	70	353	
36+	A	12	10	11	8	10	51	.08
Last move	B	140	135	136	132	130	673	

A = number of resignations.
B = total number of employees.
* Transitional probability for resignations during different career stages.

than half that of the previous group. Figure 24 illustrates this relationship.

Table 10 shows the distribution, in years of service, of the bank's employees in grade 10 at the beginning of 1982. Using the transitional probability factors, we can predict the number of resignations during 1982. This figure, based on the relationship between resignations and length of service, will be approximately 223. The calculation would be as follows: $(225 \times .10) + (320 \times .04) + (375 \times .08) + (850 \times .07) + (620 \times .10) + (460 \times .05) + (170 \times .08) = 223.4$.

Because of the significant relationships between resignations and

Figure 24.   Transitional resignation probabilities among employees at different career points in an organization.

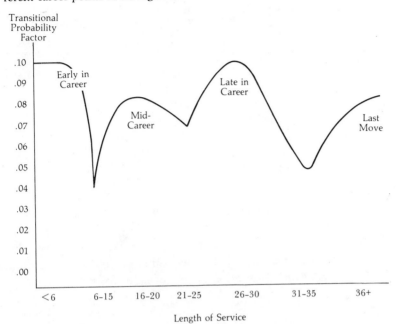

both employee age and length of service, we recommend averaging the predictions derived from the transitional probability factors for the two categories. For the sake of accurate prediction, the factors of age and length of service are treated as independent of one another. Based on this method, the probable number of resignations in 1982 will be:

$$\frac{221 + 223}{2} = 222$$

Step Five: Computing Attrition

The complete prediction of attrition is simply the sum of the employee departures for all the various causes: resignations, retirements, disability retirements, deaths, and the like. The sum of the resignations and retirements will account for over 97 percent of the attrition in most organizations. Because resignations and retirements are so significant, planners must forecast them accurately, using transitional probability factors. However, cumulative averages of

Table 10. Distribution of total number of employees in labor grade 10 at beginning of 1981, according to length of service.

Years of Service	Number of Employees
<6	225
6–15	320
16–20	375
21–25	850
26–30	620
31–35	460
36+	170
Total	3,020

deaths, disability retirements, leaves without pay, and the like should provide sufficient bases for accurately predicting these less significant causes of attrition. Subtracting the total attrition from the total number of employees at the beginning of the forecast period gives the organization's internal supply of labor for that period.

Summary

In this chapter we have discussed several methods of computing attrition in human resources in forecasting an organization's internal supply of labor. The emphasis is on methods and techniques requiring a minimum of arithmetical calculations. Data used in the turnover forecasts are from human resources data inventories already available in many organizations.

We have concentrated on resignations and retirements because they account for about 97 percent of the attrition in organizations other than the military and the paramilitary. Because of the significance of these sources, forecasters should use transitional probability factors to account for the impact of employee age and length of service on attrition. Using multiple probability factors achieves more accurate predictions than using a single probability factor, especially in forecasting resignations. Cumulative averages are sufficient for predicting attrition due to deaths, disability retirements, leaves without pay, and so forth, because these sources account for only about 3 percent of an organization's employee turnover.

CHAPTER 8

Human Resources Information Systems

The availability of relevant data on human resources is essential to any human resources system. The nature, relevance, and accuracy of the human resources data vary from company to company. Some organizations have elaborate methods for collecting and storing detailed information on their personnel, while other organizations use only the type of information found in summary job application forms. Many factors influence the amount of human resources data that organizations collect and store.

The first step in any type of planning—whether it involves a major functional area such as production, marketing, finance, research and development, and human resources, or the overall corporate strategic planning—is to determine the kinds and amount of data needed for the plans. The type of information needed and the methods of collecting the information must be determined before any significant progress can be made in planning. In this chapter we discuss the type, depth, and scope of the personnel information most relevant to HRP. We also present a method for collecting the pertinent human resources information. Finally, we provide a guideline for selecting the optimum depth and scope of the human resources data and describe the process for collecting and storing this information.

The Meaning of a Human Resources Data Inventory

A human resources data inventory is composed of any data on the personnel that have been formally stored by the organization. This could be statistical information stored in employee files. Aggregate statistical information can include such things as the number of employees, the functional distribution of personnel, and the distribution of personnel by sex, age, and rank.

Statistical data on human resources can vary according to the purposes for which the data are being collected. Thus the types of data found in different organizations may vary greatly. In some companies, personnel files may include only the sketchy outline of the personnel generally found in summary application forms. In other companies, however, personnel files may contain elaborate information not only on the employee but also on the employee's family. This information may include age, education, career path, performance evaluation results, and the type of jobs and tasks suitable for the individual. The information commonly found in personnel files concerns:

Current job title	Employee's work preferences
Current skills	Employee's aspirations
Education of employee	Number of years with company
Work experience	Summary performance evalua-
Jobs employee is qualified to do	tion(s)
	Dependents

We are interested in the types of data needed for strategic business planning and human resources planning purposes. Data on the quantity and quality of current personnel are the essence of the human resources data inventory of an organization. For SBP purposes, an organization must know whether it currently possesses the human resources needed for the planned activities, and if not, whether it is necessary and/or economically feasible to acquire these resources from outside.

The Contents of a Human Resources Data Inventory for SBP Purposes

Collecting, storing, and sorting data are expensive, but when the data involves an organization's human resources, much more must be considered: the sensitivity of the individuals and the national and local legal restrictions concerning the collection and use of demographic information.

It is possible for organizations to collect all kinds of information, within legal limits, on their employees. However, not all of this information is useful for the preparation of strategic business plans. A human resources data inventory should tell the strategic business planners the availability of the personnel required to implement their plans. To determine the availability of personnel to meet the current and projected needs of an organization, human resources data should be collected and stored in five categories: functional distribution of personnel, personal factors, education, performance, and objectives.

Functional Distribution of Personnel

The first step in developing a human resources data inventory is classifying employees by the types of jobs they perform. The purpose is to gain reliable knowledge about the number of employees and their specializations. These data can be taken from job descriptions, employee lists, and payroll information. Descriptive job titles are often sufficient for classifying current employees. This objective information is usually available in all organizations. In smaller organizations almost everyone knows how many people are employed and what the employees do. As the size of an organization increases, it becomes more difficult and perhaps too costly to make such information available to all.

The size of the organization determines the level at which job classification information should be gathered and converted into a usable form for SBP. This information generally originates at the physical location where the person is employed. That is, each operating unit or department in an organization has knowledge of how many people are employed at each type of job.

Personal Factors

The employee's current age, expected retirement age, and dependents are the most important personal factors in the human resources inventory. For instance, the fact that 10 percent of the electrical engineers in a company are scheduled for retirement in the next three years can be vital to the preparation of strategic business plans. The ages of the employees and the types of dependents can also be determining factors in the implementation of the plans. For example, the plans may call for a job and location change for 15 percent of the electrical engineers. If many of these engineers have children of elementary school age and the new location is in a remote area without adequate schools, the employees may choose not to move and may even leave the company. If the strategic business planners intend to staff the new positions entirely from internal resources and do not consider the nature of the dependents of their employees when developing the changes, they may have great difficulty implementing the plans.

Education

The employees' education and areas of specialization indicate the extent to which an organization can staff projected activities internally. Suppose that certain future projects require several highly specialized engineers. If the company plans to staff these new jobs internally, but does not review the educational background of the personnel, it may encounter some problems. The company may not have enough engineers with the required specialization. This might make internal staffing almost impossible and prevent implementation of the plan. If, on the other hand, the planners have the information, allowing them to anticipate the internal shortage, they can change the plans or make provisions for recruiting talent from outside the organization.

Employee Performance

Summary data concerning the promotability, present performance, and strengths and weaknesses of the existing personnel play an important role in determining the real human resources needs of the organization. During the SBP process, planners must know the quality of the personnel in various positions. The number of employees who can be promoted and data on them are important for SBP. Summary information on individual strengths and weaknesses can affect the direction the organization chooses for the future. A company hoping to enter a highly competitive market may wish to postpone entry because it lacks personnel with the skills and abilities needed to cope with the pressures in an aggressive field. Aggregate human resources data on employee performance characteristics can assist the planners in making realistic, feasible plans.

Many organizations initiate projects without first evaluating the quality and performance characteristics of their personnel. These organizations later experience problems in human performance when employee characteristics do not match the demands of the new job.

A stable workforce that performs well in one situation may not suit the jobs created by a new situation. Expecting high performance from employees who lack the skills or ability to succeed in the new jobs puts undue pressure on the employees and may cause the organization to fail.

In the late 1970s, a major U.S. conglomerate experienced such a problem. The conglomerate purchased an old but highly successful cement plant, primarily to have access to the raw materials and the location of the plant. The parent organization then began to build an entirely new processing plant with modern, sophisticated equipment. The old plant continued to operate until the new facility was completed. Due to its union contract, the company had to follow strict seniority rules when it closed the old plant and transferred half of the personnel to the new plant.

When the parent company made plans to build the new plant, it did not consider employee characteristics. Management thought it had complete freedom in staffing the new facility—which was not the case. The new plant was put into operation with a labor force that had little desire and almost no potential to learn the skills needed for successful performance in the modern plant. The result was catastrophic for the organization. The planned return on investment was not met and the expected profitability was never realized. At this time, the plant is still operating but only with the indirect help of the state government. If the conglomerate had utilized human resources data in the strategic planning process, it might have avoided many of its problems (too many breakdowns, slow production, and unreliable quality) in operating the new facility.

Employee Objectives

Even more important than having the required number of personnel is having personnel that are highly motivated. Therefore, data on employee aspirations and work preferences must be part of the human resources data inventory. Taking employee aspirations, objectives, and preferences into consideration during the SBP process contributes to greater employee commitment to organizational goals and missions and increases the companies' chances of success. Participative management and joint goal setting are examples of this concept, although such practices are generally restricted to the operational function and are seldom included in strategic management.

European experience with worker participation is often used to illustrate how employee input is utilized in strategic decisions. However, even in the Western European countries, where "democratic" management and worker participation in company boards have been accepted industrial practice for several decades, the inclusion of employee objectives in strategic decisions has been more political than rational. There is still no systematic procedure for including employee aspirations and objectives in the SBP process.

In summary, planners need to collect information on the five broad categories of human resources characteristics if they are to build an adequate human resources data inventory. The list below shows a human resources data inventory that uses the five categories of data.

Functional specialization:
Current job title
Previous job titles
Salary
Personal factors:
Age
Expected retirement age
Marital status
Children
Education:
Specialization
Employee performance:
Promotability
Current performance
Strengths
Weaknesses
Employee objectives:
Work preferences
Aspirations

These categories are the essence of the personal file of each employee. Organizations may collect additional information on their employees, but for strategic business and human resources planning purposes these five categories of information are sufficient. This information can be stored in summary form on computer tapes, disks, or data cards.

The Process of Aggregating Human Resources Information

A human resources data inventory represents the process of collecting and storing quantitative as well as qualitative information on current employees in the organization. Raw data are the content of the human resources data inventory. In order to be used, these data must be analyzed and sent to the strategic business planners.

Figure 25 illustrates the process of aggregating information on human resources so that it may be made available to the strategic business planners. In small companies, the human resources data can be consolidated at the plant level. This information is often more specific than the aggregation made at the corporate level. Also, if the unit is small enough, the names of individuals can be associated with each position. At the plant level, for example, human resources information for SBP may include not only the number of electrical en-

Figure 25.   Process of aggregating human resources information for SBP.

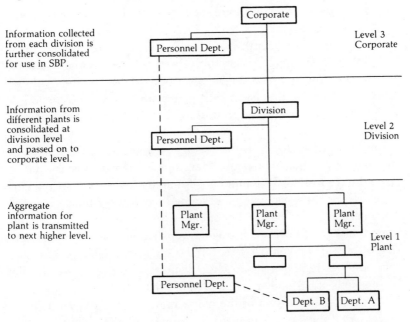

gineers but also the categorization of the engineers by their position titles.

The wealth of pertinent data collected in an organization must be able to be converted to usable forms and sent to the people who need it; otherwise, the data inventory system will be worthless. We will explore in greater detail the nature of the human resources data and the procedure for effectively using the data inventory.

Classification of Major Human Resources Variables

As we have said, five basic categories of data are used for collecting and storing information on human resources in a data inventory. The categories are defined by the major variables that describe the skills and traits of the personnel. Each organization must develop a system for classifying the data under these specific human resources variables. The categories, of course, must suit planning needs; that is, they should group the data in meaningful units for prediction purposes. The classification scheme may differ from one organization to another, but the classifications should be used uniformly within a particular organization.

For example, consider the variable *age.* The organization first must develop a classification system for the variable, such as the following age groups: 16–20, 21–25, 26–30, 31–35, 36–40, 41–50, 51–60, 61–64, and 65 and over. All departments, plants, and divisions of the organization should use these groups when classifying the employees according to age.

Suppose, now, that 60 is the average retirement age of employees in this organization. The people developing strategic business plans would have to know the number of employees nearing retirement. The classification scheme just described would help the planners if they need to know the number of employees expected to retire in the next ten years. However, the age groups would not provide meaningful data if the company required a count of the employees expected to retire in five years. More distinct age classifications would be needed, say, 51–55 and 56–60, rather than 51–60.

In short, classification of the major human resources variables is necessary if the data are to be useful in the SBP process. The type of classification system developed for a specific variable depends on the uses to which the planners will put the information as they make predictions and formulate plans.

Determining the Degree of Specificity of Human Resources Data

Extracting information for use in SBP is not easy. A major problem planners face is classifying the human resources in meaningful groups to provide summary information to strategic business planners. A straight tabulation of the categories suggested by the major human resources variables discussed in Chapter 7 will produce general, organization-wide data on human resources. However, to be really useful for SBP, the levels of specificity of the data must suit the needs of the planners. Information that is very general or very detailed is of little use in SBP. Too much information can overwhelm the planners, and too little information can frustrate them. It is important, then, to determine the level of specificity of the human resources data that suits the planners' particular needs.

Employee pay grades, for example, are useful categories because they provide planners with important organizational information without a great deal of irrelevant personal information on the employees. Table 11 illustrates the use of pay grades in grouping all positions in three organizations. The more important positions are at the top of the pay scale. Positions acquire importance for the organization according to the nature and scope of supervision and the functional specialization involved. The right side of the table shows the actual distribution of all personnel in the three organizations. The total number and percentage distribution of employees according to pay grades will differ from organization to organization, depending on the nature of the organization's business, its technology, and its management philosophy. A pyramid structure will prevail in most cases. The data in Table 11 illustrate how personnel can be grouped in a few basic levels, and how each level can be further subdivided into various pay grades.

In specifying human resources data, pay grades can be divided into job families, which are then grouped according to the location of the jobs. A scale of 1 to 4 may be used to measure the degree of specificity of data (1 is general and 4 is specific). Specificity level 1 means

Table 11. Distribution of personnel among pay grades in three organizations.

Organizational Level	Grade	Descriptive Position Title	Co. A No.	Co. A (%)	Co. B No.	Co. B (%)	Co. C No.	Co. C (%)
Top mgt.	20 19 18	Exec. V.P. Group V.P. Senior V.P., V.P.	3	(.6)	6	(.3)	15	(.15)
Upper mgt.	17 16 15 14	Gen'l. mgr. Director Specialist	8	(1.6)	20	(1)	100	(1)
Middle mgt.	13 12 11 10	Dept. mgr. Technical staff	9	(1.8)	40	(2)	300	(3)
Supervisory level	9 8 7	Supervisor Technician Staff asst.	30	(6)	200	(10)	700	(7)
Non-supervisory level	6 5 4 3 2 1	Clerical, office, and operative employees	450	(90)	1,734	(86.7)	8,885	(88.85)
		Total	500	(100)	2,000	(100)	10,000	(100)

that the data on employee characteristics are supplied for pay grades only. (For example, X percent of employees in pay grade 6 are promotable to the next pay grade.) Specificity level 2 subdivides the data into the main job families in each pay grade. (For example, X percent of the industrial engineers in pay grade 6 can be promoted to the next pay grade.) Specificity level 3 subdivides the data into the sub-jobs in each main job family. (For example, X percent of plant layout engineers in pay grade 6 can be promoted to the next pay grade.) Specificity level 4 represents nominal data, by definition the most specific data used in SBP. At this level, employee names are listed, with relevant information summarized next to each name. (For example, John Doe can be promoted to the office supervisor.)

The degree of data specificity depends on the purpose for which the data will be used in the SBP process. Once the data have been classified by the selected specificity level, they can be presented in a meaningful way to the various levels in the organization for utilization in SBP.

Analysis of Human Resources Data

Human resources data that have been collected and categorized must be converted into usable form. One way to do this is to make charts by plotting relevant human resources variables against job categories at the desired level of specificity. The broader the specificity level, the fewer variables would be plotted at a time. For example, planners might plot ten-year age categories against pay grades (a broad category) to determine the age breakdown of each pay grade; or they might want a fairly detailed profile, containing many variables, for each department manager in the company. Some of the variables that might be considered are:

Age
Expected retirement age
Number of dependents
Number of school-age dependents
Education
Specialization
Promotability
Current job performance
Work preferences
Geographical preferences
Aspirations

A straight tabulation of the information categorized under each variable will obviously provide useful input for strategic or operational business and human resources planning. However, the significance of the human resources data in the SBP process can be increased if the data can answer certain key questions about the availability of the right personnel at the right time. To answer such questions, the variables must be cross-tabulated. Usually, simple cross-tabulations will be sufficient. In a few instances, however, multiple cross-tabulations of several variables will be required. For example, the planners may want to know how many employees in pay grade 6 are between 50 and 55 years of age. This would be a simple cross-tabulation. But the planners may also want to know how many of these employees are promotable to the next pay grade. For this, the two variables *age* and *promotability* are cross-tabulated against the variable *pay grade 6.*

This technique can help planners to establish the potential availability of specified personnel for a given period in the future. Depending on the nature of the strategic business objectives, answers about the availability of internal resources can be obtained by analyzing several variables at the same time. Suppose a company is interested in determining which of its electrical engineers will be available in a few years to manage a project in a remote area of the country. All 11 of the variables listed earlier should be analyzed during the SBP process to obtain a reasonably accurate picture of the internal supply of technically qualified engineers as well as the number of persons who qualify for the job. The individuals with contrary personal preferences, due to their dependents or the location of the job, may then be separated from the group still under consideration.

Review of the Steps Needed to Analyze Human Resources Data for SBP

Step 1. Determine the degree of specificity of the data needed for SBP, and enter this factor in the vertical axis of a chart or grid. Data on the availability of personnel may be classified by broad categories (specificity level 1) or by more specific classes, such as employee names (specificity level 4). Remember, the SBP level determines the need for general or specific data. The higher the planning level, the broader is the human resources information required.

Step 2. Review the characteristics of the planned project. (a) When do we need the key personnel? (b) Where is the project located? (c) What other characteristics of this project will influence selection of personnel?

Step 3. From the list of 11 human resources variables given earlier, select those that may affect the potential availability of the desired personnel. List these on the vertical axis of the grid. (Feel free to include, and gather data about, any other variables not included in the list if they are valid for your particular project.) Generally, variables involving employee preferences and other limiting factors should be

considered. For instance, electrical engineers might have been identified as the critical personnel for a project. However, the type of degree held and the amount of managerial experience might be limiting factors to examine when selecting these engineers.

Step 4. Correlate the variable on the vertical axis with the variables
listed on the horizontal axis.

Step 5. Write the number of potentially available key personnel
(from within the organization) needed for the successful implementation of the strategic business plans.

Figure 26 illustrates the procedure for analyzing level 4 data for
SBP purposes. Let's assume that the planners are exploring the possibilities of developing a new variation of the existing product line.
The availability of certain types of human resources is being considered as one of the inputs in the decision-making process. In this example, the successful implementation of the plan depends on the
availability of enough qualified electrical engineers. Across the top
of the form, the planners can list whatever variables they consider
relevant to this particular project. By listing names of candidates on
the left and filling in the information for each of them, planners can
see at a glance how many candidates meet each criterion and also
which candidates are best qualified to work on the project. This process will give a reasonably accurate picture of whether enough qualified (and probably interested) electrical engineers will be available
from within the company.

Thus far we have identified the content of the human resources
data to be used in the SBP process. We have suggested that approxi-

Figure 26.   Form for determining availability of qualified employees from
internal sources for possible utilization in a planned project.

Name	No. of school-age dependents: None preferred	Education: Eng. D.	Specialization: Electrical engineering	Current Job Performance: Must be good to excellent	Geographical Preference: Small town, Southwest
					Relevant Variables
Matthew Robinson	0	Eng. D.	Elec.	Excellent	Prefers home ofc but would consider
Violet Hunter	0	Eng. D.	Elec./Chem.	Excellent	OK
Thomas Eng	1	Eng. D.	Elec.	Good	OK

mately 15 variables can be selected and analyzed to provide strategic business planners with the human resources data they need, and without inundating them with information that is too specific to be useful. The presentation and analysis of human resources data are a key issue to HRP. To prepare useful data, start with the assumption that planners need to know the availability of strategic human resources at a given time for a planned project. Given that need, classify the strategic human resources according to their functions and/or hierarchical level in the organization. Depending on the planning level, present the information on the availability of key human resources in terms of broad job categories or specific functions.

Many organizations have accurate data on all types of personnel, but in attempting to determine the availability of such personnel for a planned project, they do not consider the qualitative data on the employees' personal work preferences, performance, and promotability. Therefore, the human resources projections often become inaccurate. This inaccuracy convinces planners that long-term human resources availability cannot be predicted, which in turn leads them to exclude human resources data from the planning process. In this chapter, we have tried to break this vicious circle by providing a method for analyzing and using available human resources data in SBP.

A Method of Collecting Human Resources Data

Human resources data as outlined in Table 11 can generally be found in most organizations. However, the information is often scattered throughout the organization. Data collected for wage and salary administration and employee benefits may be stored in the finance or accounting departments, while other data are stored in the personnel department and in individual operating departments. Consolidating human resources data, as proposed in Table 11, is a significant step toward effective HRP.

The method of collecting data for a human resources data inventory system is as important as the data themselves. The accuracy of the data is affected by the method of collection and in turn affects the predictions of the availability of personnel for specific, planned activities. Problems with data accuracy occur not so much with objective and observable characteristics such as age, number of dependents, and current position titles, as with subjective information on employee performance, work preferences, and aspirations. Such subjective information can be gathered and used effectively.

Almost all companies use job descriptions, performance evaluations, and training needs assessments. Certain companies also record information on employee aspirations and interests. These data can often be found in unit, division, or corporate personnel departments. However, they are usually stored at the nominal level of specificity, in the form of personnel files. A particularly interesting method of gathering human resources data is being practiced successfully by one of the product divisions of a major Dutch multinational corporation. This company uses the process of job discussion, which is summarized in Figure 27, to obtain information on individuals' current levels of performance, their promotability, aspirations, and desire for movement.

The process begins at the superior/subordinate level with a discussion of the important aspects of the job, for the purpose of establishing a high degree of role clarity. Once agreement is reached on the important aspects of the subordinate's role, the process of performance evaluation begins. The immediate supervisor uses standardized evaluation forms to appraise the subordinate's performance. Following the discussion with the superior, the subordinate answers questions about personal aspirations and desire for functional, hierarchical, and geographical mobility. This evaluation, including the superior's estimate of the individual's promotability, is then forwarded to the next level in the unit. Here, a group of managers reviews the information and completes the employee's assessment. These evaluations are then forwarded to the personnel department, where they form the basis for the human resources data inventory.

The personnel department prepares summary data sheets for each individual in each department. The personnel department also prepares aggregate information on the number of promotable employees in each function or department. The department heads receive copies of these data and use them for their specific departmental purposes. The inventory can be used to answer such questions as: Whom do we employ in the organization? How good are they? How many and who can be promoted? How many and who can be transferred?

Figure 27.   Job discussion process in a Dutch multinational corporation.

Step 1 Superior and subordinate discuss	Job Content	to establish role clarity
	Job Performance	to determine whether subordinate has access to required information, has adequate authority, tools, and work areas, has job aid
	Training Needs	to improve current job performance and to broaden general knowledge level for further growth and development
	Performance Evaluation	to determine current performance level and promotability
	Aspirations and Interests	to determine aspirations and personal interests
Step 2	Review of job discussions and evaluation by management committees	
Step 3 Personnel Department	Prepares summary data sheets for each individual in each department based on reviews supplied by management committees Prepares aggregate information	
Step 4 Human resources information is used by	Personnel Department	to develop training programs, advise on promotions, job rotations, and recruitment planning
	Line Departments	to better utilize existing personnel

The personnel department also uses the same data in developing training programs; providing advice on job rotations, promotions, and transfers; and planning recruitment for vacancies. At present, little of this information is used during the SBP process. Thus we recommend that the job discussion procedure be used to gather human resources data, so that the data may be distributed to the appropriate organizational level for use in SBP.

How to Use Human Resources Information in SBP

The organizational level at which strategic business plans are prepared determines the need for either general or specific human resources data. Relevant data can be provided with respect to groups of

Table 12. Nature of human resources information for use in SBP.

| SBP Organization Levels | Specificity Level of Information Required for % of Positions in Specified Pay Grades | | | |
| | Nominal HR Information | Aggregate HR Information | | |
	S4	S3	S2	S1
Corporate level	100% for G20 80% for G19	G19	G18	Consolidated data
Division level	20% for G19 80% for G18 60% for G17	G18, G17	G16	G15 to G1
Plant level	20% for G18 40% for G17 70% for G16	G16, G15	G13 to G1	

S = specificity level.
G = grade level.

job families or to individual jobs. The problem is determining the optimum level of data as an input in the SBP process. Table 12 provides one model for selecting the appropriate quantity and the degree of specificity of data for use in the planning process at different hierarchical levels within an organization.

The data in Table 12 were obtained from interviews with the executives responsible for SBP in a major U.S. corporation. The job positions in this company were classified into 20 pay grades.

Meaningful data, as input in the preparation of strategic business plans at the corporate level, will include nominal information on 100 percent of the positions in grade 20 and 80 percent of the positions in grade 19. These data are often considered confidential and are used by only top executives. The data are not included explicitly in the formal plans.

For strategic business plans undertaken at the division level, nominal information would be needed for the remaining 20 percent of the positions in grade 19. In planning at the plant level, nominal information would be required for the remainder of the positions in grades 18, 17, and 16.

The executives who were interviewed also indicated their need for aggregate data in the planning process. For instance, at the corporate level of SBP, data may include statistical information—at specificity level 3—on employee interests, possible promotables, vacancies, and transferables, for all the positions in pay grade 19. For the positions in pay grade 18, however, a specificity level of 2 might be more useful as an input in the planning process.

As shown in the table, for business planning at the corporate level, the need for information can be restricted to pay grades 20, 19, and 18. Nominal information will be useful only for pay grades 20 and 19. Any other nominal information, as an input in the strategic business planning process, would be superfluous and difficult to include with the other inputs.

Table 12 can be used as a guide for determining the type of human resources information to be supplied to the strategic business planners prior to the formulation of specific action plans. Of course, this is a rough guideline. Companies must decide whether 20 pay grades are adequate to classify all positions. Furthermore, they must decide which positions for each pay grade should be included in nominal lists and which positions should be presented in aggregate form. Personnel with the highest rank are found in positions within pay grades 20, 19, 18, and sometimes 17. Nominal information on these individuals is often considered confidential data and should be handled with the utmost sensitivity. Permission to use nominal human resources information should be obtained from the president of the organization and the individuals concerned.

Summary

To prepare data-based human resources plans that are integrated with strategic business plans, planners must develop an adequate supply of human resources information. The first step in the HRP process is establishing human resources data inventories. A data inventory contains summary information on the characteristics of the employees, the functional distribution of employees in the organization, and the employees' job performance and objectives. The inventories can be stored at strategic locations within the organization.

The usefulness of human resources information systems is determined not only by the elaborate nature of the data they contain, but also by the manner in which the data are categorized, coded, collected, tabulated, and presented. To be useful to strategic business planners, the data must be categorized and coded at the level of specificity needed for planning. Four specificity levels are available for the tabulation of data on human resources. Lists of employees can be prepared nominally according to their job titles, or according to subjob families, main job families, and pay grades. Nominal lists are very specific and usually contain the names of every employee in the company. Pay grades, on the other hand, provide a much broader categorization of personnel. Employee lists, after being prepared according to the desired specificity level, can be analyzed to obtain information on human resources characteristics. The result of this analysis is the output of human resources data systems. This output becomes the input for the strategic planning process.

If personnel managers devote more of their time to developing data inventories and prepare summary information on relevant employee characteristics and their availability in future years, they will be taking a step forward in the direction of integrating HRP with SBP. To achieve this, data should be collected and analyzed not only for operational uses (e.g., wage and salary administration) but for strategic and policy purposes as well.

CHAPTER 9

Building Human Resources Data Inventory Systems

An organization may have an excellent mechanism for transmitting information to the planners, but if the information is not meaningful, the inventory system will be of little value. An organization may have a wealth of pertinent data, but without mechanisms for converting these data into usable form and for transmitting them to the appropriate parts of the organization, the data inventory system will be worthless. This chapter explores the reciprocal relations between SBP and HRP and presents additional formats for collecting and transmitting human resources data to strategic business planners. In a sense, we will operationalize the mechanism that integrates SBP and HRP.

Overview of the Human Resources Data Inventory System for SBP

Figure 28 presents an overview of the human resources data inventory system. The data inventory is composed of data collection, storage, and analysis elements. The system should be flexible because it must satisfy the SBP needs for data during the planning process.

The system is triggered by a demand for human resources information from the strategic business planners. For instance, during SBP, the planners may need to know the potential availability of personnel from within the organization to staff certain planned proj-

Figure 28.   Human resources data inventory system for SBP.

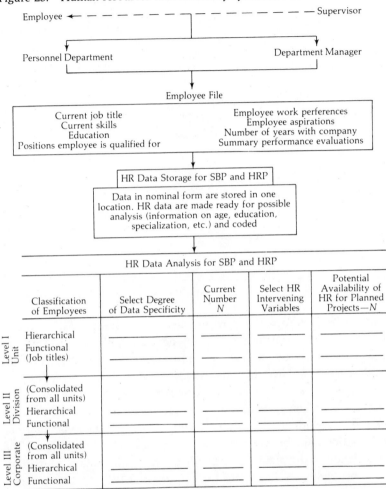

ects. SBP is not a routine function: It sets the future direction of the company. Thus, for SBP purposes, human resources information needs depend on the direction the organization wants to take, and data will be supplied only on request. For operational plans, however, the necessary human resources information will be routinely provided to the planners.

A human resources inventory system has three major components: the information itself, the methods used to build and store the inventory, and the analysis of the data. Only relevant data should be

Figure 29.   Selecting contents of human resources data inventory.

HR Data on:	Must Pass HRP Selection Criteria of:	To Be Included in Content of HR Data Inventory:
Education knowledge	Relevance to HRP	Relevant data on personnel concerning their education, knowledge, experience, skills, objectives, and work
Performance	Assistance in achieving integration between planning and utilization components of human resources management	
Experience/ skills		
Personal objectives	Cost of analysis	
Work preferences	Legal restrictions	

stored. Basic information on employee experience/skills, education/knowledge, performance, and personal objectives forms the core of the data inventory. This information can be used for both SBP and during HRP, for integrating such activities as training and development, promotions, transfers, and wage and salary administration. Whether particular data should be included in the data inventory depends on the degree to which they help establish reciprocal relationships between HRP and SBP and assist in the horizontal integration of the planning and utilization components of human resources. Figure 29 illustrates the criteria that the human resources data must meet.

The second component of the data inventory system is the method used to build the data inventory. The information on human resources is generally collected by the personnel department, the employee's immediate supervisor, the department manager, or the employee's supervisor's boss. The data contributed by the employees should include performance assessments as well as personal objective statements and demographic information.

The personnel department, immediate supervisors, and department heads are the major contributors to the development of data inventories. Immediate supervisors generally collect the evaluative,

Figure 30.   Conversion of raw human resources data into usable form for HRP.

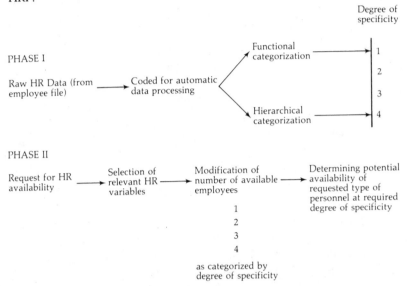

subjective, and personal information on the employees. Department heads can check the relative accuracy of this information and add their observations. The personnel department can collect the objective data usually found on job application forms and monitor the collection of data by the immediate supervisor and the department head.

The location of the data inventory is important. If the unit has a personnel department, the data should be stored there. If not, the information can be stored in the data processing department. The collected data must be transferred to cards, disks, or tapes before analysis.

Data analysis, the third component in the system, can be carried out in two phases, as Figure 30 illustrates. Phase I involves classifying the employees by their current employment—a rather routine analysis. The only problem is in updating the data as unit staffing requirements are altered and changes in human resources occur. Phase II involves a higher level of analysis because planners must select the appropriate intervening human resources variables: age, education, work specialization, and the like. The variables selected affect the accuracy of the reply to the request for the availability of human resources. This is the dynamic—and most critical—aspect of the data analysis because it involves fusing qualitative data with information on the physical availability of employees.

Gathering Human Resources Data

The first step in installing a data inventory system is developing uniform procedures for gathering and storing information. We will now present a method for gathering human resources data. Because the purpose of collecting data is to obtain accurate information on employee performance, education, work preferences, and objectives, it is logical to start with the design of a sample employee file.

Sample Employee File
Relevant information on an employee should be found in that individual's file. Various formats can be used for structuring employee files. Handling, updating, analyzing, and storing information are important considerations in building an employee file. The use of folders is discouraged because all kinds of information may be inserted into them, making handling and storing the information cumbersome. Companies with elaborate filing systems should invest in a summary employee data sheet. The summary form is also an excellent first form for companies that have little or no recorded information on human resources characteristics.

The employee data card presented in Figure 31 is recommended for recording the employee information to be used for planning. Human resources data can be transcribed on the card in summary form and updated regularly. The updating of the personnel file (or card) is the responsibility of the unit personnel department or specialist. The specialist should follow up on line managers to ensure that performance evaluations are completed on time and that changes in employee status are reported.

Information on Summary Performance Evaluation
The information on the employee data card can be routinely obtained, with the exception of data on employee performance and promotability. The job discussion procedure described in Chapter 8 can be used to obtain data on performance and promotability.

The format used for performance evaluations will vary from one

Figure 31.   Sample format of employee data card.

Personal Factors	Position Classification	
Name: _____	Labor or pay grade: Current ____ Past ____	
Age: _____	Job title: *Main job family*	*Subjob family*
Marital status: _____	Current _____	_____
Number of dependents: _____	Past _____	_____
Number of school-age dependents: _____		_____
Education: _____	Specialization: _____	
_____	_____	

Performance

Period	Job Performance Summary	Promotability
1.	_____	_____
2.	_____	_____
3.	_____	_____
4.	_____	_____
5.	_____	_____

Employee Objectives

Period	Work Preferences	Geographical preferences	Professional Aspirations
1.	_____	_____	_____
2.	_____	_____	_____
3.	_____	_____	_____
4.	_____	_____	_____
5.	_____	_____	_____

organization to the next. Some organizations will simply evaluate employee traits, such as leadership, motivation, knowledge of the job, communication, and ability to get along with people, while others will consider objective performance factors or a combination of objective and subjective factors. Policy considerations and strategic components of evaluation systems are discussed in Chapter 13. Here, it is sufficient to note that for HRP purposes the evaluation procedure must include quantifiable data. Thus some type of quantifiable summary evaluation form should be added to the performance evaluation form. For instance, the evaluator could be asked to rank the individual's overall performance on a scale of 1 to 7. Or the evaluator could use one of several specified adjectives to describe the subordinate's current job performance. We recommend using a simple, behaviorally anchored scale, such as this one:

7. OUTSTANDING: Employee performance is one of the best I have ever encountered. Certainly in the top 5 percent of all employees I have supervised.

6. SUPERIOR:	Employee performance is outstanding. In the top 10 percent of all employees I have supervised.
5. COMPETENT:	Performance meets all job expectations and exceeds expectations in some areas.
4. AVERAGE:	Meets basic requirements of the job. Acceptable performance.
3. MARGINAL:	Meets basic requirements of the job most of the time. In certain areas exhibits unacceptable performance. Substantial improvement needed.
2. POOR:	Fails to meet basic requirements of the job. Unacceptable performance. Immediate remedial action is necessary. If performance doesn't improve soon, I recommend discharging.
1. VERY POOR:	Unacceptable performance. Urgent personnel action is necessary; past remedial action has failed to bring performance to an acceptable level. I recommend discharging the employee.

This scale can be added to the existing evaluation form, with appropriate instructions. The employees' performance ratings for each period can then be transferred to their data cards.

Information on Promotability

Summary data on the employee's promotability should be transcribed on the employee data card next to the evaluation of current job performance. This information should also be recorded in quantifiable form. It can be summarized like this:

1. The employee is promotable to a position two grades higher than current position.
2. The employee is promotable to a position one grade higher than current position.
3. The employee is promotable within the same grade.
4. The employee is not yet ready for a promotion.

Summary data on promotability should indicate the type and complexity of the new positions the individual is capable of filling. Since labor or pay grades are based on the complexity and importance of existing jobs in the organization, they can be used to indicate the degree of promotability of employees. For example, the immediate supervisor's conclusion that an employee can be promoted from pay grade 5 to pay grade 6 or 7 suggests the types of jobs for which the employee would be available.

Management needs promotability data to determine the potential availability of personnel for planned projects. Current performance alone does not provide sufficient information. Employees who are currently good performers may not be able to handle higher-level jobs. Without access to promotability data, supervisors might move these employees from positions where they are successful to positions in which they would take a long time to reach an acceptable level of performance. Failure to consider the extra learning time may slow down or even prevent implementation of the strategic business plans.

Information on Employee Objectives

Performance evaluation forms can also be used to record employee objectives. For planning purposes, information about employee work preferences, geographical location preferences, and professional aspirations should be collected. If necessary, these data can be developed, refined, and adjusted during the supervisor/subordinate job discussions. There is really no prescribed way of summarizing data on employee preferences and aspirations. Employees can be asked to state their personal objectives in narrative form or to select the most representative statements from a prepared list. However, consistency is an important criterion in coding the data.

The checklist in Figure 32 is adapted from the forms used by a national bank in France to plan the career developments of its employees. The bank's central personnel office coordinates the staffing activities for all its employees throughout France. Using a standardized questionnaire, each branch collects personal data on employees above the rank of teller. This information is collected directly from the employees without the involvement of line management. In large branches, the personnel department or an officer assigned to certain personnel functions collects the data. In the smaller branches with no personnel department, an assistant manager or an administrative assistant to the branch manager collects the data. The data are coded on cards and sent to the central personnel office, where the cards are fed into the computer for storage. Information on employee prefer-

Figure 32. Checklist of employee work preferences, geographical preferences, and professional aspirations.

Hours of Work	8–5 (1)	9–6 (2)	No preference (3)

Vacations	June (4) July (5) August (6) September (7)
	Winter months (8) June/July combination (9)
	August/September combination (11)
	No preference among 4–7, 9–11 (12)
	No preference at all (13)

Type of Work

Functional	Personal (14)	Trusts (19)	Savings (24)
	Sales (15)	Investments (20)	Credits (25)
	Public relations (16)	Govmt. relations (21)	Acquisitions (26)
	Consumer loans (17)	Accounting (22)	Housekeeping (27)
	Commercial loans (18)	Mortgages (23)	Systems (28)

Managerial	Management in functional department (29)
	General management (30)
	Do not want managerial position (31)

Geographical Preferences	Prefer location in area A (32)
	Prefer location in area B (33)
	Prefer location in area C (34)
	Prefer location in area D (35)
	Prefer location in area E (36)
	No preference (37)

Professional Aspirations	Want to stay in current functional area (38)
	Want to change to another functional area (39)
	Would like to assume managerial position (40)
	Want to stay primarily in current functional area but would like to acquire experience in another functional area (41)

ences and aspirations is updated every three years, or once a year if an employee feels that some of the data should be modified as a result of changes in his or her environment.

The checklist in Figure 32 is not the complete questionnaire used by the French bank. Actually, the bank uses a more elaborate form that includes instructions to the employees. However, the checklist in Figure 32 can serve as a model for most organizations. The categories under the three headings can be altered to suit the specifics of each organization. For instance, the items under work preferences and geographical locations may be completely different in different organizations. Some companies may want to restrict the number of items an employee can check under each category. Restricting the choices to one or two items under each category improves the picture of employee preferences and facilitates administration of the system. The basic principle behind this system is that in most situations the manager should promote, among equally qualified employees, the worker whose preferences coincide most with job requirements.

Converting Human Resources Data into Input for Planning

We have looked at the possible ways of collecting and storing relevant human resources data in a usable form for planning purposes. The conversion process takes place when the current employees are classified according to their functions and hierarchical rank in the organization in terms of the four specificity levels, which are, in descending order of specificity:

Level 4. Job title: All employees are classified according to their job titles.

Level 3. Subjob family: Job titles are grouped under job families.

Level 2. Job family: Subjob families are grouped under job families.

Level 1. Pay grade: Job families are put together to make pay grades.

This categorization can take place at the unit, division, or corporate level of the organization.

Figure 33 illustrates how data can be aggregated and transformed into usable inputs in a hypothetical company. In division A, for example, each unit converts its data into four specificity levels, which describe the composition of the current personnel. Division A aggregates data from units 1, 2, 3, and 4. The aggregation of the data supplied by each operating unit begins the process of converting raw data into usable input. This input is stored at the division level. The corporate level then collects the data from its two divisions; it completes the conversion process by aggregating the data. At the corporate level, management will know how many employees the com-

Figure 33.   Aggregating human resources data categories at unit, division, and corporate levels.

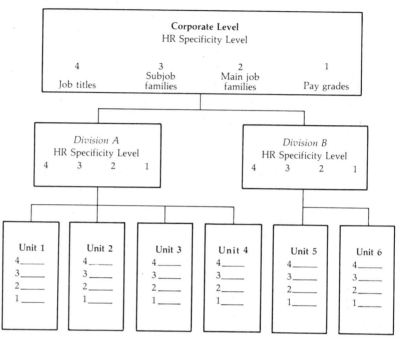

pany has, and how these employees are categorized according to job titles, subjob families, main job families, and pay grades.

The type of planning the organization is undertaking determines the specificity level needed for the human resources data. If the business plans are broad and are to be used as basic guidelines, the input needs are at lower specificity levels (pay grades and main job families). Such broad-based plans are strategic. On the other hand, if the business plans must be detailed and specific, then input needs will also be specific (subjob families and job titles). These detailed plans are operational.

Having data inventories at the three different planning levels (unit, division, and corporate) will facilitate the use of human resources input in business planning. Figure 34 summarizes how the different specificity levels of data can be used in the planning process. Business plans are classified as either strategic or operational. A percentage may then be assigned to each type to indicate the extent of their usage at each planning level. The specificity level needed for each planning level and type of business plan is also indicated.

Figure 34.   Potential usefulness of human resources input in different types
of business plans and at different levels.

Types of Plans	Business Planning at Unit Level 1		Business Planning at Division Level 2		Business Planning at Corporate Level 3	
	Strategic	Operational	Strategic	Operational	Strategic	Operational
Usage	25%	75%	50%	50%	75%	25%
Degree of HR input specificity needed	P O	P O	P O	P O	P O	P O
	2 3	4 3	1 2	3 4	1 2	2 3

P = primarily
O = occasionally

As shown in Figure 34, business planning at the corporate level is
more strategic than operational. Thus most of the human resources
data will be at specificity levels 1 and 2 and rarely levels 3 or 4. However, there are three situations in which the corporate level could require human resources input at specificity level 4. First, the company
may be highly centralized, so that even routine decisions are made at
the corporate level. Second, the corporate level of a company may
use an elaborate business planning process to prepare both strategic
and operational plans. Third, the company may occasionally engage
in the detailed planning of a specific project that is totally new to the
company.

At the unit level, business planning is mostly operational and will
require data input of specificity levels 4 and 3. Although not much
strategic planning will take place at this level, when it does take
place, it will be more specific than strategic planning at the corporate
level, and it will, therefore, use input at specificity levels 2 and 3.

In short, a human resources data inventory represents the process
of collecting and storing quantitative information on current employees in the organization. A human resources data inventory system defines the nature of the information to be collected and the
process of analyzing and transmitting this information to various
decision makers.

An inventory system can be evaluated in terms of its relevance to
the SBP process and its usefulness for analysis. Raw data are the
content of the data inventory. The inventory is used through the

analysis of these data and their transmission to the strategic business planners. The content and the use of the data inventory are equally important to SBP.

Summary

A human resources data inventory system has three major elements: the data themselves, the collection and storage of the data, and the analysis of the data. The inventory should contain only relevant employee information and should help to integrate the planning and utilization functions of HRP and SBP. The data may be collected by various segments of the organization and can be analyzed in two phases: classifying the employees and selecting appropriate intervening variables. Accurate information on employees should be found in the employee files. The files should present information so it is easy to handle, update, analyze, and store. The summary employee data sheet is one type of employee file that works well for most organizations. Pertinent information can be entered and updated on the data sheet. The data may later be transferred to computer cards for data processing and storage.

The summary employee data card should include such information as personal facts and characteristics, current position, education, and work specialization, as well as performance and promotability and data on the employee's objectives, aspirations, and preferences. A behaviorally anchored rating scale provides a useful method for quantifying performance evaluations. Pay grades can be used to indicate the employee's degree of promotability. The employee data card stores all the important employee information—both subjective and objective—and allows for the further collection and updating of the information.

Human resources data are converted into usable input for SBP at the unit, division, and corporate levels of the organization. At the unit level, the employees are classified in four specificity levels, from specific job titles to general pay grades. Once aggregated, the data may be used at the unit, division, or corporate levels. The type of planning to be undertaken determines the specificity level of the data. Strategic planning, which is broad, requires general data. Specific operational planning, however, requires specific data.

The human resources data inventory is generally found at all three planning levels in the organization. At each level, a percentage of both strategic and operational plans is used. For each type of planning and at each planning level, there is a certain specificity level required for the data.

This chapter has emphasized the link between HRP and SBP. The collection of human resources data for the preparation of the data inventory provides a significant input for SBP. Much human resources information can be found in most organizations. However, because the information is often disorganized, little of it is used in planning. Before engaging in HRP and SBP, then, organizations must develop practical human resources data inventories and procedures for processing the information meaningfully.

CHAPTER 10

Planning Structural Changes

Strategic business planning defines an organization's missions and broad goals. It allocates, in a general way, the limited resources available to the organization. Human resources planning is primarily concerned with the availability and utilization of personnel to accomplish the organization's missions and goals. Both SBP and HRP determine the shape of the organization (its structures and procedures) that best suits the accomplishment of the business's product market mission.

In most situations, organizational planning is a gradual process associated with the changes inside and outside the organization. In simple form, organizational planning is the first logical step in HRP. Once an organization develops a strategy, it can make the necessary structural adjustments by creating new jobs, consolidating some others, and perhaps eliminating a few. Next, the organization develops forecasts and identifies recruitment and training needs. However, the relationship between organizational planning and HRP is not a one-way, sequential process. The shape an organization takes depends in part on its existing personnel, personnel policies, and management philosophy. In other words, ongoing HRP activities influence the organization's future shape.

Organizational planning is not a simple process of grafting a few new jobs onto the existing structure and adjusting the number of hierarchical levels and the span of control. A simple, incremental process may be adequate for minor or short-term changes. But organizational planning is essentially a long-term activity concerned with major or long-term changes, over a period of three to five years. In this sense, it is a strategic activity heavily influenced by the availability and readiness of suitable personnel during the contemplated time period.

The Meaning of Strategic Organizational Planning

We use the term strategic organizational planning (SOP) to describe long-term adaptations an organization will have to make in its structure because of the alterations in its internal and external environments as clarified in strategic business plans. SOP includes broad policies and important structural and procedural alterations affecting the entire organization. The concept of SOP can be illustrated through an analogy to different levels of structural designs.

Organizational theorists often refer to macro-, meso-, and micro-organizational designs. Macroorganization theory deals with the design of structures for the entire organization. Microorganization theory deals primarily with job design and the relationships of personnel to jobs. Mesoorganizational theory deals with the operations of departments—an intermediate level between the two extremes.

SOP refers to macroorganizational design affecting the developments and changes at the meso and micro levels. A top–down approach, however, should not be construed to mean that changes at the meso and micro levels can occur only after a macrolevel change. On the contrary, changes in job designs (bottom–up influences) often force an organization to make major structural changes.

SOP covers changes, and/or adaptations, of the entire organization, or of a large and important section of the organization. These changes and adaptations can be either internal or external. They are expressed as broad policies that restructure decision-making procedures and levels, spans of control of the president and/or key vice presidents, and the like. The adjustments and changes, which deal with long-term issues and problems, usually are made by the highest authorities in the organization. These are policy decisions, not routine decisions. The effects of SOP decisions may take some time to be felt by the organization, but the impact can be long-lasting. Errors—difficult to discern immediately—generally will affect many people.

Factors Affecting SOP

The SOP process can either be reactive or proactive, depending on the type and the philosophy of SBP. In a sense, SOP is a strategy for achieving the goals set by the strategic business planners.

Internal and external pressures constantly act on an organization. These forces, emanating from changes in the economic, social, legal, political, technological, and competitive environment of the organization, are at first broad. Broad or general internal pressure may also come from such areas as personnel, stockholders, major power blocks, and changes in employee productivity. These pressures are analyzed and are often expressed in the form of strategic business plans. This is the first phase in the analysis of the forces creating a need to change.

The second phase of the analysis is more specific: The sources of the internal and external pressures take the shape of specific factors directly affecting the organization. For instance, organizations will respond to changes in the environment by expanding or contracting existing operations. The decision to expand or contract, as well as the perceived strengths and weaknesses of the current structure, rather than the gross changes in the organization's internal and external environments, creates the need for SOP. In other words, certain intervening variables modify the impact of the brute forces inside and outside the organization.

Business Forecasts

A major component of SOP is business forecasting. Organizational missions are set and adjusted against predictions about inflation, costs, wages, raw material supplies, energy sources, and so forth. On the basis of these predictions, organizations alter their structural characteristics. If, for instance, forecasters predict that wages in several employee categories will continue to increase drastically over the next two years, a restructuring of certain departments to reduce requirements for employees in these job categories may be necessary. SOP is influenced highly by the fluctuations of general economic business cycles. The restructuring that took place in the U.S. auto industry in 1980, which resulted in the laying-off of over 100,000 employees, clearly illustrates how business conditions affect organizational planning.

Expansion or Retrenchment

SOP is often undertaken in anticipation of future organizational expansion or retrenchment. Most organizations expect to grow in size and scope. Such expansions can include mergers, acquisitions, new units, and enlarged existing units. Irrespective of how an organization expands, expansion will have an impact on its shape and structure.

Retrenchment presents another set of pressures on the organization. Cutbacks, layoffs, shortened working hours, total disinvestment in certain areas, and other forms of retrenchment create the need to adjust and modify the current organizational structure.

Technology and Product Mix Changes

Changes in the product mix and/or services produced by an organization and changes in the manufacturing or operating technology may require new organizational structures. An expected move to a higher technology operation may make the existing structure obsolete in the light of the different skill composition of the new workforce.

Different technologies require different organizational structures. The impact of technology on the organizational structure is moderated by many factors. Some of the more relevant ones are the changes in employee skill composition, time requirements, the need for coordination, centralization/decentralization of the operations, and feedback time. Introduction of a new piece of equipment or process can also create the need to realign the existing organizational structure. For instance, the introduction of an automatic data processing system may exert pressure on the existing information channels and may require the creation of a new department or the modification of an existing one. In short, changes in technology, regardless of their causes, will strongly affect the existing structure. An actual case will help to dramatize the importance of technology in shaping the future structure of an organization.

In 1978, a medium-sized bank with 27 branches decided to use automatic data processing systems in its consumer loan departments. Before the computers, processing a loan application followed certain predetermined steps. First, a clerk in the loan department gave the client a form to complete; second, a credit checker reviewed the information on the form for correctness; third, the applicant saw an assistant loan manager. In clear-cut cases a decision was generally made by the assistant loan manager. However, exceptions and difficult cases were forwarded to the next higher level, and the manager of the loan department made the decision. The introduction of the computers in 1978 altered the process as follows. First, as before, the client receives the application form from the clerk; second, the information on the form is reviewed for correctness by a credit checker, as before, and then it is fed into a computer. The computer, programmed to make the routine decisions usually made by the assistant loan manager, separates the clear-cut rejections and the clear-cut approvals from the rest of the applications.

At this point about 20 percent of the applications receive a positive or a negative answer. The client is then contacted. The original clerk handles the remaining formalities and the customer receives the loan.

The clerk refers exceptional cases to the manager of the loan department. This procedure has made the assistant loan manager's job obsolete. This person had to be trained and promoted to make the exceptional decisions or taught to use the computer, thus becoming a technician rather than a manager. Another alternative was to encourage these employees to leave the organization.

This technological change has eliminated entirely one managerial layer. Figure 35 depicts the original and the current shapes of the branch organizations, three years after the change. The number of departmental managers and clerks actually increased. Because of anticipated increases in business, some of the assistant loan managers were promoted. Top management of the bank hoped that by handling only the exceptions, the managers would be able to spend

Figure 35.   Impact of automatic data processing on structure of branch banks.

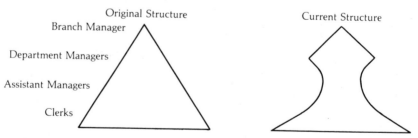

more time with each client, therefore increasing customer satisfaction. In most branches, business increased within a year of the change. Job satisfaction among the clerical personnel also improved noticeably.

Management Philosophy

Another important factor influencing organizational structure is the changing values and philosophies of managerial personnel. In general, the concept of close supervision is on the decline. More and more responsibility and authority are being delegated to lower levels in the organization. Such changes certainly influence the managers' span of control. Managerial philosophies are becoming more flexible and participative. SOP attempts to incorporate the changes in the philosophy of the managers into new and more accommodating organizational structures. The need for tall organizational structures with an elaborate chain of command reflecting the belief that a narrow span of control is necessary to achieve organizational goals is giving way to flatter organizational structures with a rather wide managerial span of control. Such changes are a result of the development of a management philosophy in which personnel are seen as mature and not in need of close supervision.

Leadership Styles

As key top managers in organizations are replaced, or new managers are added to the existing team, leadership styles usually change. A new president or vice president brought in to guide the organization into new arenas requires a change in the structure of the organization to accommodate his or her leadership style. Effective organizational structures differ under different leadership styles. An authoritarian president will be uncomfortable with a permissive and laissez-faire structure. There will be pressures to start the SOP process.

Role of the Union

A previously non-union organization may change its structure to combat or accommodate the new unionization. Personnel departments may be enlarged, and their locations in the organizational hierarchy may be changed. Working with a contract may require a new style and attitude from the managerial personnel. The managers of major divisions could be replaced with people more experienced in labor-management relations. Certainly, the emergence of a union within an organization creates new pressures to which an institution will react by making structural alterations.

Impact of the Law

The changing role of government also necessitates SOP. Some organizations that receive government contracts or that otherwise have substantial contact with government agencies have created departments within their organizations to coordinate government relations and comply with government regulations.

Personal Demands

Powerful individuals and various employee groups often attempt to modify an organization's structure so that it fulfills the individual's or group's needs. Personalizing the organization to meet individual objectives is a common and continuous phenomenon. Through whatever available means—including infighting and power plays—individuals often attempt to put their personal imprint on the organization that employs them. It is not uncommon to see the president of an organization restructure the organization to consolidate his or her powers. Key personnel are shuffled within the organization, not necessarily for objectively sound reasons but because of different power plays. Regardless of the means used or the degree to which it is accomplished, personalization of the organization creates a need for SOP.

Marketing Mix

Changes in marketing mix often require changes in the marketing strategy. Increasing retail sales in proportion to wholesale sales may be possible only by building a new, or altering the existing, marketing organization. In a large organization, for instance, the functional division of labor in the marketing department at the corporate level may be reorganized according to geographical divisions due to the increased number of retail sales personnel. A company marketing its product through wholesalers does not need as elaborate a sales force as if it were marketing its products through retailers. A centralized marketing division might be quite adequate in the first instance. However, moving into retail business not only will require a substantial increase of marketing personnel but also the reorganization of the marketing personnel according to the different geographical areas they serve.

Similarly, planned changes in the composition of clients affect the structural characteristics of the organization. A company shifting from household clients to institutional clients is very likely to contract its marketing division and realign the geographical areas covered by its sales force. SOP helps assess the impact of these changes and provides for controlled institutional reaction.

Perceived Strengths and Weaknesses of the Current Structure

Managers often see their own organizations as possessing unique strengths or weaknesses. Thus they justify the fact that their organizations differ structurally from other organizations of similar size in the same industry. Perceived weaknesses create pressures for structural changes. Similarly, management's desire to exploit perceived strengths prompts structural changes. Capitalizing on perceived strengths is one way to create a competitive advantage over other organizations. Often an important segment of the organization is built around a perceived strength.

Business organizations often advertise their products or services as being of high quality, reliability, and dependability. To ensure high quality, reliability, and dependability, management may make the organization's structural characteristics different from those of other organizations. For example, the decision to move the quality control department outside the manufacturing department and give it status equal to manufacturing may be the result of SOP.

The difference in the organizational structures of Martin Marietta Corporation's cement and aerospace divisions exemplifies this thinking. The company decided to compete in the cement market by lowering its product prices. To achieve this objective, an efficient manufacturing process technology was built. In every cement plant, all organizational functions are subordinate to manufacturing, and everything is aimed at achieving an efficient, continuous flow of products.

On the other hand, the one-job-at-a-time technology used in the aerospace division is designed to achieve high reliability and dependability of the products. The quality control department has become omnipotent in the organization because the management of the division believes that a single defective product would be one too many.

International Factors

One of the most dramatic and significant trends of the last three decades has been the rapid and sustained growth of international business. Of all the factors mandating the need for SOP, the impact of international considerations is one of the strongest. The impact of international business is important because the mere process of becoming international eventually forces the corporation to develop new policies, structures, and procedures for effectively pursuing its objectives.

Many of the domestic pressures that create an organization's need for SOP can be extended to cover international business activities. However, the unique problems that develop when an organization crosses national boundaries cause international SOP to differ from domestic SOP. Special elements of risk, conflict, and operating environment influence SOP functions and thus require new orientations, attitudes, and knowledge from the executives involved with SOP.

Firms entering international business experience special risks in finance, politics, government regulations, and taxation. These risks derive from the different currencies, monetary standards, and national goals that characterize the world marketplace. Unforeseen changes in fiscal policy, different legal systems, overlapping jurisdictions, balance-of-payment considerations, fluctuating exchange rates, and differential inflationary trends produce unique needs for SOP.

A common type of potentially explosive conflict results from the disparity between the interests of the national sovereign states and the goals of the organization engaged in international business. One example is the organization's desire for factor mobility. An organization starts operations in another country to gain an advantage over its competition. The corporation, depending on the economic exigencies, would like to move its operations to a more advantageous location. However, once the initial investment decision is made, the company loses its ability to freely transfer funds, technology, and personnel from one country to another because of unwanted learning costs and political pressures exerted by the host country's government.

Conflicts also arise when a corporation's product is considered vital for the national interest and security. The management of such organizations faces problems of national allegiance. When business activity becomes international, its environmental influences become more complex, diverse, and significant than before. Multiple environments broaden the range of SOP problems, thus requiring new tools, concepts, analytical methods, and types of information. The shape and structural characteristics of multinational companies need to be modified to cope with the problems of operating in multiple environments.

A multinational corporation must enter into contractual arrangements with host country governments before it can operate in businesses restricted to public economic enterprises, such as transportation, publications, and natural resources. The executives of companies operating in a single environment are seldom versed in the management techniques needed to operate smoothly in situations where a major portion of ownership is in the hands of the government. Legal, political, economic, and social institutions vary throughout the world. Some are based on democratic or capitalistic principles; others are based on socialistic, communistic, or totalitarian concepts. Laws not only differ, but they develop from different philosophical, cultural and theoretical foundations that management should appreciate.

In summary, international business succeeds by operating within different societies and by pursuing comparative advantages on an international scale. To deal with pressures not encountered in the domestic setting, multinational corporations must change the components of traditional SOP.

The SOP Process

The SOP process has three stages. The first stage is the analysis of the present shape of the organization and its structural characteristics. The second stage involves planning the shapes and characteristics that management envisions may be needed to achieve organizational objectives. The third stage involves developing strategies for implementing the agreed-upon changes.

Organizational Analysis

Organizational analysis is the review or audit of key structural characteristics by top management, in light of the direction in which the organization wants to move, as specified in strategic business

Figure 36.   Form for ranking important influences on SOP.

Influences on Shape and Structural Characteristics of Organization	Relative Impact of Influences*				
	1	2	3	4	5
General economic conditions					
Market and competition					
Expected expansion					
Expected retrenchment					
Technology					
Product mix					
Managerial styles					
Laws and government regulations					
Union					
Employee demands					
International conditions					

*Relative impact ranges from no pressure to change current shape or structural characteristics (1) to extreme pressure to change current shape or structural characteristics (5).

plans. There are many ways of reviewing the current structural characteristics of an organization and assessing how well they will meet the demands mandated by anticipated changes in the organizational environment.

The first step in an organizational analysis is assessing the strategic issues that may necessitate structural changes. The chief executive officer or a select group of managers first reviews the probable impact of each of the factors discussed in this chapter and illustrated in Figure 36. Assessing the relative impact of each factor gives top management an idea of why the current structure needs adjustment and allows management to concentrate on a few of the significant factors. The cause for the need to change must be diagnosed before an appropriate change can be prescribed. For instance, a change in top-level department structures caused by expected changes in product mix could be different from a change necessitated by recent unionization or international competition.

The analysis may help management establish the priority for structural changes. For instance, because of deterioration in general economic conditions, the organization may want to combine two departments. However, simultaneous pressure from international competition may require just the opposite. For instance, management may be considering the consolidation of domestic and international sales in one department and allowing the same staff to handle both types of sales. This move might be expected to save the company operating costs and to enable it to coast through poor domestic market conditions. However, conditions in the international market may be such that if even for a few years a high degree of individualized attention is not given to foreign operations, the company's international competitors may make drastic inroads into its international sales and erode its competitive advantage for many years to come. Ranking the degree of pressure from the different sources and considering its long- and short-term impact may enable management to resolve the conflicts.

Alternative Organizational Structures

The second phase in SOP involves designing alternative structures to meet present and future challenges. The crucial need key executives are constantly confronted with as they deal with current and forthcoming issues is to eliminate structural weaknesses and enhance organizational strengths.

SOP can cover the same planning period as SBP, or even a period several years longer. However, the first 12 months of the SOP period are critical. The organization must have a clear picture of what its structure will be like in the 12 months immediately ahead. Without a clear projection of its key structural characteristics, the organization cannot accomplish meaningful HRP.

Top management may spend too much or too little time and effort adjusting the organization's structure. Executives may indulge in elaborate exercises, devising alternative structures for every conceivable business scenario. The problem is that there are no set rules on how to determine appropriate solutions to the organization's structural problems. Consequently, management must act cautiously. Before selecting an alternative solution, the executive should be satisfied that the alternative indeed solves the problem. Once the executive has established an objective relationship between the solution and the problem, he or she should reconsider the problem. Is the problem real? How acute is it? Is it properly identified and analyzed?

Organizational planning decisions are made by a select group of people. Very few individuals within the top management group are involved. The executive must not only seek the optimum economic solution, but must also consider the political consequences of the decisions. Too often strategic decisions involving vital organizational interests are made during managerial power plays. A sound economic solution may be discarded for internal political reasons.

Implementing SOP

Decisions to restructure an organization have broad, long-lasting impacts on the organization's policies, procedures, and personnel. Obviously, the success of SOP depends on its being accepted by those organizational members affected by the changes. Conceivably, personnel will resist implementation of the changes. The resistance may derive from either real or perceived problems in the change cycle. To anticipate the resistance to change, management must anticipate the problems.

Reactions by the organizational members to structural changes are based on a three-dimensional evaluation of the change.[1] These three dimensions or factors are the logical, psychological, and sociological. The *logical* dimension is a cost/benefits analysis of the structural change based on available economic evidence such as increased profits or reduced costs. It is the individual's assessment of the benefits to the organization provided by the new structure. The *psychological* assessment is the consideration of how the change influences the individual. It concerns the expected qualifications or denial of personal needs as a result of the changes brought by the impact of the new structure. The *sociological* dimension of the evaluation assesses the impact of the structural change on the interaction of the organization members.

These three dimensions of the individual's assessment of change are determined by three factors. The first is the nature of the change itself. The second factor is the means and the process by which the structural change has been introduced into the organization. The third element is the perceptual base or cognitive map of the individual, the value pattern that guides the individual's perception of the world. The three factors just described interact to determine the logical, psychological, and sociological dimensions of the person's reaction to a structural change—which, in turn, determine whether the person will resist or accept the change.

Resistance to change can also be viewed as being caused by faulty diagnosis of the problem, improper or inadequate solution of the problem, the manner of intervention, and assessment of the change.

The actual diagnosis and the process of diagnosing the problem could cause resistance. Affected individuals may perceive that the organizational problems have not been properly diagnosed or that proposed solutions are directed to superficial rather than real problems. Executives may differ in their assessments of the real problem. For example, is it a marketing or a production problem? The process of diagnosing the problem can also cause resistance. How was the diagnosis done? Were the affected people involved? Was the problem identified and presented to the rest of the organization unilaterally, by a single or a select group of executives? Was the problem diagnosed by an outside consultant hired by the top management? Depending on the circumstances, the answers to such questions may reveal areas of resistance associated with the diagnostic phase of the change process.

The selected change itself, of course, may be a major cause of resistance. For real or imaginary reasons, people react negatively to the intended solutions. After all, their professional lives and organizational roles are affected. Again, the reaction may be to the solution itself and/or to the process of determining the necessary change. An executive may agree with the basic premises of the intended solution but may resent it because of his or her lack of involvement in its selection. This does not mean that everybody wants to be involved to the same degree with impending organizational changes. But avoiding surprises is a good policy.

The actual implementation of the new structure or policies can coincide with the implementation of the strategic business plans. Or to provide lead time, the change could be implemented ahead of the strategic business plans.

The organization should carefully review and evaluate the change. After a change has been implemented, people may begin to react negatively, not because they dislike the solution itself but because it fails to solve their problems. Such reactions can be eliminated if management monitors the change and makes adjustments along the way.

How to Analyze Reactions to Structural Change

The reactions to structural changes can range from very negative to very positive. It is as important to predict positive reactions as it is to predict negative ones. Individuals will react to change because of

Figure 37.   Form for macroanalysis of employees' potential reactions to structural changes.

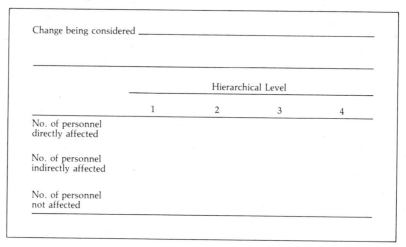

its perceived impact on matters important to them. Before undertaking any structural change, executives should diagnose its potential impact on personnel.

The form shown in Figure 37 can assist executives and staff specialists in diagnosing the general reactions of the people affected by a proposed change. Changes in hierarchical structure, span of control, centralization or decentralization, functional specialization, and general personnel policies could all be analyzed in this way. After filling in the form, the executive can get a general picture of who, at what level(s) in the organization, will feel the impact of the proposed change the most.

From this macroanalysis the executive can move to a microanalysis. Having isolated possible impact areas, the executive can predict how selected individuals will react to the proposed change. The analysis could be in terms of how important factors in the work environment of the individual(s) will be affected by the change. By important elements in the work environment we mean those factors influencing job satisfaction: wages, job security, advancement opportunities, working conditions, task autonomy, power, position with peer group, relations with supervisor(s) and subordinates, and the content and nature of the job itself.

Employee satisfaction with economic rewards is an important

facet of organizational climate. Traditionally, wages have been considered to be the most important motivator of employee behavior. Money has a universal appeal and may be used in countless ways to satisfy our various needs. In actuality, however, money is limited in its usefulness as a motivating force. It can eliminate sources of dissatisfaction, but in itself will not increase employee satisfaction.

Satisfaction with the job itself is a significant motivational factor. Employees are motivated to perform more effectively if they consider their jobs to be interesting and meaningful. If the employees perform isolated tasks that are distantly related to the overall work structure, their motivation to produce may be quite low. It is important that employees receive a form of built-in satisfaction from their jobs.

Another important facet of climate is whether the employees feel reasonably secure in the organization. Job security (especially in industries affected by adverse economic and competitive factors) plays a very significant role in how employees behave and perform on their jobs.

Perceived opportunities for advancement also tend to influence employee motivation. A high percentage of turnover problems occur because of the lack of advancement opportunities. Also, the "I don't care" attitude and unwillingness to put in a little extra effort are directly related to an individual's long-term commitment to the organization.

The need for status and recognition—to stand out among our peers—affects employees at all levels. The extent to which employees feel that their accomplishments and good task performance are being recognized by management is an important contributor to the employer's perception of the overall climate of an organization.

Similarly, the power of the individual and his or her relations with peers and subordinates as well as with superior(s) are important contributors to job satisfaction or dissatisfaction. The impact of the structural change on the individual could be indicated by assessing how the change is likely to affect each of these facets of job satisfaction.

Before deciding on strategies to introduce change, the executive may have to consider the specific aspects of each of the factors that influence job satisfaction. At this point, however, the kind of micro-picture suggested in Figure 38 should be sufficient. Each element of this simple job satisfaction instrument could be rated for each of the

Figure 38.   Form for microanalysis of impact of a change on a selected individual.

Name of Person Reuben Hayes	Position Machine shop supervisor

Change Being Considered_____Reorganization of manufacturing division_____

Work Factors Important to This Person	Degree of Impact of Considered Change*
Wages/salaries/benefits	−2
Job security	+1
Advancement opportunities	0
Working conditions (office space, parking, secretary, etc.)	0
Task autonomy	+1
Power	−1
Relations with peer group	0
Relations with supervisor(s)	+1
Relations with subordinates	−1
Content and nature of job itself	−1
Total	−4

*Negative: −3, −2, −1   Neutral: 0   Positive: +1, +2, +3

key personnel indicated by the macroanalysis as warranting individual consideration. The impact of the change on each of the specific factors could be estimated on a simple positive-to-negative scale. Once this form is completed for all the key personnel affected by a change, the numbers can be averaged to get a composite picture. This can be done either horizontally (on a factor-by-factor basis) or vertically (by department, pay grade level of employee, and so on).

People generally resist change when they see it having a negative impact on their organizational roles: their autonomy and authority on the job as well as their relations with peers, superiors, and subordinates. Perceived status is an important element. Many factors— private offices, secretaries, assigned parking spaces, and the like—influence an individual's perception of his or her status in the organization. Such status symbols are grouped together in our instrument under the heading of "Working conditions."

Users of the microdiagnostic tool must keep one key point in mind: The questions must be answered from the point of view of the person affected by the change. In other words, the executive must measure the impact of the change as it would be perceived by the person in question. Executives must therefore develop accurate perceptions of the peers and subordinates with whom they are in close contact. From time to time, then, executives might test their perceptions of others' reactions to possible decisions.

Obviously, the diagnostic instrument presented in Figure 38 could serve as a questionnaire distributed to persons identified by the macroanalysis. The impending change could be outlined in terms of several alternatives. The participants in the survey could then speculate about how such changes might affect their job satisfaction. In small companies such explorations could be conducted informally over a period of time. The questionnaire or the formal interview approach would be more useful in large organizations where the chief executive or the executive contemplating a strategic structural change has little access to the people who will be affected by the change.

The results of the analyses—macro and micro—should help top management decide whether or not to implement a change. If the macrochange will have limited impact, the executive may decide to stop at this level of analysis and go ahead with the change. However, if the change affects many people, the executive should consider the nature of the impact and then decide whether or not to implement the change and what strategy to use for implementation.

A good implementation strategy minimizes resistance and increases acceptance by the members of the organization. The information generated by the microanalysis provides the basis for the proper implementation strategies. The executive takes the first step toward developing an effective implementation strategy by asking: "*Why* will the change have a negative impact on a particular aspect of an individual's job satisfaction?" The next obvious question is: "*What* can be done to reduce this negative impact?" Answers to these two questions form the essence of implementation strategies.

Summary

Strategic organizational planning defines the structural changes an organization must make in response to changes in its operating environments. SOP may be a part of either SBP or HRP. SOP is related to SBP in many ways. First, the need for reorganization is often stimulated by the analysis that goes into the making of strategic business plans. Second, SOP can be an inherent part of strategic business plans. That is, at the moment of their formulation, new business objectives may alter the structure of the organization. In a sense, SOP is a strategy for achieving the goals set by strategic business planners. As such an organized activity, SOP can provide an effective link between SBP and HRP.

To enable adequate treatment of organization planning at the executive level, we have emphasized its strategic rather than its operational aspects.

SOP describes long-term adaptations an organization will have to make in its structure because of the alterations in its internal and external environments. The SOP process can be divided into three phases. The first phase is the analysis of the current structural characteristics of the organization. This phase involves an assessment of the strategic issues that may necessitate structural changes. The second phase involves the design of alternative structures to meet present and future challenges. The third phase deals with the implementation of the decision to restructure the organization. The success of SOP depends heavily on its acceptance by those organizational members affected by the change.

CHAPTER 11

Recruitment and Selection Policies

This chapter explores the policy decisions that influence recruitment and selection, and the processes by which an organization obtains the number and types of employees it needs to accomplish its objectives and plans. Recruitment and selection involve the actual process of going out to find individuals to do the jobs, attracting them to the organization, and building methods for deciding which applicants to hire.

An organization's recruitment and selection system communicates the broad characteristics of the organization and its management philosophy to potential employees. Uncoordinated recruitment and selection processes often send incorrect messages, turn off potential employees, or build incorrect stereotypes. Poor recruitment and selection practices make subsequent utilization of human resources difficult.

The first questions to answer in human resources acquisition are where and how to look for job applicants. A system that produces unqualified employees, or one that produces qualified employees only after long delays and at a very high cost, needs to be reexamined. In recruiting new employees, management must consider the nature of the labor market, sources of employees, methods of reaching the sources of employees, and, finally, the legal and cost restraints on hiring.

Figure 39 illustrates the complete recruitment process. It is important to remember that every step of this process is affected by budget constraints and by legal considerations, such as the EEO Act and immigration laws.

Within the recruitment process certain important policy decisions

Figure 39.   Recruitment process.

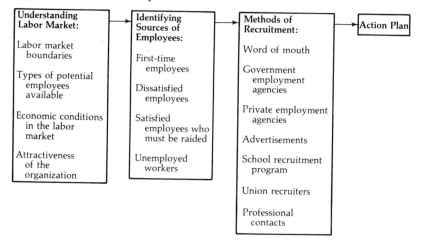

must be made. These decisions will have a long-term impact on the organization's recruitment activities. Because such decisions involve strategic planning, they are made at the top level in an organization, by a high-level functional executive and/or the chief executive officer or a group of senior executives. In this chapter we discuss the aspects of recruitment policies that require strategic planning. To facilitate our analysis, we will consider separately each of the major activities found in the normal recruitment process.

Understanding the Labor Market

Labor Market Boundaries

Knowing the boundaries of the labor market enables management to estimate the potential supply of human resources from which the organization may recruit. Technically, a labor market is the geographical area in which people looking for work and employers seeking personnel interact. The decision to establish the boundaries of the labor market for certain categories of personnel is critical because it affects the price of labor. The actual geographical boundaries of any labor market depend on the nature of the skills sought. For certain skills the labor market could be the entire country. At the other extreme, students seeking part-time clerical employment may be unwilling to take jobs that are not within 10 miles of their universities.

To begin a successful recruitment program, one must define the labor market. Data entering into this decision are highly technical and specific. The decision is influenced by such information as the organization's long- and short-term objectives. Decisions to increase or decrease labor market boundaries are made according to business objectives and human resources plans.

Available Potential Human Skills

Organizations do not hire labor; they hire specific kinds of workers with particular skills. Knowledge of the type of skills that are available and where these skills are located is critical to an organization's efforts to recruit the desired number of qualified employees. This information acquires strategic characteristics when it is used in establishing company objectives and making future plans.

Economic Conditions

The economic situation in the labor market can affect recruitment. A new plant moving into a depressed area, where the supply of labor far exceeds demand, may have no problem filling positions. Knowing where such areas exist can be critical for an organization in a labor-intensive industry. The decision to expand the boundaries of the labor market to include such a depressed area can also affect the success or failure of the organization. These are policy decisions involving strategic planning with significant long-term effects.

Understanding labor market conditions is the first step in designing a successful recruitment program. The recruitment process requires advance planning, some of which is strategic. Forecasts of demographic characteristics of the future labor force and predictions of the degree of labor force mobility and the boundaries of labor markets certainly have significant impacts on an organization's human resources situation in the future. Future conditions of the labor market often are projected in broad employee categories. Most small or medium-sized organizations with undeveloped personnel departments pay little attention to this phase of recruitment. At best, they base their projections on government research and forecasts. The U.S. Department of Labor is a good source of information on labor markets. The Bureau of Labor Statistics publishes monthly and yearly data on the current and expected conditions in different labor markets.

Identifying Sources of Employees

In the second phase of the recruitment process, the organization determines what sorts of employees are available in the labor market, and how these employees search for jobs. In general, we can classify available employees into four categories: first-time employees, dissatisfied employees, satisfied employees who must be "raided" from other companies, and unemployed workers.

The First-Time Employed

The first-time employee is generally young and inexperienced, and is often just out of school or military service. This category also includes some older employees, such as women who are entering the labor markets for the first time. Young, inexperienced employees are likely to be mobile, both in their willingness to seek employment in a broad job market and in their willingness to change jobs within the first five years of their employment.

Older inexperienced employees are generally less mobile in their search for and acceptance of employment. They tend to define narrow geographical boundaries for their labor market, but tend to stay in their jobs.

The Dissatisfied Employee

Most employees are somewhat dissatisfied with their jobs because any job has its disadvantages. Consequently, a number of employed persons will be looking for better jobs. However, only a small percentage of all employed persons are actively seeking another job. Dissatisfied employees are perhaps more receptive to tips, rumors, and actual job offers than satisfied employees, but they may not engage in an active search for work.

Satisfied Employees Who Must Be Raided

Raiding is the practice of hiring employees from other companies. Satisfied employees constitute a different source of workers because the company actively seeks them, not vice versa. These employees have not made their intention to move to another job known to others. They are usually very successful in their current jobs and seem content with them. Often, the particular individual is known personally by the potential employer or by the recruitment agency acting on behalf of the company.

The Unemployed Worker

Unemployed workers could be individuals who have involuntarily lost their jobs because of reduction in the labor force, permanent plant closure, or some infraction of company rules. Organizations are generally careful, even reluctant, about tapping this source of potential employees for fear that they will return to their previous jobs, where they have accumulated seniority benefits. If the employee was discharged for the infraction of a company rule, the potential employer has suspicions about the employee's ability, motivation, and even character.

Tapping the different sources of employees involves certain strategic decisions. For instance, an organization may establish a policy of not raiding another company. An organization may require a minimum number of years of experience for certain or all job categories. Such a policy virtually eliminates first-time employees. Because such decisions have a significant impact on the future, they influence human resources planning. In practice, many organizations try to remain flexible by refraining from making categorical policy decisions. They may become more restrictive as the economic conditions in the labor market deteriorate.

Currently there seems to be abundant labor for many job categories. In such cases, some organizations make a priori decisions restricting the sources of employees they are willing to consider for employment. Although such a decision may not have an immediate negative impact, it could jeopardize an organization's sources of future personnel. Or a company may find itself subject to a lawsuit under the Equal Employment Opportunity Act.

Methods of Recruitment

Even in depressed labor markets an organization hardly receives a steady stream of applicants. With a few exceptions, even companies with a reputation for offering good jobs must engage in active recruiting. Once again, the organization has an opportunity to make certain policy decisions that affect the availability and quality of its present and future supplies of human resources. The decision in this case may emphasize or deemphasize the use of a given recruitment method.

Word of Mouth

Word of mouth is an effective method of recruiting. Individuals currently working in the organization, or those who are otherwise associated with it, recommend the organization to other people as a good place to work. Although this method is effective, it may lead to nepotism, particularly in management positions. It may also be inconsistent with affirmative action programs aimed at reducing disparity in the employment of racial minorities. Word-of-mouth recruitment tends to maintain the current characteristics of the labor force.

Employment Agencies

Both private and public employment agencies play an important role in attracting candidates to an organization. Private employment agencies tend to specialize in particular occupations and skills while state employment agencies do not.

For highly specialized job categories, private employment agencies are a good recruitment source. They often have access to employees who have indicated a willingness to change jobs under the right conditions. Because the decision to recruit through agencies is tactical and operational, the use of employment agencies does not involve strategic planning.

Advertisements

Newspaper, trade journal, and professional magazine advertisements tend to attract a large number of applicants. Because the characteristics of the applicants are so varied, making it difficult for the company to distinguish qualified applicants from unqualified ones, many companies have discontinued the method. In recent years, however, organizations have increased their use of this method, not to generate more applicants but to indicate their compliance with EEO and affirmative action programs.

School Recruiting

Recruiting at schools is a good method for reaching individuals seeking their first jobs. Selecting schools and timing visits to them are operational decisions that are best made by personnel specialists. However, there are still certain strategic considerations. The most common one is the company policy to include a new employee on the recruiting team who has recently graduated from the school. Such a policy decision is usually made by the chief executive officer, the president of the division, or the general manager of an operating unit.

Professional Contacts

The use of professional contacts to develop sources of applicants resembles word-of-mouth recruitment. The same tactics are used, but the contacts are among professionals and often occur at trade association meetings, professional society conventions, and executive development sessions sponsored by industry groups and universities.

Organizations can use professional contacts to attract highly skilled and specialized employees. However, effective use of this method involves a policy decision: The organization must encourage its professional employees to attend meetings and develop contacts. For instance, the primary method employed by universities to recruit professors in business administration is through professional contacts at association meetings. A few years ago, when a major university restricted its professors' trips to conventions, it immediately experienced a sizable drop in the number of recruits for available positions. The policy decision adversely affected the college's human resources plans.

Union as a Recruiter

Unions play the roles of employment agencies and recruiting offices for many job categories in certain industries. Unions act as clearinghouses for jobs in the heavily unionized maritime and construction industries, where employment is cyclical. The same is true, though to a lesser degree, in the printing, entertainment, restaurant, and hotel industries. In Western European countries, government agencies often provide this service. A company's personnel department sends its request for employees to the union or to a government agency, and the union or agency selects and sends the employees to the company.

The policy decision with this method is whether or not, or to what extent, the organization is willing to use the union or other outside agency as a recruiter. Even in companies operating in highly unionized industries, management is often reluctant to accept the union's role in recruitment because it sees recruiting as the function and right of management. In these cases, company policies prohibit the personnel departments from directly using union hiring halls.

Legal and Cost Constraints

Both recruitment and the ensuing selection processes take place within the constraints imposed by the law and by costs. Certain methods of recruitment, such as direct personal contacts or sending line executives on recruiting trips to schools, may be totally abandoned or substantially restricted because of their high costs. Personnel departments' budgets generally cover all the direct costs of recruiting but not the hidden, indirect costs. The hidden costs include the time spent by company recruiters from departments other than personnel and the time spent by line executives in making strategic decisions concerning any particular phase of the recruitment process.

As important as costs are in the establishment of many company hiring policies, recent legal requirements have had an even greater influence on personnel recruitment decisions. The employment-related legal restraints in the United States derive primarily from Child Labor laws, Social Security laws, and Section VII of the Civil Rights Act of 1964. These and other pertinent laws are discussed in Chapter 4.

Laws against discrimination are particularly stringent for employers involved in government contracts. In such cases, the contractors are not only prohibited from discriminating in employment, but are also forced to take affirmative action to identify and analyze their employment practices to see if they present problems. Where problems exist, the contractors must develop programs that ensure equal opportunity. The contractors must set specific goals and timetables for achieving equal employment opportunity. In the past, affirmative action meant eliminating artificial barriers to the employment of women and members of minority groups. Today the concept includes equal compensation as well.

Antidiscrimination legislation has had a significant impact on the recruitment and selection practices of organizations. Many organizations are altering their recruiting methods to include ways of reaching minority groups. Such legislation has also begun to affect labor market boundaries, forcing organizations to expand the areas in which they search for employees. For example, consider the organization that traditionally has recruited its plant and clerical personnel from a small labor market. If the EEOC finds the results of such recruiting to be discriminatory, it may force the company to search for applicants in a wider labor market, where minority groups are more likely to be found.

Strategic Selection Planning

The recruitment process brings the candidates to the organization; the selection process enables the organization to decide who should be offered the job. Essentially, selection involves predicting who, among the various applicants, best suits the job being filled. The selection process has three components:

1. The organization's overall philosophy of selection.
2. Techniques and instruments used to gather information about the applicants.
3. The selection decision itself.

The Organization's Overall Philosophy of Selection

There are two extreme orientations in the selection process: One is eliminating applicants who do not meet the company's image, and the other is fitting jobs to the available applicants. By eliminating applicants who do not fit the company's image of a good, reliable employee, the organization is, in effect, trying to find the "right type" of employee. The right type of employee is defined in terms of desirable or appropriate physical characteristics, motivation, background, age, and personality traits similar to those of individuals already in the organization. Such a policy may favor, for example, graduates of Ivy League schools. The organization may not set formal restrictions; rather, it tries to make the organization attractive to the desired types of applicants.

Because applying the "right type" criterion can lead to irrational discrimination, it is unethical and may be unlawful. However, it is a strategic option available to an organization. Some organizations genuinely believe that maintaining a homogeneous workforce improves their effectiveness and efficiency. Their policies necessarily affect their methods and processes of collecting information on the applicants and making the selection decision. Organizations with preconceived ideas of the ideal type of employee will spend time and money to justify their positions ethically and legally and to devise selection criteria that appear to be general.

At the other extreme, some organizations attempt to adjust the jobs to fit the characteristics of the available applicants. Such management philosophy has ramifications beyond the selection process. The organization may spend large sums of money redesigning jobs to meet the characteristics and the demands of the individuals. Great progress has been made in the area of job enrichment, which is essentially a motivational tool, to attract people who otherwise might be reluctant to seek employment in a particular organization. The famous job-redesign experiments of Volvo and Saab originated in an attempt to make the assembly-line jobs attractive to native Swedes; otherwise, the companies would have had to rely increasingly on foreign labor.[1] Similarly, companies attempting to develop new sources of labor are redesigning jobs to permit their performance by blind or otherwise handicapped workers.

Certainly, the two orientations are strategic and have a tremendous long-term impact on the acquisition and utilization of human resources.

Techniques and Instruments for Gathering Information

The most common selection instruments are preliminary interviews, application forms, follow-up interviews, physical examinations, formal tests, and assessment centers. Their design and use are technical issues beyond the scope of this book. However, there are strategic considerations in the selection and use of these instruments that affect the entire organization.

Legality is one of the most important strategic considerations in the design and use of selection instruments. Legal issues primarily involve the kinds of questions asked in applications, tests, and interviews. Consequently, the organization's top management group, as well as its personnel executive, should be familiar with the predictive validity and the pitfalls of the interviews, tests, and other data gathering instruments. Top management does not need to be completely knowledgeable on the technical aspects of these instruments, but it should know the legal do's and don'ts that must be followed during the selection process. More than one old-school manager who has casually disregarded legal requirements has been unpleasantly surprised with a discrimination charge.

There is no built-in conflict between the equal opportunity employment laws and merit selection and promotion programs. Both the law and merit selection and promotion philosophy require selection and promotion of individuals without regard to their religion, sex, color, and race. Such laws are forcing organizations to validate their selection criteria against performance on the job. The short-term impact of the legislation and EEOC practices may be to reduce the use of selection tests by organizations. In the long run, however, the legislation may cause the organization to establish higher validity between selection instruments, jobs, and employee characteristics needed for job proficiency.

As a result of the civil rights decisions, organizations must be aware of the types of information that can be gathered from job applicants. To request information on age, sex, race, national origin, and the like is considered discriminatory unless the employer can demonstrate the pertinence of the information to task performance. For example, employers are prohibited by law from obtaining information on a candidate's religious affiliation unless it is for the purpose of hiring clergy.

Test validity is also becoming a central legal problem in the selection process. The legality of any test rests on how well it predicts job success. Similarly, invasion of privacy has become a legal issue. In particular, personality tests have recently come under attack for probing into such personal areas as sexual preferences, family life, and hidden fears and urges. On occasion, applicants have charged that they were forced to reveal aspects of their private lives that have little relevance to job performance and that their test results were evaluated by individuals not qualified to use personality tests.

In conclusion, using tests to prevent allegations of discrimination in hiring or promotion practices is not an answer in itself. Tests can only be used as one of several instruments and only if they have proven validity. Indiscriminate use of tests can be devastating, both legally and economically.

Final Selection Decision

The selection decision should be based on information pooled from many sources and gathered by a variety of techniques. Determining the final authority for selecting among several candidates is a strategic consideration.

In general, the immediate supervisor of the potential employee has the authority and responsibility for making the final decision. Personnel specialists usually act as advisors. The role of the personnel department increases with the number of positions to be filled. For routine jobs in organizations with traditionally high turnover, the personnel department may play a direct role in the selection process. However, as jobs and positions increase in complexity and/or responsibility, the involvement of the line executive in the selection process also increases.

Summary

This chapter has reviewed the strategic and legal considerations crucial to recruitment and selection planning. We have presented the long-term policy issues that management must consider before it operationalizes any recruitment and selection plan. The first questions management must answer are where and how to look for job applicants. More specifically, in recruiting new employees, the nature and characteristics of the labor market, different sources of employees, methods of reaching potential employees, and, above all, the legal and cost constraints on hiring must be considered.

Strategic planning for recruitment and selection should include a decision on the institutional image to be projected in attracting potential employees. This image should be painted differently for the different categories of personnel the organization is attempting to recruit. Other broad policies involve the organization's overall philosophy of selection, the use of employment tests, and the final authority for selecting candidates.

Human resources planning cannot be treated properly without an adequate perspective on organizational policies concerning hiring. Existing hiring policies may necessitate acceptance of alternative human resources plans. Conversely, specified human resources plans may require an alteration of existing hiring policies.

CHAPTER 12

Planning for Employee Training and Development

Training and developing new employees are crucial to the effective use of human resources and are, therefore, integral parts of human resources planning. Both training and developing involve teaching employees the skills and behavior they need to perform their jobs well. The main differences between training and development are in their time frames. Training focuses on immediate needs, while development achieves long-term objectives. Training has a "now" and "how to" perspective. Employee development, on the other hand, helps employees acquire the abilities and characteristics needed for the future and thus helps both the employee and the organization cope with change.

All employees in an organization need training at one time or another. New employees may need training before they can perform their work; existing employees may require training to improve their performance. Training is stimulated by the organization's desire to improve its effectiveness and individual performances. In progressive organizations, training is a continuous process, not a one-shot activity. Such training becomes development. New employees, new jobs, new problems, and changes in the environment, technology, and knowledge require both a planned approach to training and development and its integration with other personnel administration functions under the HRP umbrella. A discussion of specific activities in training and development programs is beyond our scope. Our concern is with strategic planning for training and development: the establishment of broad policies in conjunction with the overall HRP.

The Need to Integrate Training with HRP

Since training is often used to facilitate the implementation of strategic plans, it should be built around organizational goals as specified in the plans. For instance, if an organization plans to introduce a new product, human resources plans must include provisions for training employees in the production and marketing of this product. Training can be crucial to attaining specific organizational goals.

One strategic decision might be to limit all training activities to specific organizational goals. Many organizations attach their training programs to organizational objectives as defined by specific products or services. Such policies obviously require that training activities be planned in advance.

Strategic business and human resources plans are devices for coping with changing environmental demands. For example, a new ruling on the Occupational Safety and Health Act or on an EEOC decision may stimulate the need for training. Plans must be made for training all production supervisors in the requirements of the new rulings, thus bringing the training process to the center of the HRP.

A shift in organizational goals or newly imposed environmental restrictions and requirements may prevent employees in certain job categories from satisfactorily completing their tasks. For instance, on short notice the supervisors in a food processing plant were required to complete forms on the quality specifications of the product. The supervisors, who were not used to such forms, had difficulty completing them accurately. A training program for completing the forms was instituted. In another part of the same company, several supervisors participated in an accident prevention program that was stimulated by a sudden increase in the accident rate in their departments.

Training programs that deal with these and other problems often require contingency planning. Although training plans are not by nature strategic, there may be a need to create a broad policy just to cover such contingencies. For example, certain large multinational corporations plan for emergency training programs and maintain funds and other resources at the corporate level to provide assistance in the design of a specific, problem-oriented training program anywhere in the world.

Specific Training Programs Within the HRP Context

Training is generally directed toward organizational goals, environmental changes, and specific problems created by the changing goals and environmental demands. In practice, organizations define their training objectives more specifically than this suggests. The specific objectives include orientation training, new skills training, remedial training, training for advancement, training to aid displaced employees, and apprenticeships. Each type of training is guided by a variety of policies defining the boundaries within which the activities may take place. These policies are generally drawn within the basic framework of HRP.

Orientation Training
Many organizations have long recognized the need for formal orientation programs that introduce new employees to their jobs. The programs not only familiarize the employees with the expected tasks and roles, but also provide individuals with information on company rules, personnel policies, and the like. Such inductions can be left to individual supervisors or personnel departments in multi-unit operations, or they can be a matter of company policy requiring a certain degree of strategic planning. Whether to have formal orientation programs is itself a strategic decision having a long-term impact on the company. The organization that wants to institute formal induction programs must also plan the implementation of these programs. The strategic plan may involve, for instance, designing and producing employee handbooks, making provisions in the organization's budget, and issuing the necessary directives and follow-up mechanisms.

Figure 40 describes how to differentiate between the strategic and the tactical planning involved in orientation training. The process starts with deciding whether to have formal induction methods and procedures. Because this is a strategic decision, the organization should first consider the following factors:

- Would a formal program improve the informal induction process?
- How much will the program cost?
- What benefits will it provide?

- Is a uniform policy feasible?
- How specific should such a policy be?

The last two considerations depend on the organization's homogeneity. The more heterogeneous the organization is, the less likely it is to have inclusive policies with specific instructions. In such cases, policies express the desirability of formal induction programs but leave the content and methods of delivery of the programs to the discretion of the local units.

Skills Training

Jobs change and thus require new employee skills. Consequently, even organizations that attract and select the best applicants and put them through excellent induction programs must develop human resources plans that provide for employee retraining and new skills acquisition.

Skill training involves technical, human relations, and conceptual skills. Skill composition changes according to the managerial level of the employees. Personnel occupying top management positions need more conceptual and human relations skills than technical skills. Conversely, front-line managers require more technical and human

Figure 40.   Strategic and tactical planning in orientation training.

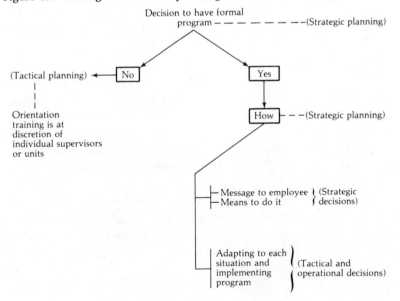

relations skills than conceptual skills. Most middle management personnel require fairly equal amounts of technical, human relations, and conceptual skills.

Skill composition is also affected by the nature and characteristics of the jobs. A marketing research specialist may require more conceptual and technical skills than human relations skills, while a salesperson may need more human relations and technical skills than conceptual skills to be effective on the job.

A major policy question is: How much of the skills updating process should be the organization's responsibility and how much the individual's? The greater the organization's direct involvement in skills updating, the greater the need for planning. Generally, the updating of technical skills specific to the jobs in the organization is an organizational responsibility. Most of the time these skills are provided through some kind of in-house training program for employees new to the job, such as on-the-job, apprenticeship, or vestibule training programs. (Vestibule training gives employees preliminary training prior to placement in the actual job; it takes place in a separate location and uses equipment specifically designed for training purposes.)

Effective performance in top management and professional jobs often requires the development of cognitive abilities. Many organizations use outside resources to train employees in these skills. For example, in the greater Philadelphia area, 75 percent of the medium-size and large companies encourage their employees to enroll in local colleges or technical institutions through a program of reimbursement for the educational costs.[1]

The cost of updating conceptual skills is borne by organizations that require individuals to attend specific programs or encourage them to take approved courses offered by educational institutions. In comparison to updating technical and human relations skills, however, updating conceptual skills requires less of a commitment from an organization. Employee initiative plays the greatest role in improving conceptual skills.

Strategic planning for skills training is twofold. First, it forecasts gradual changes in individual jobs and the relationship of these changes to other jobs. Second, it identifies the type of skills updating that must occur in the organization as a result of the changing nature of the jobs.

Dynamic organizations include forecasts in their human resources plans that predict how existing jobs will evolve in the future and how the organization will meet the requirements of the changed jobs. At the strategic level, human resources plans may point out the direction of the change and the new employee skills needed to meet the change. At the tactical and operational level, each unit may develop its own plans and timetables for updating the skills of its current employees.

Remedial Training

Skills training can also be in the form of remedial training. Remedial training aims to overcome existing deficiencies in employee performance, rather than to develop new skills. The difference between remedial and skills training may be slight. This is especially true in professional jobs, where skills and knowledge unused for some time need to be refreshed by additional training. Remedial training is often tailored to meet the needs of specific individuals rather than occupational groups. Some organizations emphasize remedial training over new skills development. This pragmatic approach, however, can have negative effects on employees. If employees are sent to training programs to overcome a deficiency, they may develop feelings of resentment, thus undermining the purpose of the programs.

Distinguishing between remedial and new skills training is a strategic decision. Identifying needs for remedial training can be part of organizational HRP. It becomes strategic when it leads to organizational policies that define the nature of the training programs in the operating units.

A major oil company, for example, has a policy that requires all employees in its refineries throughout the world to be evaluated to determine their training needs. The forms used to identify training needs are developed in the international training department at the corporate headquarters. The forms describe the individual jobs in detail and identify the specific skills needed to perform each aspect of the jobs. The unit supervisor evaluates the employees in terms of the skills they need to perform their jobs. Next, the unit personnel department categorizes the information on each employee according to skill similarities. The personnel department then cross-references information on the skills needed with information on available training programs. A training program is then planned according to the type of skills the employees need to improve.

Aiding Displaced Employees

Organizations contemplating or anticipating technological changes may train employees to meet the future demands of their jobs. Without training, these employees may be displaced by the technological changes. Not only do such programs help employees keep their jobs, they also reduce resistance to change. Human resources plans should include forecasts of how various technological changes will influence current jobs and what types of training programs the organization may need.

An organization that has flexibility in using its employees may not need strategic HRP. When technological changes occur, such an organization keeps the employees who have the necessary skills to meet the requirements of their changed jobs, lays off those who do not, and hires new employees with the necessary qualifications as replacements. In reality, however, hardly any organizations have this flexibility in human resource acquisition and utilization.

Examples of two companies, one that engaged in a retraining program before a major technological change and one that did not, illustrate the need for considering training in HRP.

Before adopting new microwave transmission technology, a dynamic telephone company retrained its personnel by sending them to courses in electricity, applied mathematics, telephone equipment, and circuitry. The company paid the cost of the training programs. As a result, the company achieved the technological change with minimal disruption and resistance.

At about the same time, the cement division of a large conglomerate was also undergoing a major technological change. The company had decided to replace its old plant with a new facility. The construction took several years. On completion of the project, the employees from the old plant were transferred to the new facility on the basis of seniority. The company undertook extensive on-the-job training programs provided by the various suppliers involved in the construction of the new plant. There was no earlier retraining program. It took the company three years to reach the specified production level, which was supposed to be achieved within three months of the start-up of operations. No matter how much remedial training the employees received, their performance level was far below that of employees at comparable cement plants.

Extensive studies, made by corporate specialists and outside consultants, have converged on one primary cause for the poor perform-ance: the negative employee attitudes toward change and the com-pany's strategic mistake of not retraining the employees during the construction of the new facility. The old-timers who were trans-ferred to the new plant as a result of seniority resented being told by their foreman, a young college graduate in electronic engineering, that they couldn't do their jobs. The jobs in this department had changed drastically. The once-skilled cement makers found their know-how and experience outdated, and they had to depend on people half their age for guidance.

The entire informal work structure was reversed, and the older cement makers had lost their status in the organization. The restruc-turing and the change in technology had eliminated the need for the cement makers' skills. Previously, to control the quality of the ce-ment, a skilled craftsperson, dressed in an asbestos suit, would enter the kiln to check on the uniformity of the flames and make necessary adjustments. Now, the cement quality is controlled electronically from a room resembling the cockpit of an aircraft. Television cam-eras monitor the interior of the kiln. A single technician in the con-trol room can, by pushing a few buttons, adjust the uniformity of the flames without going near the kiln.

After three years, when performance reached the established standards, the consultants and top management could not determine how much of the increased performance was due to employees' im-proved skill levels and how much was due to employees' simply having adjusted to the new situation.

Employee Development

HRP aims to help an organization solve its present and future per-sonnel problems. In the short run, HRP focuses on current organiza-tional problems, such as how to recruit and select the best candidates and how to train personnel to cope with new government regula-tions. Most of the activities are accomplished through tactical and operational planning and, as has been said, are beyond the scope of this book. However, the issues are strategic when human resources plans must come to grips with long-range, fundamental problems of job structures, with long-term personnel policies for improving employment stability and worker performance, and with policies for reducing the workforce through natural attrition, layoffs, and discharge.

Personnel and organizational development goals cannot be reached with a haphazard, on-off approach. Development processes must be tied to other organizational procedures. Planning for personnel and organizational development is strategic. Personnel information gathered for developmental activities—such as information on the current and future availability of human resources—can help make strategic business plans realistic.

Career Paths

Career path planning is the key element in planned personnel development. Career paths are crucial to the blending of employee needs and aspirations with organizational goals. This leads to compatible personnel and organizational development activities. Unfortunately, career path planning has been a neglected area of personnel management for many years, and it still is. At best, career path planning is a frustrating exercise for several reasons. First, the instability of employees in the early years of their employment makes career planning a futile exercise. Young employees often do not have clear ideas about which career path to follow. Even if they are sure of their future careers, they may not remain in an organization for more than a few years. Second, future business conditions are uncertain. The range of human resources plans seldom goes beyond five years. Career paths have much longer time perspectives.

These two problems summarize many issues that make career path planning a difficult and limited activity. Thus in many organizations planning career paths is not a priority and is seldom done for nonmanagerial personnel. Career path plans are more readily predictable for higher-level personnel in their middle thirties and older.

Experiments with career path planning in several major European multinational corporations clearly reflect these problems. HRP managers from these companies point out that career path planning is workable only for managers and professionals who have been with the company for at least five years and who are likely to remain with the company. These executives operationalize the two limitations by converting them into an age requirement. They believe that career path plans can be effective only if the employee is at least 35 years old and occupies a managerial or professional position in the middle of the organizational hierarchy. Given these limitations to career path planning, we will restrict our discussion to managerial and professional positions and to strategic considerations.

Pressure for Career Path Planning

The April 1977 issue of *Forbes* reported that most organizations have fewer good managers than they need and that in some cases these managers command six-figure salaries. Developing and retaining good managers, even at such salaries, is an ever-growing organizational concern.

Equal employment opportunity and affirmative action legislation have also contributed to the importance of career path planning at higher organizational levels. Although there are many qualified minority and female workers in entry-level positions, most major U.S. and European organizations do not have proportional representation from those groups in their middle and top management ranks, because opportunities for promotion are limited. To remedy such situations and to conform to affirmative action legislation, organizations are beginning to focus on career path planning.

Further, the growing recognition that an organization's objectives may not coincide with individual interests is contributing to the development of career path planning. Recent evidence shows that increasing numbers of college graduates are choosing business careers, but that the majority of them are critical of the organization's objectives and are highly committed to their own self-fulfillment.

Sources of Confusion About Career Path Planning

Many of the difficulties encountered in career path planning stem from the planners' inability to distinguish between career planning that is organizationally oriented and career planning that is individually oriented. From the organizational perspective, career path planning involves job families and career ladders designed to help individuals progress through jobs. The organization's primary concern is to ensure an adequate supply of people to fill positions at any given time. The key to successful career path planning is the thoroughness with which the organization has identified its future human resources needs.

In individually oriented career path planning, planners consider the individual's total experiences in and out of the organization. Individually oriented career planning includes procedures and diagnostic exercises that help employees identify their abilities and potential. When planners combine individual and organizational perspectives, they achieve a realistic picture of career planning. Consequently, career planning involves more personnel functions than just defining a career ladder and planning training programs to groom individuals for a sequence of jobs. The initial recruitment and selection process, for example, is critical in harmonizing organizational demands and individual aspirations.

Strategic Considerations in Career Planning

Length and breadth of career paths. Important strategic considerations here are whether to promote employees within specialized or narrow career lines or to expose them to a variety of jobs and broad career lines. Narrow career paths quickly lead individuals to dead-end jobs. Human resources planning experts agree that narrow and short career paths demotivate employees and damage employee morale. Broad career paths, on the other hand, provide employees with a range of job opportunities. But broad career paths also have distinct disadvantages. If the career ladder leads to very different and complex jobs, the organization may face a double-barreled problem. First, the organization, when hiring employees, may take broad career paths into consideration and select candidates who are distinctly "overqualified" for their entry-level jobs. These employees may experience morale problems while passing the time until they can be promoted to positions that require their special abilities. Second, if the employees at the entry-level jobs are not overqualified and need extensive training and development before moving into higher positions, they can cost the organization much money.

Clarity of career paths. Should career paths be sharply defined or allow some ambiguity? Toward which end of the continuum should an organization strive?

A clearly defined career ladder might state, for example, that a bank teller is always selected from among trainee tellers and the head teller from among tellers. In contrast, ambiguous career paths might allow upward, diagonal, or even downward movement. For instance, in a given organization the traditional route to the position of executive vice president has been through sales, but the current

Table 13. Clarity in career paths.

Age	Stage	Characteristics of Career Path
20	"Ex-student"	High mobility among employees; thus general training and development
30	Young promotable	Contingency planning for groups of employees No individual plan; high ambiguity
40	Mid-career	Individual contingency plans Grooming for management position
50	Late career	Sharply defined, precise individual plans
60	Pension age	"Freed"

executive vice president is from finance. The career path has become ambiguous.

Sharply defined career paths are generally advantageous, but they tend to add rigidity to occupational and hierarchical mobility in an organization. Clear career paths have the advantage of providing tangible objectives for which employees can strive. Each promotion for achievement-oriented individuals could be considered a mark in their progress toward an identified objective. Thus clear career paths are feasible in stable environments. In periods of high environmental uncertainty, ambiguous career paths are generally useful to the organization.

Clarity of career paths is often a function of age. As one advances in a career path, the path becomes sharper. Table 13 illustrates how career paths may be flexible in the early stages of employees' careers but become sharply defined late in their careers.

The Number of Promotional Steps

The length of career paths is determined by the number of promotional steps between the entry-level and the top position. For instance, in most university teaching jobs there are no more than 2 to 4 steps between the top and bottom jobs. On the other hand, there could be as many as 20 steps in the promotional ladder in the data processing department of a large company. How can the optimum number be determined? Too few steps in a specific career path may not serve the purpose of career path planning; too many steps may create excessive red tape and administrative nightmares. The number of promotional steps must be realistic and consistent with the differences in the responsibility, complexity, and overall nature of the jobs. The decision to establish the number of promotional steps in given career paths should be based on objective job evaluations.

Promotion from Within or Recruitment from Outside

An organization's philosophy on filling its vacancies relates closely to its career path planning. Organizations that are committed to career path planning necessarily emphasize promotion from within. Otherwise, these organizations would find it difficult to practice career planning. Only on very rare occasions would a company with extensive career planning look outside to fill a vacancy, especially in a managerial position. The more sharply defined a career path is, the greater is the tendency to promote from within.

An organization's emphasis on employee development also contributes to its career path policies. If there are no formal programs for employee development—even when career paths are sharply defined—organizations tend to look outside when filling key managerial or professional positions.

Organizations with federal contracts often engage in nationwide recruitment efforts to fill vacancies in middle management positions. In many cases, this is necessitated by conformity to EEOC and affirmative action requirements.

Both promoting from within and recruiting from outside have many advantages and disadvantages. They depend on the organization and the organization's operating circumstances. The purpose here is not to elaborate on each but to show how the decision to go outside or to stay within depends on other personnel policies.

Selecting the Person to Be Promoted. An important strategic consideration in career planning deals with organizational policies regarding promotion on the basis of seniority or merit. Policy decisions on selecting the person to promote involve evaluations of merit, ability, seniority, and family relations (nepotism). There are arguments for and against promotions based on any one criterion.

If an organization wants promotions to be incentives, it must promote the employee with the best performance record. However, because differences in individual performances are difficult to measure, a person bypassed for promotion may feel that favoritism was involved in the decision. It is also difficult to select an individual on the basis of high performance when his or her job reflects the coordinated efforts of many people.

Another problem is in predicting ability. That is, what is the person's potential for performing well in the next job? A person may perform poorly in a current job but exhibit high potential ability to perform well in a higher-ranking job. Similarly, an employee may be performing very well in a current job but show little or no potential for performing well in a higher-level job. What should the organization do? Should it promote the good performer to his or her level of incompetency or reward the poor performer with a promotion to a higher job?

Ability, as a function of performance, is also very difficult to measure. It involves individual traits, attitudes, personalities, and skills. Because the characteristics of ability are ambiguous, many organizations prefer to rely on objective measures of performance, such as relevant education and years of experience on the job.

In many small and medium-sized private enterprises, and in some large companies, nepotism still plays a very important role in promotion decisions. Promotions based on nepotism can lead to power imbalances and career blockages and thus to company stagnation—especially if many family members seek powerful managerial positions.

Every organization must develop a policy on how to combine merit, ability, and length of service in its promotion decisions. Promotions in the private sector often depend more on merit and ability than they do in the public sector. An organization should locate its current promotion policy along a continuum, ranging from pure merit to pure seniority, and set an objective as to where on this continuum the organization wants to be. Figure 41 provides a spectrum of criteria from pure seniority to pure merit for promotion decisions.

Figure 41.   Merit/seniority continuum for promotion decisions.

Pure Seniority	• Seniority is the only determinant of promotion.
↑	• Senior employee is selected if not truly incompetent.
	• Consideration for promotion is given only after employee fulfills minimum length of service requirements.
	• A senior employee is bypassed only if the most meritorious employee is head and shoulders above the senior employee.
	• If there are equally qualified employees, the most senior one is promoted.
↓	• In addition to performance on current job, future potential is assessed.
Pure Merit	• Promotions are based strictly on merit.

Sample of Current Career Planning Practices

General Electric

Career planning at General Electric is tied in with its human resources plans. General Electric, in its management development institute in Crotonville, New York, has designed forms, procedures, and manuals to be used for career planning. Workbooks and workshops assist individual employees in exploring life issues that affect career decisions. Managers are made aware of the company's long-term objectives and the career paths open to managers and professional employees.

The essence of GE's program is decentralization. Career paths are formulated within the scope of each operating unit. When an employee reaches the end of a specific path in a given unit, he or she is shown a spectrum of opportunities available elsewhere in the company.

Top management encourages strategic career path planning in all the business units. However, the effective range of such plans seldom exceeds three years, because the average stay in most managerial and professional positions is about three years. As a result, the employee seldom knows what his or her next job will be, although a general career path exists. It is company policy to monitor the career paths of its employees and periodically revise the plans through superior/subordinate conferences. These revisions are based on information on the unit's human resources needs and the changing aspirations of the employee.[2]

Syntex

Career planning at Syntex is done from the employee point of view. Workshops and published materials provide employees with descriptions of various functional areas and the experience, education, and skills needed for positions in each of the areas. Syntex also has an assessment center that provides individual employees with inputs on their capabilities and develops career path plans for the participants. As at GE, Syntex's career path planning provides specificity and company commitment to employees in higher positions. The rank-and-file employees and front-line supervisory personnel are given career counseling but not formal career plans.[3]

IBM

IBM's corporate employee development policies provide voluntary annual supervisor/subordinate conferences about career, personnel growth, and development interests. The company provides information on opportunities, a supportive environment, and training facilities. IBM has created a supportive environment by taking the career development plans of its employees into consideration in transfers and promotions. The manager provides specific information on the job and counsels and assists the employee in developing his or her plans. The employee, on the other hand, is responsible for self-assessment and for acquiring the necessary skills to advance along the selected career path and to implement the plans.[4]

3M

In 1977, 3M inaugurated a career path planning program and established a career information center. In the center, employees can find information on company jobs and career paths and literature on the career planning and career counseling available to employees. Career counseling workshops help employees to assess themselves and make career plans.

Like the career development programs at most major companies, the 3M program offers the individual few planned, long-term objectives. Except for a few top and middle management positions, employees of these companies are offered no specific career paths. The individual employees must take the initiative in devising and implementing their plans. For instance, instead of designing specific career paths for middle management employees, 3M will assist the employees in their search for jobs within the company in accordance with their personal career plans. The job search is oriented toward existing or pending vacancies. This practice makes career planning very broad. It does not provide individuals with advanced knowledge on the type and nature of the specific job that they might be holding five years hence.

In conclusion, most existing career path plans are reserved for selected individuals in top and middle management positions, or for certain professionals in jobs important to the company. When a broad group of employees is considered, the meaning of career path planning changes. It becomes an operational tool that managers use to improve the quality of their employees' work life and help them reach their career objectives. It is hoped that this will be accomplished within the organization, but there is no commitment from the organization that any specific career path will be followed or implemented. Career planning used from the employee's point of view has very little strategic meaning because its practice is individual and its impact local. The first strategic decision is, of course, whether an organization should commit itself to career planning and attempt to develop the kinds of formal career paths common in many government jobs and in the military. If the decision is yes, all positions in the organization become parts of specific career paths, and the company must provide entry-level specifications for each career path and the requirements for progression.

Even career path counseling with no real commitment by the organization toward an individual's specific career ladders and job progression is a significant step in the right direction. We believe that career path planning will grow in the 1980s and that it will emerge as an important management tool for improving productivity and increasing employee satisfaction.

Summary

Training and development policies cannot be formulated in isolation from other critical human resources considerations. What an organization does in training and development influences its recruitment and selection policies, and vice versa. HRP provides the mechanism for putting these organizational considerations into practice. We have concentrated on strategic problems, alternative solutions, and the criteria that can be used in choosing among the solutions. Programs that introduce employees to the organization and that teach and improve skills and prepare employees for future jobs are crucial to the organization's achievement of its goals.

Career path planning has received much attention because it is one way for an organization to coordinate strategic planning for recruitment and selection with strategic planning for training and development. Career path planning can reinforce the desired compatibility between organizational goals and employee aspirations. Career path planning can be a powerful tool for increasing employee commitment to an organization and reducing worker alienation.

Career path planning beyond employee counseling is often restricted to the very top levels in the organizational hierarchy. Many organizations that claim to practice career planning are at best doing so only in theory, since they make no specific commitment to individuals who have not yet reached or passed the middle management level.

Broad-based career path planning is made difficult by the unpredictability of future supplies and demands for labor and by the career instability of young employees. High turnover among young employees discourages organizations from making career paths, which in turn fuels turnover by causing employees to experiment with new jobs before settling down.

Nevertheless, even limited career path planning is a significant step. Career path planning is likely to increase in the 1980s and to emerge as an important management tool.

CHAPTER 13

Performance Appraisal

Performance appraisal is a formal evaluation procedure by which an organization documents its employees' job performances and development potentials. Properly designed, performance appraisal systems can serve a variety of HRP functions, providing management with essential information for making strategic decisions on employee retention, advancement, and separation. A good performance appraisal system links training, development, and career planning programs with the organization's long-term human resources needs. Specifically, managers can use appraisal procedures to:

- Assess the potential of employees for future jobs and suggest appropriate training and development programs.
- Design and implement merit and incentive wage systems.
- Determine whether employees receive appropriate compensation for their particular functions and positions in the organization.
- Identify and modify dysfunctional work behavior.
- Provide documented evidence to support disciplinary and separation actions.

Decisions to design, introduce, and use formal performance appraisal systems are strategic because they are made by top management and have widespread impact on the organization. Conceptually, at least, a well-developed performance appraisal system is a powerful tool for generating useful information on the current and potential availability of the organization's human resources. A well-planned system helps management predict personnel requirements, diagnose strengths and weaknesses in human resources utilization, and plan remedial and future actions. Used this way, a performance appraisal system is a crucial link to the long-term human resources needs of the organization.

Specific Uses of Performance Appraisal Systems

Performance appraisal is an old managerial process. Surveys indicate that nearly 80 percent of major corporations have developed performance appraisal systems. However, most of these systems do not achieve their objectives. Problems may result from faulty designs in the systems themselves, from the inability of managers to write objective appraisal reports, or from poor communication of the reports to subordinates. The detrimental effects of poorly designed and implemented systems can be significant and long-lasting. Even at the operational level, the potential impact on wide segments of the organization is much greater than that of most operating decisions made by individual superiors.

Forecasting Human Resources Supply

Performance appraisal records reveal the characteristics of an organization's internal supply of labor. Human resources planners can analyze this information and produce functionally correlated age distributions, retirement forecasts, illness and absenteeism patterns, work preferences, and so on. The planners can then extrapolate from these data what the labor force will be like in the future and identify potential problems, such as groups of employees approaching expected retirement age and gaps in certain technical specializations. This information helps management introduce preventive measures.

Assessing Employee Potential and Promotability

Planners can use information from performance appraisal records to match employee potential with the performance requirements of certain jobs. Employee lists prepared according to degrees of potential can form the basis for special training and development programs for fast-track people. Planners can also use the records in assessing the promotability of employees. This, of course, is the major purpose of performance appraisals.

Stabilizing the Internal Labor Market

Relatively large organizations may want to transfer employees from one operating unit to another, or from one job to another. In their attempts to transfer personnel, they often find that their internal labor market is not functioning smoothly. Information collected through performance appraisals about career and geographical preferences of personnel can give the organization a clear picture of its internal labor market. When information is also fed into existing personnel models, forecasts of the labor force flows in the organization are more accurate than is otherwise possible.

Succession Planning

Data from performance appraisals are also used for succession planning. Planners can use an employee's suitability for a given job or jobs, as determined through performance evaluations and correlated with career and location preferences, in preparing lists of successors for positions from the top down to any level in the organizational hierarchy.

Salary Planning

When performance and remuneration are related, planners can use appraisal systems in forecasting future payroll costs in an organization. Performance ratings can be analyzed to establish trends for the entire organization or for certain divisions. Based on these trends, planners can predict future payroll costs and implement merit or incentive wage systems.

Organizations can also establish norms for performance ratings. Certain managers may be more generous than others in evaluating employees, causing payroll costs to be proportionately higher in those units than in others, and perhaps creating equity problems. By analyzing performance appraisal reports, top management can treat such deviation from the standard at the policy level.

Identifying Trouble Spots

Many personnel departments use automatic warning systems that enable them to note sudden changes in employee performance and to suggest corrective action. The information revealed by such systems can be categorized in appropriate units for monitoring. The HRP department of one large computer manufacturing company, for example, employs a relatively simple warning system. Past trends indicated that when employees had two conservative lateral moves, and stayed in the positions longer than normal, their next move was usually downward, leading to separation from the company. Now the early warning system pulls out the names of employees who make consecutive lateral moves, enabling management to review the employees' places in the organization and offer special career counseling. Already the system has saved the company much money and has helped it retain many employees it might otherwise have lost.

The applications of information obtained from employee appraisal systems will increase as HRP becomes more sophisticated. There are already systems in which "soft" qualitative data are stored, ready to be used in subtle forecasts and analyses.

Characteristics of a Performance Appraisal System

Formal appraisal systems—and most appraisal systems are formal—have three basic phases:

- *Appraisal planning*—development of individual performance standards.
- *Evaluation*—regular, objective, written evaluations of the subordinate's performance.
- *Action*—superior/subordinate discussions of the subordinate's evaluation and career opportunities.

Each phase of the appraisal system requires its own strategic and operational considerations. Figure 42 illustrates the overall performance appraisal process.

Phase I, appraisal planning, ties together business plans and the job objectives of departments and individuals. Without this link, performance appraisals may be worthless. The decision to link performance appraisal to employee functions, individual jobs to department activities, and department objectives to organizational goals—as determined by business plans—is strategic. The decision sets the tone of the appraisal process, gives it a long-term orientation, and makes possible the tying together of employee performance, compensation, training, development, and career planning.

Top management must approve the form the evaluation process takes, even though the actual work may be done by personnel specialists. Selecting the most appropriate appraisal process and deter-

Figure 42.   Performance appraisal process.

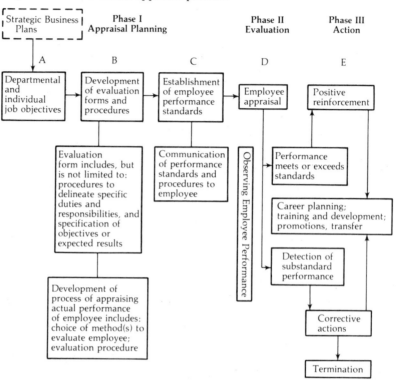

mining the format require considerations that may be beyond the scope of specialists. Specialists may prepare alternative procedures and evaluation methods, but top management must approve their implementation. What personnel specialists consider an optimal performance appraisal system may not be optimal from a general management perspective.

Actual implementation of the evaluation process takes place in Phase II. This phase is operational. Carrying out the performance appraisal is the responsibility of the superior, and as such it is localized. However, performance appraisal decisions can have greater long-term impact than most other localized decisions. Personnel decisions derived from performance appraisals can affect the employees' present and future work behavior. For instance, improper identification of a subordinate's dysfunctional work behavior can reinforce the behavior and perpetuate poor performance.

Implementation problems often cause performance evaluation

systems to fail. Many supervisors find it difficult to write useful and objective performance appraisals. Supervisors often submit subjective, impressionistic appraisals that defy comparison with the evaluations of other raters.

Moreover, supervisors with high standards may do injustice to their good employees if they compare them to the subordinates of an appraiser who has low evaluation standards. In practice, low evaluation standards result in evaluations highly inflated with superlatives. Such evaluations have little or no validity in decision making.

Organizations can take steps to improve the validity, and thus the usefulness, of their performance appraisal process. A strategic decision is to train all supervisors in the techniques of performance evaluation. An operational decision is to determine the needed contents of training programs and then ensure their delivery.

Phase III, evaluation, involves more strategic decisions. Management puts the results of evaluations into action through positive reinforcements or corrective measures. Strategic decisions include organizational policies regulating the schedule and nature of reinforcements and corrective actions. Defining individual managerial responsibilities and authorizing implementation of the results of performance evaluation are also strategic decisions. Decentralized Phase III decisions that offer front-line supervisors flexible guidelines help guarantee successful performance appraisal systems.

The Scope of Performance Appraisals

Determining the scope of a performance appraisal system is a policy decision. The purpose may be specific or general, depending on top management's philosophy.

Performance appraisals can be primarily evaluative. Just as final examinations in a school can provide the basis for final grades, performance evaluations can serve as the basis for promotions, salary increases, and the like. An organization using performance appraisals primarily for evaluative purposes is likely to view the system narrowly, for its usefulness in promotion and compensation matters. The emphasis is likely to be on separating the superstars from the good and the not-so-good employees. Performance standards are likely to be short-term results-oriented and will concentrate on the current job.

On the other hand, performance appraisals can emphasize developing the employees' overall performance abilities. Such appraisals are more like midterm exams than final exams. Superiors and subordinates determine relative strengths and weaknesses from the results. Consequently, developmental performance appraisals are good for more than just determining salary increases. The superior can diagnose the subordinate's strengths and weaknesses so that the weaknesses can be corrected and the strengths reinforced. The emphasis is on training, development, and career planning. Because such appraisals often lead to counseling, they can contribute to improved superior/subordinate relations.

Managers must carry out the dual function of evaluating their subordinates' performances and developing their capabilities. Problems occur when the supervisor attempts to carry out both functions at the same time. Performance appraisals designed to combine evaluation and developmental coaching in the same interview may not work. Managers often lack the skills required to integrate these functions and to criticize constructively.

One must consider, then, the compatibility of the two functions. Can performance appraisals be evaluative as well as developmental? The answer is no if merit raises and promotions are directly tied to the results of formal performance appraisals. When merit raises and promotions immediately follow formal performance appraisals, the evaluation results have little developmental value. On the other hand, evaluation and development are compatible when there is sufficient time between the interview and the remuneration decision. Management must allow subordinates sufficient time to improve their performance.

What Should Be Appraised?

Should appraisals measure traits or results? Evaluations that emphasize traits determine and measure employees' general aptitude and ability, their potential for advancement in the organization. These evaluations stress such factors as employee optimism, ability to learn, motivation, initiative, and decisiveness.

Evaluations that emphasize results objectively measure employees' on-the-job performance. The popularity of management by objectives reflects the trend toward evaluating performance on the basis of tangible, measurable standards. Performance standards establish objectively how well a job is to be done.

Performance standards have two basic elements. First, they include a description of the key result areas or important aspects of the job that should be measured. Second, they define an acceptable quantitative or qualitative level for these measurements.

Criteria for Sound Performance Standards

Performance standards must be established according to specific guidelines: (1) Performance standards must be tied to key result areas of the job. In this sense they must be significant, results-oriented, and economical. (2) Performance standards must reflect the recurring, problem-solving, and creative aspects of the job. The recurring aspects are the ongoing daily routines of the job. The problem-solving elements include finding and implementing solutions to problems so that the job reverts to normal. The creative aspects of a job include innovation and change in solving problems and performing tasks. The standards set for these three aspects of a job should be balanced. This balance may differ from job to job, but all three aspects should affect the performance standards. For instance, a performance standard for sales personnel that includes dollar sales but excludes problem solving and innovativeness would not provide complete or adequate job performance information. Problem solving and innovation can also affect short- and long-term sales results. (3) Performance standards must be consistent and fair.

Who Should Evaluate Whom?

All employees, from the highest to the lowest in rank, should be evaluated. However, in many organizations, the formal evaluation of employees tends to decrease as the hierarchical rank of the employees increases. Performance evaluation systems for nonsupervisory employees and personnel below middle management are more common than for employees in higher echelons. We believe performance evaluations should cover all employees. The strategic consideration here is the organizational readiness for an all-encompassing performance appraisal system.

Top management must decide who, in any performance evaluation system, will appraise employees. The most common method is evaluation by immediate supervisors. However, it is normal to find peer evaluation, self-evaluation, evaluation by subordinates, evaluation by other supervisors, evaluation by the personnel department, evaluation by an outside consultant, or any combination of these methods. An organization may stipulate one appraisal method for all personnel, or several methods of evaluation, depending on the type of employee. For instance, a policy may state that all production employees will be evaluated by their immediate superiors, but that all superiors will be evaluated by their immediate superiors and a committee composed of the production manager, personnel director, and plant manager. The use of more than one appraiser can reduce bias due to discrepancies between appraiser perceptions and actual employee behavior.

How Often Should the Employee Be Evaluated?

The specific purpose of performance appraisals is probably the most important determinant of the frequency of evaluations. Because most formal evaluations are used for promotion and remuneration decisions, the frequency of formal evaluations should be tied to the frequency of the changes in such major personnel actions as promotion and compensation.

Two or three formal evaluations a year may be necessary in organizations characterized by frequent personnel changes: promotions, transfers, layoffs, retirements, and the like. By providing accurate, up-to-date information, the frequent appraisals enable management to keep up with the changes. An annual performance evaluation may be sufficient in a stable organization.

Another important factor in determining the frequency of evaluations is the length of time between an action and the observation of its consequences. If the performance outcome of the employees can be observed in a relatively short time, frequent formal performance appraisals are worthwhile. If the time span between action and observation is long, frequent performance appraisals are not advantageous. For example, the consequences of a decision made by an employee at the lowest level of the hierarchy can sometimes be noticed immediately, and most of the time within days or weeks. But the consequences of decisions made by the plant manager may not be observed for many months or even for several years.

Since evaluation frequency depends on several factors, it may not be advantageous for an organization to have a uniform policy on this. Obviously, performance evaluation must be recognized as an ongoing process. Managers must make every effort to communicate the results of their observations on the performance of their subordinates as soon as possible, without waiting for the formal performance review. Feedback is most useful when it closely follows the behavior it is about. In deciding on the frequency of formal performance appraisals, management must keep in mind the continuing nature of the evaluation process itself.

If appraisals are to promote employee development, they must be relatively frequent. Such appraisals are directed at specific aspects of the employee's overall job performance. They often focus on one or two issues. These appraisals constitute a large part of a manager's supervisory responsibilities.

Where Should the Appraisal Take Place?

Evaluators often do their appraising alone, not in the presence of the employee. The employee's immediate supervisor may fill out the formal evaluation form in the office or at home. However, the interview between the appraiser and the employee may take place at one of several locations: the immediate supervisor's office, the subordinate's office, the office of a third party, or in a conference room if an appraisal committee is used. Whichever location is chosen, privacy must be ensured.

How Should Employee Performance Be Evaluated?

Each organization must consider its unique situational factors when designing and implementing an employee appraisal system. These factors include products, production methods, existing legal requirements, remuneration policies, employee needs, and organizational structure. Consideration of these factors helps ensure a more valid and reliable appraisal system.

Management must also understand the major similarities and differences between the various evaluation methods. A method applied to nonsupervisory employees may not be appropriate for managerial employees. A review of the most commonly used evaluation methods follows.

Person-to-Person Comparison

Person-to-person comparison, or ranking, is a simple, low-cost appraisal technique. In the absence of performance standards for key results areas, the appraiser identifies the best performer in the unit, the second best, and so on, until all personnel are ranked.

The straight-ranking method utilizes a certain standard, such as performance or effectiveness, and appraises each employee in relation to that factor. If the appraiser is very familiar with the employees and their efforts and is able to reduce personal bias, this method can yield good results. A major problem occurs with the employees who fall in the bottom half of the ranking. Since most employees view their own performance as average or above average, ranking may lead to dissatisfaction and hostility within the group.

Forced distribution is a variation of the straight-ranking method. Forced distribution requires an appraiser to distribute the employees among different categories, in a pattern that approximates a normal frequency distribution (e.g., 10, 20, 40, 20, 10 percent categories). The distribution pattern used may vary from organization to organization.

Paired comparison is a ranking method in which the evaluator compares each employee with the others. The paired comparison technique can take many forms. In general, a paired comparison method considers two employees at a time, compares one with the other, and chooses the best of the two. This method becomes cumbersome when there are many employees.

The alternate-ranking method begins with a list of the employees to be ranked. The appraiser identifies the best employee and puts his or her name on the top of a new list. The worst performer is then identified and placed at the bottom of the new list. The best and worst employees from the original list are alternatively chosen until all employees have been ranked.

Employee comparisons measure overall performance and evaluate one individual against another. They are not useful for developmental purposes. They are, however, suitable in determining the size of merit compensation, such as bonuses, and to some extent in selecting employees for promotion. Employee comparisons are more suitable for low-level, nonsupervisory employees than for high-level personnel. The use of person-to-person comparisons is declining rapidly in the face of the rapid development of job-related performance standards.

Rating Scales

Rating scales provide one of the most common, and easiest to administer, methods of evaluating employee performance. The appraiser evaluates an employee according to a number of factors related to job performance, such as quantity of work, quality of work, job knowledge, decisiveness, cooperation, dependability, and initiative. Next to each factor is a scale indicating the degree or quality of the performance factor (e.g., from low to high or from poorest to best).

The appraiser chooses an appropriate scale—either continuous or discontinuous—by which to evaluate the employee. The appraiser places a check at the point or interval that best identifies the employee's degree of performance for that factor. With a continuous scale, the location of the check on the continuum determines the point score. The employee may receive any score between the lowest and highest scores. Here is a continuous scale:

1	2	3	4	5	6	7	8	9	10
Very poor				Average					Best

A discrete or discontinuous scale has specific evaluation points. The appraiser checks the one item, among five or ten distinct evaluations, that best describes the employee's performance. Here is a discontinuous scale:

1	2	3	4	5	6	7
Poorest	Poor	Below average	Average	Above average	Superior	Best

Most performance appraisal rating scales include five to ten value-identification points. Fewer than five intervals may omit valid measures of performance. However, there must be meaningful differences between the identification points. Too many intervals (more than ten) prevent discrimination between the points. An odd or even number of interval points may be used. An even number of intervals forces the appraiser to designate a value slightly above or below average, thus inhibiting reliance on average value.

Some organizations use behaviorally anchored rating scales (BARS). With this method, specific, illustrative behaviors accompany each rating. Behavioral terms are used to describe a complete range of actions, from the most negative to the most positive. The actions relate to a performance dimension of the job being described. Each behavioral description in the range determines an interval to which points may be assigned. This provides a ranking order or scale for the demonstrated behavior. For example, here is a behaviorally anchored rating scale used in evaluating the performance of supermarket checkout clerks:

7. EXTREMELY GOOD PERFORMANCE:	By knowing the price of items, this checker would be expected to look for mismarked and unmarked items.
6. GOOD PERFORMANCE:	You can expect this checker to be aware of items that constantly fluctuate in price.
	You can expect this checker to know the various sizes of cans–No. 303, No. 2, No. 2½.
5. SLIGHTLY GOOD PERFORMANCE:	When in doubt, this checker would ask the other clerk if the item is taxable. This checker can be expected to verify with another checker a discrepancy between the shelf and the marked price before ringing up that item.
4. NEITHER POOR NOR GOOD PERFORMANCE:	When operating the express checkstand, which is supposed to be for 10 or fewer items, this checker can be expected to check out a customer with 15 items.
3. SLIGHTLY POOR PERFORMANCE:	You can expect this checker to ask the customer the price of an item that he or she does not know.
	In the daily course of personal relationships, this checker may be expected to linger in long conversations with a customer or another checker.
2. POOR PERFORMANCE:	In order to take a break, this checker can be expected to block off the checkstand with people already in line.

1. EXTREMELY POOR
   PERFORMANCE:

This checker might treat customers rudely or make frequent errors in ringing up items.

More accurate ratings may be obtained when the BARS relate to work behaviors that are readily observable by the appraiser and are under employee control. A major drawback to BARS is the expense and difficulty of developing the instrument, due to the number of behaviors that must be identified and described.

BARS are no more reliable than other rating instruments. However, BARS offer an excellent method for providing an organization with accurate information on both job requirements and job performance. The more structured the job is, the greater the benefit of using BARS. Descriptions of behavior patterns used in the scale can form the basis of a training program, thus increasing the developmental value of the appraisal process.

Checklist

The checklist is another method of evaluating employees on the basis of certain desirable and undesirable behaviors. The supervisor is given a list of statements describing effective and ineffective behavior or performance. The checklist statements are developed by many individuals who are familiar with the job. The appraiser checks the statements that best describe the behavior of the person being appraised.

More sophisticated forms of checklists may be used. For example, a weighted checklist can be developed, in which a weight or scale value is ascribed to each statement according to its degree of importance to performance. Both positive and negative performance items may be included.

Another checklist method utilizes forced choice. In this method, checklist statements are combined into groups. The items within a group appear to be equal in value. Again, the statements may describe behaviors that are acceptable or unacceptable. However, some of these items may have an impact on performance, while others may not. In certain instances, the appraiser may be asked to view a group of statements and choose the most *and* least representative items.

Checklists do not present serious "halo effect" problems. A halo effect occurs when the evaluator generalizes one characteristic to all other characteristics. For instance, an employee may be voted average on all dimensions because the evaluator perceives the person as average on just one dimension and carries this perception onto the remaining dimensions. Although special scoring procedures can be developed to reduce a leniency effect, checklists do not control the effect any more directly than other rating scales. A leniency effect takes place when an evaluator consistently overrates the employees appraised. Checklists make it difficult for raters to give feedback to the subordinates because the raters do not see the scale value of the items they have checked to describe the subordinates' behavior.

With the checklist method, raters are reporters more than evaluators of job-related behavior. Thus the checklist method helps to minimize appraiser bias. Since ratings are descriptive, they are likely to be more reliable than evaluative ratings. Checklist items can be scaled and evaluated in the personnel department. Checklists are useful when it is possible to identify specific behaviors that are highly correlated with success or failure in job performance. These behaviors should also be reasonably stable over some period of time. The objectivity and the ease of usage of checklists account for their widespread use in organizations.

Critical Incidents

The critical incident method of performance evaluation is a procedure in which important requirements of a job and employee behaviors are identified that will make a significant difference between doing a job effectively and doing it ineffectively. By observing employee work behavior, the appraiser collects information and records events related to the productive or unproductive performance of subordinates. At appraisal time, these specific incidents, reflecting aspects of critical job requirements, provide the basis for evaluating the performance of each employee.

A major advantage of this method is its objectivity; all ratings are based on specifically defined instances relating to actual job behavior. The use of critical incident observation can increase the accuracy of appraisal ratings through the documentation of significant behaviors. The observations are also helpful when the appraiser provides performance feedback to the employee.

The major drawback to the critical incident method is that it requires considerable time and effort. Moreover, critical incident observation can degenerate into detailed supervision, causing employees to feel that everything they do is being observed and recorded. Appraiser bias may persist, especially if the rater is inconsistent in recording or describing similar events for different employees. To some degree, all managers should collect critical incidents that justify their evaluations. But care must be exercised in collecting and recording the significant incidents associated with various key result areas.

Free-Form Write-Ups

With this method, the supervisor writes impressions of the subordinate without the assistance of rating scales, checklists, or any other standard evaluation forms. The appraiser describes the employee in relation to several general categories, such as the employee's strengths and weaknesses, promotability, and training and development potential. Free-form write-ups may be used in combination with other appraisal methods.

Free-form appraisals often depend for their meaning on the supervisor's writing abilities rather than on the employee's performance and ability. Collecting the information and writing a thorough appraisal may be time-consuming. Free-form appraisals are useful for evaluating top management and specialized professionals, but they are unsuitable for evaluating the majority of employees.

These traditional appraisal methods are often used to evaluate the means of getting a job done rather than the results of performance. The usefulness of these methods increases when the means of getting a job done correlate with successful job accomplishment. Encouraging a specific method of completing a job when several ways exist may stifle individual creativity, reduce job satisfaction, and in the long run impede overall organization performance. Means-oriented evaluations may be good for traditional jobs where there is a historic relationship between type of behavior and expected results, but for jobs demanding initiative, ingenuity, and specialized knowledge and ability, their usefulness diminishes. For instance, on a traditional assembly-line job where quantity of performance is regulated by the speed of the chain, attendance and tardiness may be the two most important factors in employee performance. Therefore, a behavioral evaluation form measuring these two factors would be appropriate. However, the same factors would not measure appropriately the performance of an R&D scientist.

Results-Oriented Evaluations

Results-oriented performance appraisal, or management by objectives (MBO), offers an alternative to the traditional methods for evaluating employee performance. Unlike the traditional systems, which stress such means of performance as personal traits and operating methods, MBO focuses on results. MBO is based on the assumption that establishing clear, understandable performance objectives leads to improved organizational performance.

A results-oriented appraisal system is composed of three elements: job description, performance standards, and appraisal interviews. The manner in which these elements are used in the performance appraisal process distinguishes one system from another and accounts for the relative success and failure of the various systems.

Most written evaluations include a descriptive list of the tasks to be accomplished in a particular job. This job description can be developed to spell out specific performance objectives, for example, the work output expected from the job over a certain time. MBO is based on the quantitative performance objectives that are decided on in a superior/subordinate conference. Each employee, with his or her supervisor, establishes short-term performance goals. These goals are adjusted to make them consistent with the goals of the other employees in the department and of the unit as a whole. Ways of measuring progress toward achieving the goals are also discussed in the conference. Periodically, supervisor and subordinate meet to discuss progress and, if necessary, adjust goals.

Better than the traditional appraisal methods, MBO increases superior/subordinate interaction. Mutual goal setting and agreement on performance criteria lead to productive teamwork. Thus MBO-based performance appraisal systems help management integrate long- and short-term plans. Its built-in planning elements help managers clarify responsibilities, organize the job, iron out problems in advance, and select and evaluate the means available for performing the job. Because of its participative, self-determinative philosophy, MBO can be motivational. It provides continuous feedback and facilitates employee self-appraisal because the individual helps set the appraisal standards and evaluates his or her own performance.

Although MBO clarifies working objectives and offers potential for integrating organizational plans with career goals, it has limitations that, if not understood, can cause disillusionment with this potentially powerful appraisal process. An MBO system provides no way of evaluating the difficulty or the qualitative aspects of achieving an objective. When MBO is used to compare one individual's performance against another's, managers must ensure comparability of objectives—a difficult task to accomplish. Moreover, objectives may be too easy or too difficult, too vague or too specific, or simply not measurable.

Another limitation is that the accomplishment of the set objectives may not be under the employee's control. For example, a salesperson's dollar volume of sales, used as an objective performance measure, may be influenced by such factors as territory, location, number of accounts in the territory, distance between accounts, nature of competition, price and quality of the products, and the like. Most of these factors are often beyond the control of the individual salesperson. The purpose of performance appraisals is to evaluate an individual's performance, *not* the factors beyond the individual's control.

To conclude, MBO is a useful performance appraisal tool when its limitations are understood. With well-written objectives, an MBO system can integrate strategic business and human resources plans (long-term) with operational plans (short-term) and career objectives. Through MBO, it is possible to translate operational plans derived from strategic business plans into individual actions consistent with the overall business and human resources strategy of the organization. The following are a few sample objectives for personnel managers.

- Select 5 candidates in the third quartile from 15 trainees following their successful completion of the supervisory training program. These candidates are to be appointed for six months at the new division.
- Reduce the cost of recruiting each engineer from $2,500 to $2,000 while meeting requisition totals and dates.
- Complete within three months a general attitude survey of labor-management relations among all employees for under $4,000.
- Complete for distribution by the end of 1983 fiscal year a 20-page, 10-topic industrial relations policy manual for newly hired employees.

A Pragmatic Appraisal System

Making a choice among alternative appraisal methods available to an organization is a strategic decision. The major problem with this selection is management's desire to consider both measurable results and the intangible, qualitative aspects of task performance. For many years MBO has been viewed as a possible alternative to more subjective performance evaluations by results-oriented managers. But for the reasons mentioned earlier and because of its indiscriminate application, many companies have become disillusioned with MBO. Nevertheless, the ideas and the concepts associated with MBO, if selectively implemented, have excellent potential in an appraisal system.

In designing a task-oriented appraisal system, we will diverge from the traditional MBO format by deemphasizing its time-bound specific objectives for which individuals are held accountable and by which their performances are measured. A task-oriented appraisal system has job descriptions and performance standards as its two basic components. We suggest a method for preparing job descriptions that promises more objective performance appraisals than can be attained with MBO. This task-oriented system can also be used as an effective management tool in recruitment, selection, training, and development.

Job Descriptions for Effective HRP

Job descriptions are the primary source of information for all aspects of HRP. If used properly, job descriptions can provide relevant inputs to computerized human resources data systems. Creating job descriptions is the first important step in translating the goals of the organization into employee work activities. Each job description can be composed of five elements, as listed on the next page.

The summary description of a job—element 1—commonly states the mission, purpose, or primary function of the job. Element 2, the detailed description of the job, covers the specific activities, duties, tasks, or functions of the person doing the job. Most traditional job descriptions include these two elements only (see Figure 43). To develop a useful job description for a task-related performance appraisal process, however, management should use all five elements. Elements 4 and 5 are considered performance standards.

Job Description

1. *Summary Description*
   Purpose
   Mission
   Primary function

2. *Activities*
   Duties
   Work
   Tasks
   Functions

3. *Key Result Areas*
   Major Responsibilities
   Effectiveness Areas
   Output Areas
   Key Tasks

4. *General Measurement Criteria*
   Indicators
   Measurement Techniques

5. *Standards of Performance*
   Specific Outputs
   Rating Scales
   Results

The third element groups together, under several key result or output areas, all the activities involved in a job. Because these areas are often distinct from one another, they can almost be considered part-time jobs. For example, an office secretary may be receptionist, typist, and telephone operator. Activities involved with each of these roles are generally listed haphazardly, with little regard for their major purposes. The secretary's three roles are the key result areas of the job. Duties, when grouped under meaningful headings (key result areas), help relate the job to the goals of the unit, clarify what is expected of the individual, and enable the individual to realize what the outcomes of the job may be. Of course, the duties or tasks of various key result areas are not totally isolated. An activity leading to the accomplishment of one key result may also lead to the attainment of a second key result. An important activity may even contribute to all key results.

Our experience with organizations using this job description system shows that jobs can be divided into three to six key result areas. Fewer than three key result areas indicates a narrowly defined job and may cause job dissatisfaction. More than six key result areas may indicate a misgrouping of activities or a job that is too broad and that therefore needs to be split up. In identifying key result areas, planners should ask: What is the outcome of this activity?

Figure 43.   Elements 1 and 2 of personnel manager's job description.

JOB TITLE: PERSONNEL MANAGER

ELEMENT 1. PURPOSE (SUMMARY DESCRIPTION)

The purpose of this job is to provide the highest-quality personnel possible and the best possible work environment in order to influence the productivity, product quality, and morale of employees, while maintaining budgetary limitations and actively encouraging affirmative action and humanistic principles of management.

ELEMENT 2. ACTIVITIES (DETAILED DESCRIPTION)

1. Determine job requirements.
2. Develop recruiting resources.
3. Write employment advertising.
4. Place employment advertising.
5. Telephone and screen candidates.
6. Interview candidates in person.
7. Administer candidate testing.
8. Analyze interview and testing data.
9. Check references.
10. Make recommendations to department head.
11. Formulate job offer.
12. Make job offer.
13. Sign up employee and perform orientation.
14. Listen to employee grievances.
15. Write company manual for personnel policy.
16. Counsel employees on interpretation of company policy.
17. Arrange relocation of employees and families.
18. Review employment practices within the labor market.
19. Provide competitive employment practices and program.
20. Provide employment practices and program that comply with government regulations.
21. Enforce EEO and OSHA regulations.
22. Train subordinates in various job functions.
23. Administer merit compensation program.
24. Analyze results of merit compensation program.
25. Upgrade merit compensation program.
26. Provide personnel and organizational development program.
27. Install personnel and organizational development program.
28. Scrutinize progress of personnel and organizational development program.
29. Analyze results of personnel and organizational development program.
30. Solicit and listen to employee suggestions on company policy.
31. Provide for company-sponsored recreational programs.

What is its purpose? Where does it lead? What other activities must be performed to obtain a meaningful result? In our example of the personnel manager's job description, the 31 activities listed in Figure 43 could be grouped under four key result areas, for example:

- Organizational Development
- Customer and Employee Satisfaction
- Departmental Budgetary Control
- Government Regulation Compliance

Figure 44 illustrates how specific activities lead to key results. Successful attainment of key results, in turn, is expressed as successful

Figure 44.   Results-oriented analysis of job (element 3).

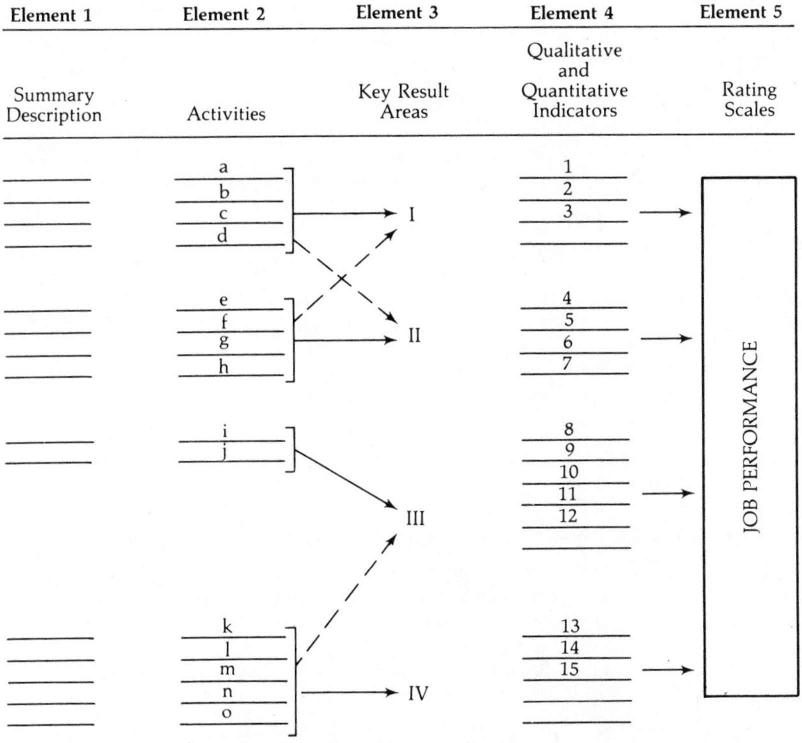

Element 1	Element 2	Element 3	Element 4	Element 5
Summary Description	Activities	Key Result Areas	Qualitative and Quantitative Indicators	Rating Scales

job performance. Certain activities may contribute to more than one key result.

Element 4, general measurement criteria, directly ties the appraisal process to the job. This is shown in Figure 45. The general measurement criteria indicate whether a key result has been attained. A general measurement criterion can also be viewed as a performance indicator that can measure observable outcomes of work activities. Indicators must be identified for each key result area. For example, resignations and mobility flow rates, absenteeism/time ratios, accident profiles and rates, number and settlement of disciplinary cases, and recruitment and placement costs can be used as performance indicators for a personnel manager. The purpose of general measurement criteria is to quantify, or at least to create a tangible means to measure, task performance and to indicate whether key results, and consequently the overall job, are successfully attained. For example, the number of exempt employees in training or development

Figure 45.   Element 4 of personnel manager's job description.

ELEMENT 4. GENERAL MEASUREMENT CRITERIA

I   Organizational Development Indicators
   1. Number of exempt employees in training or development programs.
   2. Number of internal promotions.
   3. Number of employees upgrading their overall performance rating.

II   Customer and Employee Satisfaction Indicators
   4. Turnover rate.
   5. Number of employee grievances settled.
   6. Number of labor-days/positions remaining open.
   7. Number of terminations within probationary period.

III   Departmental Budgetary Control Indicators
   8. Number of employees over planned number.
   9. Cost per hire ratio.
   10. Actual consultant fees compared to planned fees.
   11. Deviation of benefits and salaries costs from planned costs.
   12. Deviation of all other expenditures from planned expenditures.

IV   Government Regulation Compliance Indicators
   13. Number of citations for noncompliance.
   14. Dollar value of assessments for noncompliance.
   15. Quantitative evaluation by Corporation Affirmative Action Officer of programs and compliance.

---

programs might serve as a performance indicator in organizational development, a key result area for a personnel manager (see Figure 45). In other words, one way of measuring the performance of the personnel manager in this key result area is to estimate the number of employees in training and development programs.

Element 5 is generally referred to as MBO. Many of the problems associated with MBO result from setting objectives without giving due consideration to the first four elements. We do not ascribe to the total philosophy of MBO in performance evaluation. Rather, we set objectives and use them as standards of performance or rating scales. The general measurement criteria (element 4) tell what to measure, while performance standards (element 5) tell how to measure. Performance standards are used to determine what is poor, acceptable, or superior performance. The standards may use a continuous or a discontinuous scale to indicate the measurement. Under MBO, this measurement would be specified within a given time, for example: "50 percent of all hourly paid exempt employees should be involved in training or development programs by the end of FY 1982." With such a rigidly set standard, there is often no incentive to exceed the objective. Further, the objective could be unrealistic (too high or too low).

Under our system, each indicator is expressed as a rating scale, not as an objective. For instance, a performance standard for the organizational development area could be designed with the following continuous scale of five items:

1. *Poor* (less than 20 percent of all exempt employees involved in training or development programs within one year).
2. *Below average* (20 to 39 percent).
3. *Average* (40 to 49 percent).
4. *Above average* (50 to 69 percent).
5. *Superior* (70 percent and over).

The personnel manager's performance is then compared to the standard for this key result area, and judged as being poor, below average, average, above average, or superior. Each key result area would have its own scale (see Figure 46).

This method of performance appraisal has the advantage of relating evaluations to objective measures of task performance, without rigidly specifying the objectives.

Illustration of a Job Description and Evaluation

What follows is an example of a job description of a personnel manager in a small electrical appliances manufacturing plant with 2,000 employees. In our example, 60 percent of the personnel manager's evaluation is based on the objective criteria identified in Figure 45. In this case, quantitative measures for organizational development, customer and employee satisfaction, departmental budgetary control, and government regulation compliance are used to evaluate the personnel manager's performance in each of the key result areas. Rating scales are developed for each of the 15 general measurement indicators, as in Figure 46. Indicators used to measure performance in each key result area can be weighted to reflect their degree of importance. For instance, the three general measurement criteria for the key result area of organizational development can be weighted as follows: 1.1 = 50 percent; 1.2 = 30 percent; 1.3 = 20 percent.

Going back to our example, let's say that the personnel manager receives the following ratings on the three key indicators for key result area 1, organizational development: 3 (1.1), 4 (1.2), and 5 (1.3).

Figure 46.   Element 5 of personnel manager's job description.

ELEMENT 5. STANDARDS OF PERFORMANCE

1.1 Number of exempt employees in training or development programs.
(Degree of importance: 50%)

1._____   Poor (less than 20% of all exempt employees
              involved in training or development programs
              within one year)
2._____   Below average (20 to 39%)
3.__x__   Average (40 to 49%)
4._____   Above average (50 to 69%)
5._____   Superior (70% and over)

1.2 Number of internal promotions. (Degree of importance: 30%)

1._____   Poor (less than 20% of all exempt employees
              involved in training or development programs
              within one year)
2._____   Below average (20 to 39%)
3._____   Average (40 to 49%)
4.__x__   Above average (50 to 69%)
5._____   Superior (70% and over)

1.3 Number of employees upgrading their overall performance rating.
(Degree of importance: 20%)

1._____   Poor (less than 20% of all exempt employees
              involved in training or development programs
              within one year)
2._____   Below average (20 to 39%)
3._____   Average (40 to 49%)
4._____   Above average (50 to 69%)
5.__x__   Superior (70% and over)

On a scale of 1 to 5, and with the degree of importance (as shown in Figure 59) factored in, the personnel manager's objective evaluation in organizational development is:

$$(3 \times .5) + (4 \times .3) + (5 \times .2) = 3.7$$

The personnel manager's overall evaluation in all key result areas (KRAs) equals the sum of the individual KRA evaluations, with each KRA evaluation weighted according to its degree of importance. Assuming the following degrees of importance for each of the key result areas and the following ratings for each of the key indicators for the KRAs, the computations are:

Organizational development (degree of importance = 40%):

$$.4 [(3 \times .5) + (4 \times .3) + (5 \times .2)] = 1.48$$

Customer/employee satisfaction (degree of importance = 35%):

$$.35 \ [(4 \times .2) + (5 \times .5) + (4 \times .2) + (3 \times .1)] = 1.54$$

Departmental budgetary control (degree of importance = 15%):

$$.15 \ [(4 \times .1) + (4 \times .3) + (5 \times .1) + (4 \times .3) + (4 \times .2)] = .62$$

Government regulation compliance (degree of importance = 10%):

$$.1 \ [(3 \times .4) + (4 \times .2) + (5 \times .4)] = .40$$

Total objective KRA evaluation:

$$1.48 + 1.54 + .62 + .40 = 4.04$$

Our personnel manager receives a score of 4.0 on a scale of 1 to 5 for this part of the evaluation. These measurable task elements account for 60% of the manager's total performance evaluation. To add developmental value to the performance appraisal, however, certain qualitative performance factors such as initiative, supervisory ability, and job knowledge also have to be considered. The most common qualitative performance factors for supervisory personnel are:

Job knowledge (JK)
Decision making and judgment (DM)
Planning and organizing effectiveness (PO)
Leadership effectiveness (L)
Communication skills (C)
Self-improvement efforts (SI)

In our example, these factors are given a 40% weight in the personnel manager's overall performance appraisal.

Each performance factor can be evaluated on a scale of 1 to 5. This scale, however, does not need periodic readjustments because the factors on the scale are universal and stable. Each performance factor can also be weighted. Usually job knowledge weighs the most, and self-improvement efforts the least. Using the personnel manager's position as an example, we might have the situation shown in Table 14. The total qualitative factor evaluation equals the average of the total means: in this case, 3.28. In this hypothetical situation the per-

Table 14. Qualitative factors in the performance evaluation of a sample personnel manager, weighted according to importance.

	% Weight Distribution of Factors						
	30	15	15	15	15	10	Weighted
Key Result Areas	JK	DM	PO	L	C	SI	Mean
Organizational development	4	5	3	4	3	2	2.57
Customer and employee satisfaction	5	5	3	3	3	3	3.90
Departmental budgetary control	2	3	2	3	4	4	2.80
Government regulation compliance	4	4	4	3	4	4	3.85

sonnel manager receives an overall evaluation of 3.7 on a scale of 1 to 5.

$$\text{Performance KRA: } 60\% \times 4.0 = 2.4$$
$$\text{Qualitative factors: } 40\% \times 3.28 = \underline{1.3}$$
$$3.7$$

Management can use this overall score for developmental purposes or for awarding bonuses or promotions. The personnel manager's immediate supervisor can concentrate on individually scored items during an appraisal interview. The low scores in the qualitative evaluation were for poor self-improvement efforts in organizational development and ineffective planning and poor job knowledge in departmental budgetary control. Once indicated, poor performance in these areas can be corrected. For instance, to improve in organizational development, the personnel manager might join professional societies or participate in short programs at universities, activities that would acquaint the personnel manager with the latest developments in the field.

By presenting this method of describing jobs and setting performance standards, we mean to alert management to a viable alternative to the MBO approach. This pragmatic approach can be used to quantify performance appraisals without setting overly specific, time-bound goals. The format enhances the method's potential as a management tool in employee recruitment, selection, training, and development, as well as in organizational development and policy setting.

Summary

Evaluating personnel is one of the most troublesome aspects of human resources management. Employee performance has long been recognized as a prime contributor to an organization's overall productivity. Not until recently, however, has management stressed measuring employee performance accurately and using the information to improve productivity. Job performance appraisal has become a cornerstone of HRP.

Before managers can influence performance, they must measure the level of employee performance. This evaluative function of the appraisal process provides the basis for strategic managerial decisions concerning employee promotion, remuneration, and separation. Development, the second appraisal function, aims at improving performance by identifying employee strengths and weaknesses. Programs for reinforcing strengths and correcting weaknesses can then be devised. The dual appraisal functions give supervisors two closely related but sometimes incompatible roles: judge and coach.

There are many methods available to help managers appraise employee performance. Such traditional methods as person-to-person comparisons, rating scales, checklists, analyses of critical incidents, and free-form write-ups are relatively easy and inexpensive to administer. However, these traditional methods evaluate the means by which a job is performed, not the results of the performance.

Management by objectives, a results-oriented system, assumes that establishing clear, understandable performance objectives leads to improved organizational performance. Because MBO involves considerable supervisor/subordinate interaction, it helps management to motivate employees and to integrate long- and short-term plans. However, misunderstanding the limits of MBO or applying it indiscriminately can lead to disillusionment with the system.

A pragmatic, task-oriented appraisal method that stresses job description but that deemphasizes specific, time-bound objectives provides a viable alternative to MBO. Values and degrees of importance are assigned to the key result areas. Quantitative measurements of performance can thus be derived. For development purposes, qualitative factors such as employee initiative and job knowledge can be considered as well.

Job performance appraisal systems provide top management with powerful tools for improving productivity and integrating organizational and employee career goals. Regardless of the system used, however, the performance standards must be tied to the key result areas of the job; they must reflect the recurring, problem-solving, and creative aspects of the job; and they must be consistent and fair.

CHAPTER 14

Compensation Policies

Decisions concerning the design, implementation, and maintenance of an effective compensation system are among the most important ones made by top management. Because compensation systems, including employee benefits packages, are significant policy issues in all organizations, they are an important segment of any human resources planning and utilization system.

HRP and compensation policies are directly related. Decisions establishing overall pay levels, payment methods, types of incentives, individual pay, and benefits packages affect and are affected by the availability of human resources. Competitive wages, including benefits, are one of the most powerful means of attracting and retaining qualified employees. Compensation policies have a strong impact on the institutional image of an organization. An organization reputed to be a good place to work is often perceived by the public as offering above-average starting wage levels or providing reasonable job security and opportunities for advancement.

Strategic decisions about pay levels, pay structure, job evaluation systems, individual pay, incentives, benefits, payment methods, and wage and salary criteria influence the future of an organization. Compensation policies that are an integral part of HRP become proactive rather than reactive. Long-range strategies replace a patchwork approach to solving problems as they occur.

The Need for a Comprehensive Compensation System

An effective compensation system provides the backbone of all policies influencing the acquisition and utilization of human resources. This is true in both the private and the public sectors for two primary reasons: (1) Employees must be compensated as equitably as possible for the services they render; that is, the organization should not overpay or underpay its employees. And (2) without an effective compensation system, an organization has difficulty creating and maintaining a supportive climate that motivates employees to achieve the desired level of performance. If employees do not perceive a compensation system as being equitable, they will not produce to their capacities and will not be fully committed to the organization—despite the organization's otherwise good supervisory practices and personnel policies.

The Importance of the Compensation System to the Employee

Employees want a positive relationship between the skills, efforts, and expertise they contribute to the organization and the pay and other rewards they receive from the organization. This relationship can be expressed in the following equation: Input (employee contributions) = Outcome (organizational remunerations).

If the outcome is below the employees' expectations, the employees experience a feeling of inequity. If the employees perceive that they are contributing more to the organization and/or are more qualified than other employees receiving the same or more pay, they may seek to reduce the difference. The employees may lower their contributions or input through absenteeism, low-quality work, less cooperative attitudes, or reduced activity. Any of these methods could be detrimental to the organization.

On the other hand, if there is an objective way of determining the relative worth of each job and each person's performance, and for making the person aware of this determination, employees are less likely to perceive themselves as victims of inequity. Although motivation is an internal, personal phenomenon, one of the primary objectives of instituting an effective compensation system is to increase or maintain an acceptable level of employee motivation or at least to prevent a decline in motivation by reducing perceived inequities of the existing compensation system. A closer look at how money motivates employees will highlight the important issues in compensation policies.

The Role of Money in Motivating Employees

Motivating employees in today's business world is a more difficult task than it has ever been. Managers face pressure from labor unions, stockholders, consumer groups, and minority groups in a complex and increasingly unpredictable world. Nevertheless, motivating employees to accomplish company objectives is a very important function. The prices we pay for worker alienation are staggering: underproduction, low-quality work, sabotage, turnover, and absenteeism are just a few. Keeping employees motivated to produce is an ever-increasing challenge.

The role of money in motivating employees can best be understood within the framework of the motivation theories that form the basis for many policies on human resources planning and utilization. Chapter 3 reviews the aspects of motivation theory that affect strategic decisions about remuneration. These considerations are matters of organizational policy because they are beyond the control of individual supervisors. Individual managers can motivate or demotivate subordinates, but their ability to do so is limited by the work climate of the organization. Among the factors contributing to organizational climate are policies and strategic decisions on all the key elements of contemporary human resources planning and utilization processes. Strategic decisions and overall policies governing employee compensation are particularly important.

Wages are the most common reward organizations provide for their employees. If there is little relationship between rewards (money and promotion) and successful task accomplishment, employee motivation will be low. Organizations that tie promotion and salary increases to a strict seniority system generally face acute motivation problems. Performance and compensation should be closely aligned, and the relationship should be clearly understood and accepted at all levels. Salary increases often fail to motivate because employees see them as something to which they are entitled rather than something they must earn. If an increase is not given on schedule, disappointment and bad feelings result. If the delay is prolonged, the employee may look for another job, or complain not only about the delayed raise but about petty annoyances that might otherwise have been overlooked. If the increase is smaller than expected, the employee may feel deceived. Properly designed compensation systems help prevent some of these problems.

Expected Results from a Compensation System

The adequacy of a compensation system can be measured by how well it helps attract, retain, and motivate employees. An effective compensation system must provide a systematic method of job analysis, including descriptions/specifications that clarify the employee's function, authority, and responsibility. Furthermore, it should lead to a comprehensive and consistent method of evaluating and classifying jobs; and it should ensure a fair and equitable method of providing wage/salary increases. The compensation system must include provisions for disseminating definitive information concerning jobs, so that complaints due to employee misunderstandings and/or lack of information can be reduced. Finally, it should provide a comprehensive analysis of each job that enables all departments in the organization to select, train, and transfer employees as well as to administer wage and salary policies.

The Coverage of an Effective Compensation System

An effective compensation system must address at least five issues. First, the compensation package should be perceived by the employees as being equitable. If employees believe their pay is "out of line," discontent—eventually leading to unacceptable rates of turnover—often results. Organizations must try to develop pay structures that provide pay based on internal comparisons of jobs as well as on market rates. Compensation should be commensurate with the relative worth of jobs in an organization. To ensure internal equity, jobs should be analyzed and evaluated.

Second, the compensation package should be externally competitive. In creating its compensation system, an organization must consider what other organizations pay their personnel. Unless an organization's compensation is competitive, its employment advertising will go unanswered and its turnover will be high. Through wage/salary and benefits surveys, organizations must determine what other relevant organizations are paying for comparable jobs.

Third, in deciding on wage structure, benefits, and other forms of employee compensation, the organization must consider its own economic means. Personal, financial, and budgetary requirements must be analyzed in relation to one another.

Fourth, compensation structure must be legal. Minimum wage laws and the provisions of the Equal Employment Opportunity Act must be observed. Furthermore, particularly in larger organizations, compensation structure should be tied to the organization's affirmative action plans.

Figure 47.   Schematic description of effective compensation system.

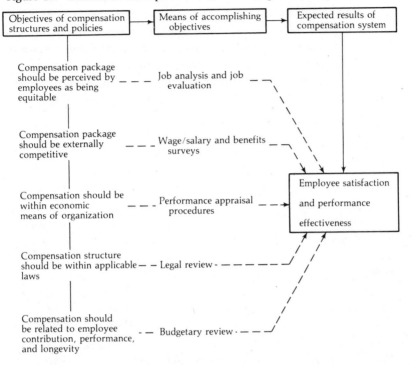

Finally, compensation should reflect employee contribution and productivity as well as longevity. This objective may be achieved through performance appraisal policies and procedures. Figure 47 presents the major components of a compensation system.

The primary objectives of an effective compensation system are to attract, retain, and motivate employees. There are alternative ways of attaining each one of these objectives. Determining the means for attaining and refining objectives is a matter of top management policy and is strategic by definition. Management, in order to hire the kind of people it thinks the organization needs, may decide to set compensation levels that are high in relation to those of competitors and other relevant organizations. Certainly, this is a strategic decision that affects human as well as other organizational resources.

The remainder of this chapter discusses strategic considerations that make a compensation system internally equitable and externally competitive. Job evaluation and compensation surveys have traditionally been considered to be specific technical issues and have been treated in isolation from the other components of the HRP process. It is true that they are specialist activities, but so are the other HRP elements. By highlighting the strategic aspects of job evaluation and compensation surveys, we can illustrate their interrelatedness with other human resources policies of an organization and thus move toward integrating human resources policies under the umbrella of HRP.

Internal Equity

Achieving internal equity among jobs generally involves two strategic activities: job analysis and job evaluation. The output of job analysis and job evaluation is the job, or position, classification. By *class*, we mean a group of jobs sufficiently alike in duties and responsibilities that they justify common treatment in selection, compensation, and other personnel matters. The jobs so classified are sufficiently different from jobs in other groups to justify different treatment.

A job classification is not a pay plan, but it provides the basis on which management structures and administers a compensation plan. Compensation can be changed, and classes of jobs can be rearranged on a pay schedule, without affecting the job classification system.

Job Analysis
Job analysis is the process of obtaining information on the duties and responsibilities of the job, and the knowledge, skills, and physical attributes required for performing the job. To collect this information, the analyst must answer three basic questions:

1. *What does the employee do?* What are the employee's physical and mental responses to the work situation? Job descriptions often provide this information.
2. *How does the employee do it?* What methods does the worker use to accomplish the tasks? What machinery, tools, measuring instruments, and other equipment are used, and what procedures and routines are followed? What are the movements of the other workers?
3. *What skill is involved?* What skills, knowledge, abilities, and other characteristics does the job require of an employee, re-

gardless of whether the job is manual, skilled, clerical, professional, or managerial?

A strategic decision here is whether or not to ask the employee and/or the employee's immediate supervisor to contribute information that will be used in the job evaluation. The criteria for this decision include the nature of the job and the evaluation method used. Objective job evaluation procedures have traditionally been applied to blue-collar jobs, which have been well defined and extensively studied. Generally, industrial organizations have no difficulty in ranking skilled and unskilled blue-collar jobs on the basis of predetermined job specifications. For evaluating these traditional jobs, the organization generally does not seek information from the employee. On the other hand, supervisory, professional, and to some extent office and clerical positions lack standardized job descriptions and job specifications. For instance, two jobs entitled "office manager" may entail very different duties and require different employee skills and attributes. Consequently, analysis of managerial, professional, and often clerical positions usually dictates that the analyst solicit accurate data on job specifications and compensatable factors from the employees. If the evaluation method is quantitative, it is especially advisable to ask the employee and the employee's immediate supervisor to contribute data on various compensable factors.

Job Evaluation

Management can determine the relative worth of a job by comparing the whole job to other jobs in the organization or by rating key factors in a job according to a scale derived from certain "benchmark" jobs. Comparing jobs is a qualitative evaluation method; rating job factors is a quantitative method. We discuss four methods here—two qualitative and two quantitative. The information should help management choose the best evaluation method for its particular organizational circumstances.

Ranking method. Jobs can be ranked according to their relative worth in much the same way that employee performances can be ranked comparatively. The appraiser examines the job as a whole and then ranks it, on a list of jobs, in relation to the most important job. The various ranking methods discussed in Chapter 13—simple ranking, paired comparisons, and the like—can be used.

Ranking is the oldest and simplest evaluation method, but it is also the least specific and objective. It indicates the relative worth of jobs, but it does not distinguish the degrees of importance among the jobs. Consequently, its usefulness is limited to small organizations in which the jobs are more or less homogeneous. For example, the manager of a restaurant could determine the relative worth of the jobs by ranking them between the chief cook and the dishwasher.

Classification method. Classification involves arbitrarily establishing a number of job classes or wage groups and defining their boundaries. The appraiser then examines each job as a whole and assigns it to its proper class. The appraiser can compare the undifferentiated specifications of each job to the descriptions of the job classes. The job class descriptions form a kind of scale against which the jobs can be evaluated.

Classification is more precise than ranking, and it can accommodate the numerous jobs in large organizations. One of the oldest examples of classification is the U.S. government's salary schedules. The Civil Service uses 18 job classes, or general schedules (GS 2 to GS 18). However, classification does not consider the specific conditions of a job. Attempts to eliminate subjectivity lead to centralization and reliance on job descriptions only, which in many organizations are soon outdated. Moreover, it is usually difficult to change classification systems. Like ranking, classification is far more subjective than the quantitative evaluation methods discussed next.

Factor-comparison method. Factor comparison is an analytical evaluation method that is more precise than ranking or classification. The appraiser chooses as benchmarks clearly definable key jobs that are neither underpaid nor overpaid. The appraiser analyzes these benchmark jobs to reveal the key factors defining the jobs' importance and assigns portions of the job's pay rates to each selected factor, according to the factor's degree of importance to the job. The result is a rating scale that matches pay rate to key factors, rather than to whole jobs. All other jobs can then be analyzed in terms of the selected factors and rated, or evaluated, according to the scale derived from the benchmark jobs.

Factor-point method. Like factor comparison, the factor-point method is analytical, but it is more precisely quantitative than factor comparison. The factor-point method enables the appraiser to rate the demands of a job: the degree of importance of the responsibilities and duties of the job, the relative complexity of the decisions made on the job, the depth of knowledge required to perform the job, and the like. The appraiser analyzes the job in terms of these key diagnostic factors and then rates the factor by assigning it points, according to its relative importance, complexity, and so forth.

The factor-point method has become the most popular job evaluation method, especially for evaluating blue-collar and traditional industrial jobs. Widely accepted manuals explaining how to use the method have been available for more than 50 years. The manuals for evaluating blue-collar, office, and clerical jobs adopted and refined by the National Metal Trades Association provide an excellent basis for an effective job evaluation system.

The factor-point evaluation method has been adapted successfully to white-collar jobs, but more work needs to be done, primarily because white-collar jobs lack precise definitions. We will concentrate on the development of manuals for nonindustrial jobs. The factor-point method provides the best basis for evaluating such jobs because its rating scales are stable. Moreover, employee acceptance of this method has been high. It also enables management to involve the employee in the job evaluation.

Selecting the key diagnostic factors and assigning them weights involve strategic decisions. Table 15 presents the results of a survey aimed at revealing the factors contributing to the perceived impor-

Table 15. Some commonly used job factors that reveal the importance of a management job.

Factor	Degree of Importance: Mean Response*
Experience	80
Supervision exercised	75
Impact of the decision expressed in terms of financial or operating objectives	70
Complexity of decisions made as measured in terms of the range of alternatives available	65
Depth of knowledge required to effectively perform in the position	60
Supervision received	55
Stress imposed on the position	35
Relationship with the public and/or clients	30
Intracompany relationships	25
Working conditions	20

* 100 = highest rating.

tance of white-collar jobs. Alpander asked 175 personnel managers from major New England corporations to list what they considered to be the factors that best distinguished the relative importance of management jobs.[1] As requested, the personnel managers rated the degree of importance of each factor on a scale of 1 to 100.

Not surprisingly, the experience needed to perform the job, under normal supervision, scored the highest. Supervisory responsibility and the complexity of the decisions made—the key job-related factors to which the experience is applied—ranked nearly as high. The depth of knowledge, or education, required to perform the job satisfactorily scored relatively high as well. Supervision received, the degree to which the employee's work is checked by others, seems to indicate a falling-off in the perceived importance of the job. Supervision received measures the degree to which a supervisor outlines the objectives and procedures of the job and monitors the employee's progress. The remaining factors—stress, public/client and intracompany relations, and work conditions—are significant enough to be included in a white-collar factor-point evaluation, but, as the survey indicates, they should receive significantly lower rates than the other factors.

Because task environments tend to be unique to an organization, management should assign to each job factor a point value that reflects the nature and character of the task environment. Once the relative weight of each factor is determined, specialists can work out the details of the evaluation system, including the degrees of complexity within each factor. Normally, each factor can be subdivided into five to seven degrees of complexity. Two examples of the point-factor method of job evaluation, one as used by a major fiduciary organization and the other by a county government, are presented in the Appendix.

A major drawback of the point-factor method, especially when it is applied to white-collar jobs, is its design and implementation complexity. Defining degree of importance, complexity, and the like within specific job factors is difficult and time-consuming. However, the precision with which it enables management to compare jobs and the potential it offers for involving employees justify its cost.

Analysis of Job Evaluation Data

Once the jobs have been evaluated (preferably by the factor-point method), they can be compared in terms of their worth and the sal-

Figure 48.   Distribution of points and wages for 75 managerial and professional jobs in medium-size leather manufacturing company. The three lines
represent the minimum, median, and maximum amounts for the pay
grades.

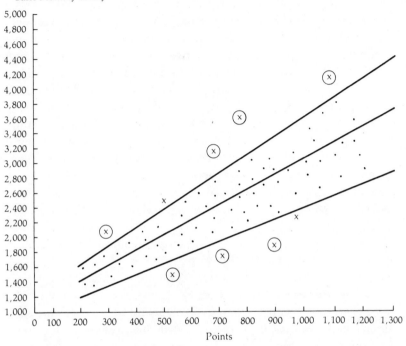

aries received by the incumbents. Frequently, this analysis—conducted by specialists—is expressed in a chart that plots salary data
against the points that have been assigned to each job. Figure 48 illustrates the distribution of points and wages for 75 supervisory and
professional positions in a medium-size leather manufacturing company. The horizontal axis in Figure 48 represents the relative point
value of each job evaluated, using the point-factor method. In this
particular case, the point-factor method is similar to the examples
presented in the Appendix. The maximum point value that could be
assigned to any given job was 1,400 points. However, in this illustration, the maximum value assigned to any job did not exceed 1,200
points.

Using a statistical technique such as the least-squares method,
wage and salary specialists can draw the line that best fits the data.

Frequently, the specialists also draw the lines that establish acceptable salary/point ranges—generally 10 to 20 percent of the median. This operational analysis provides management with the data it needs to take into account the concepts of relative worth and internal equity.

Setting the actual pay range and pay grades for jobs involves strategic decisions. Management at the leather manufacturing company decided on a 40 percent spread between the minimum and maximum pay in a given grade. Figure 48 illustrates how the pay grades are superimposed on the data. Handling overpaid and underpaid jobs (those circled in the figure) is a policy matter also involving strategic decisions. Decisions on salary variations—the minimum and maximum for each pay grade—should not be completed until management has considered pertinent external factors. Before management can establish its wage and salary policies, it must have information on its relevant external environment, and it must consider its external competitiveness as well as the worth of each job.

External Competitiveness

The second ingredient in effective strategic compensation decisions is external competitiveness. To obtain information on prevailing pay rates and trends in fringe benefits, many organizations conduct their own compensation surveys to supplement or replace the annual Bureau of Labor Statistics survey of professional, administrative, and clerical salaries.

Designing the survey questionnaire and collecting the data are primarily specialist activities. However, to evaluate the quality and the relevance of the compensation information obtained, management must know who was surveyed and what questions were asked.

Whom to Survey

Organizations seek information on the market from which they draw their human resources and in which others compete for employee services. For office, clerical, and/or semiskilled production jobs, the market may be local. For highly technical jobs, the market could be within a given industry. For other jobs, the market could be national or even international, thus necessitating a broad-based survey. The organization should identify locally or nationally relevant organizations that offer alternative employment possibilities. Normally, to get an accurate picture of the market value of any given job, data from at least seven organizations should be obtained.

What to Survey

In addition to basic salary data, management needs a complete picture of the overall compensation packages of other relevant organizations before it can complete its organization's wage and benefits policies. Information obtained from the organization's environment should include current pay rates, type and nature of employee benefits, changes in cost of living, conditions of human resources supply and demand, and, where relevant, union bargaining power.

How to Evaluate the Quality of a Compensation Survey

In reviewing a compensation survey, management should consider the degree to which the following key points have been properly dealt with.

1. *Coverage.* Does the survey cover all jobs in the organization or only a select few? Most job surveys are based on key or benchmark jobs, not on all the jobs in an organization. Ideally, the survey should include all jobs. However, cost and time often make a complete survey unfeasible. An adequate survey requires a methodical selection of key or benchmark jobs. Benchmark jobs should be immediately recognizable with brief job descriptions. They should represent the complete range of jobs, from the lowest to the highest paid. They should serve as reference points for comparison with other jobs in the organization. These jobs should be relatively stable over time. Benchmark jobs should also employ large numbers of people.

2. *Comparability of the job.* Brief but adequate descriptions highlighting the key duties and responsibilities of the benchmark jobs are necessary to ensure their comparability with jobs in other organizations. Rarely do job titles alone adequately describe the jobs.

3. *Selection of organizations for the survey.* The location of the organization's labor market in terms of the jobs to be surveyed is the most important criterion. The second criterion is the existence of comparable jobs in organizations located within the same labor market.

4. *The number of organizations to be surveyed.* The number of organizations to be surveyed is directly related to the number of responses desired for each benchmark job. Obviously the greater the response to each benchmark job, the greater the significance of the survey. We

have found that a minimum of seven organizations must provide information on any given benchmark job for the results to be significant.

Analysis of Employee Benefits

Since total compensation policies cannot be completed without an analysis of employee benefits, organizations should gather information on benefits packages as well as on wages and salaries. Designing this survey is also a specialist activity that need not be gone into here. However, management must determine the kinds of data it needs, and it must evaluate the adequacy of the survey itself.

The most complete method of gathering employee benefits data is to ask organizations to send copies of their employee handbooks, insurance plans, and the like. However, this presents logistic problems because most personnel departments do not have the resources necessary to sort through and analyze such large quantities of data. Also, many organizations may not have employee handbooks. For these reasons, most organizations seeking employee benefits data use questionnaires to collect such information. The question then becomes: What type of information should be collected? Our experience shows that management needs information on the following benefits before it can make strategic decisions on employee compensation:

- Paid vacations.
- Paid holidays.
- Type and coverage of medical insurance.
- Type and coverage of life insurance.
- Type and coverage of dental insurance.
- Other types of insurance (e.g., legal insurance).
- Major miscellaneous benefits (college tuition, flexible working hours, etc.).
- Sick leave.
- Bonuses.
- Incentive pay.

Employee benefits specialists can rate their organization's benefit packages against those of the organizations surveyed. The specialists' summary evaluation should give management the information it needs for making compensation policy.

Management should take into account the rating of the benefits package when considering changes in total compensation or just in wages or salaries. An organization with a superior employee benefits package may be able to attract and maintain highly qualified employees even though the wages for many positions may be lower than those offered by other organizations.

In the recent past, direct wage and salary outlays constituted a significant part of the total compensation package. Today, the share of direct wage and salary payments is declining as benefits increase. Employee benefits are financial supplements usually providing extra leisure, extra income, better working environments, and added protection against accidents, unemployment, illness, and other possible losses of income. It is difficult to measure indirect employee compensation because there is no agreement on what benefits or services should be standard. Therefore, more value judgments go into the determination of employee benefits packages than into the design of direct payment systems. Nonetheless, management must be aware of the relative increase in the proportion of benefits or indirect payments in the total compensation package.

Further, management should note the emerging trends in new employee benefits. For example, legal assistance is rapidly becoming a popular benefit. A study conducted by Alpander and Kobritz revealed that although few legal assistance plans have been adopted to date, the number of such plans established through collective bargaining is likely to increase significantly in the near future.[2] Representatives of the 86 largest independent and AFL-CIO–affiliated unions rated prepaid legal services number 2 in desirability, just below prepaid dental services. (The union representatives' preferences among several new forms of benefits were, in descending order of preference: prepaid dental insurance, prepaid legal services, birthday holidays, early retirement, flexible working hours, portable pensions, and educational benefits for the entire family.) Recent amendments to the Taft-Hartley Act and the Internal Revenue Code, as well as the provisions of ERISA and several Supreme Court decisions, may account for the attractiveness of the benefit of prepaid legal services.

As new forms of employee benefits develop, preferences among employees for different types of benefit packages become more diversified. Some companies have responded to the divergent employee preferences by adopting the "smorgasbord" or "cafeteria" compensation package: Each employee, depending on personal needs, designs his or her own indirect compensation program. The organization provides a collection of company-wide benefits (e.g., life insurance, health insurance, accident insurance, vacation, dental insurance, legal insurance, educational assistance, holidays, pension, and profit sharing), and the employees, within given financial limits, choose their own packages. The cafeteria compensation concept has been in existence for about 20 years now, but it has not been adopted freely because of practical problems.[3] The major problem is financial; small organizations, especially, have difficulty obtaining low group rates for their few employees.

Finally, management should base its benefits decisions on the cost of the package, the organization's ability to pay, employee needs and preferences, tax considerations, social responsibility, and public relations. However, management should also evaluate the benefits in terms of their contribution to employee satisfaction and to the stability of the labor force.

Summary

Compensation policies and systems are among the most important ingredients of the HRP process. (Policy decisions establishing overall wage levels, payment methods, and benefits packages affect and are affected by the availability of human resources.) Without an effective compensation system, an organization has difficulty attracting and retaining a productive labor force.

An effective compensation system has at least five major objectives. First, compensation systems should be perceived by the employees as being equitable. Second, the compensation package should be externally competitive. Third, in designing an equitable and competitive wage and benefits structure, the organization must consider its own economic means. Fourth, compensation policies should be within the applicable laws. Finally, compensation structure should take into consideration the employees' contribution (merit) as well as their longevity (seniority).

We have presented managerial tools and techniques, such as job analysis, job evaluation, and compensation surveys, from the policy makers' perspective, rather than from the technician's point of view. Actual examples were provided to illustrate (1) how organizations can undertake a job evaluation program, (2) the policy implications of such programs, and (3) how management can evaluate their quality. Based on our experience, we have recommended the point-factor method of job evaluation to establish internal equity. To achieve external competitiveness, organizations gather relevant data through wage and salary benefits surveys. Here, too, the emphasis was on the strategic considerations rather than on the operational issues. We have looked at how management can evaluate the quality and the relevance of data collected through these surveys. Attention was also given to the use of such data in generating policy actions or recommendations.

Finally, compensation policies should consider internal equity, external competitiveness, existing legal requirements, and the economic means of the organization. They should also contribute to increased employee satisfaction and performance.

Appendix

===

Position Rating Manual for a Fiduciary Organization

The following manual was designed for a fiduciary organization before its planned expansion into 15 additional states. The jobs are evaluated using a total of 1,000 points. The actual weight of each position factor is obtained by interviewing a representative sample of employees and line managers at supervisory, middle, and top management positions, and by actually observing employee and managerial performance at a dozen key jobs.

Position Factors and Degrees

1. *Experience* (Maximum 80 points)
   This factor measures the amount of experience required to perform the duties effectively under normal supervision with the specified background of knowledge.

1st degree (10 points)	Up to and including 6 months.
2nd degree (20 points)	More than 6 months and up to 2 years.
3rd degree (30 points)	More than 2 years and up to 5 years.
4th degree (50 points)	More than 5 years and up to 10 years.
5th degree (80 points)	More than 10 years.

2. *Supervision* (Maximum 120 points)
   This factor measures the number of people for whom the incumbent is responsible.

1st degree (5 points)	Does not supervise, or supervises 1 person.
2nd degree (20 points)	Responsible for up to 5 persons.

    3rd degree   Responsible for 5 to 10 persons.
    (40 points)
    4th degree   Responsible for 11 to 25 persons.
    (80 points)
    5th degree   Responsible for 25 or more persons.
    (120 points)
3. *Stress* (Maximum 50 points)
   This factor measures stress, which as used here is defined as pressure,
   strain, or tension imposed on the position in terms of meeting deadlines.
    1st degree   Predictable, 3 to 4 times a month.
    (10 points)
    2nd degree   Predictable on a daily basis.
    (20 points)
    3rd degree   On an unpredictable basis, 3 to 4 times a month.
    (35 points)
    4th degree   On a continuing but unpredictable basis.*
    (50 points)
4. *Knowledge* (Maximum 200 points)
   This factor is measured by combining two independent elements.
   Element A = *Depth* (80 points)
   This element measures the depth of knowledge required to perform
   effectively in the position.
    1st degree   Requires knowledge of basic office routines, simple
    (10 points)   accounting tasks, or operations of basic office
                      equipment gained through experience, training, or
                      education.
    2nd degree   Requires knowledge of more complex office rou-
    (20 points)   tines, accounting procedures, or general office/data
                      entry equipment gained through experience, train-
                      ing, or education.
    3rd degree   Requires knowledge of a broad variety of general
    (30 points)   office procedures/practices, accounting practices, or
                      complex office equipment gained through extensive
                      experience, training, or education.
    4th degree   Requires expert knowledge in a wide variety of
    (50 points)   business procedures gained through extensive ex-
                      perience, training, or advanced education.
    5th degree   Requires specialized knowledge of a specific nature
    (80 points)   applicable to one area gained only through exten-
                      sive experience, training, or advanced education.
   Element B = *Complexity* (120 points)
   This element measures the complexity of knowledge in terms of the
   diversity of activities and responsibilities of the position.

*This is found in only a few positions.

1st degree (25 points)	Routine and homogeneous activities using clearly defined instructions or procedures. Subordinate employees (if any) would perform repetitive tasks using basic skills.
2nd degree (50 points)	Activities that are diverse but governed by standard policies and procedures. Subordinate employees (if any) would perform somewhat varied tasks using skills acquired through experience and/or training.
3rd degree (80 points)	Varied or specialized activities for which procedures may not exist. Subordinates would perform advanced technical, professional, or managerial functions.
4th degree (120 points)	Highly diverse activities for which policies very often do not exist. Management environment may be quite unstructured, requiring development of guidelines, policies, and procedures. Subordinates would perform senior-level technical, professional, and managerial functions.

5. *Decision Making* (Maximum 350 points)

This factor is measured by combining two independent elements.

Element A = *Complexity* (200 points)

This element measures the complexity of decisions required in terms of the range of alternatives available.

1st degree (25 points)	Activities or decisions when required are made based on routine or repetitive information. Alternatives are precisely defined.
2nd degree (60 points)	Decision making requires processing varied information that requires some interpretation. Alternatives exist and are reasonably well defined.
3rd degree (125 points)	Decision making requires analysis of complex information often requiring assumptions or manipulation. Alternatives are numerous and not well defined.
4th degree (200 points)	Decision making involves using incomplete, unrelated, or contradictory information requiring hypotheses. Alternatives are not defined. Innovation is required to put the decision into effect.

Element B = *Impact* (150 points)

This element measures the impact of the decision expressed in terms of financial or operating objectives.

1st degree (10 points)	Incorrect decision will have little impact on customer relations or profitability.
2nd degree (40 points)	Incorrect decision will cause minor delay in processing or customer dissatisfaction, small effect on profitability.
3rd degree (150 points)	Incorrect decision will cause significant loss of revenue, resulting in failure to meet company objectives.

6. *Public and Intracompany Relationships* (Maximum 170 points)

This factor is measured by combining two independent elements.

Element A = *Diversity* (50 points)

1st degree (10 points)	Relationships are almost always limited to the individuals in a specific work group.
2nd degree (20 points)	Relationships extend to members of other departments within either the regional or headquarters location.
3rd degree (35 points)	Relationships extend to other regions, headquarters departments, or outside the company to customers, vendors, and consultants.
4th degree (50 points)	Relationships extend to other subsidiaries, the holding company, and regulatory agencies.

Element B = *Purpose of Relationship* (120 points)

This element measures the purpose or reason for the relationship and the impact.

1st degree (20 points)	Relationships involve providing and/or receiving information or documents. Impact is minimal on the customer/company.
2nd degree (50 points)	Relationships require explanation or interpretation of information, company policies/procedures, programs and services. Impact is moderate and usually confined to a single customer/vendor.
3rd degree (80 points)	Relationships usually involve business development or maintenance/service of business sources. In addition, relationships may require negotiation or recommendations on issues regarding policies, programs, etc. Impact is considerable but primarily limited to individual departments or regions.
4th degree (120 points)	Relationships usually involve broad business decisions involving key personnel and requiring negotiation on corporate issues. Impact is considerable and may affect several areas within the company.

7. *Unique Working Conditions and Other Factors* (Maximum 30 points)

This factor measures unique elements that may be found either singularly or in combination in positions. There are no degrees indicated; if the element exists in the position, the point value is added.

(15 points)	Primary responsibility for security of confidential data, disclosure of which could be detrimental to individuals or the company.
(15 points)	Long periods of extreme mental and/or visual concentration and/or physical effort required more than 50% of the workday.
(15 points)	Periods of extended travel and/or adversary relationships with others.
(15 points)	Working conditions that are not found in the normal office environment and that exist on a permanent basis.

Position Rating Manual
for Medium-Size Nonprofit Organizations

This manual was designed for several county governments and a nonprofit community action agency established pursuant to the provisions of the Economic Opportunity Act of 1964. About 150 different jobs in each type of organization were evaluated using the manual. As in the preceding manual for the fiduciary organization, 1,000 points in total are used to evaluate the jobs. These points are divided among 14 factors, with the highest weight of 150 points given to experience. The complete manual follows.

Position Factors and Degrees

1. *Experience* (Maximum 150 points)
   This factor measures the amount of experience required to perform the duties effectively under normal supervision with the specified background of knowledge.

1st degree (20 points)	Up to and including 2 months.
2nd degree (30 points)	More than 2 months; up to and including 6 months.
3rd degree (40 points)	More than 6 months and up to 1 year.
4th degree (60 points)	More than 1 year and up to 2 years.
5th degree (80 points)	More than 2 years and up to 3 years.
6th degree (100 points)	More than 3 years and up to 5 years.
7th degree (120 points)	More than 5 years and up to 8 years.
8th degree (140 points)	More than 8 years and up to 10 years.
9th degree (150 points)	More than 10 years.

2. *Supervisory Responsibility* (Maximum 120 points)
   This factor measures the number of people directly supervised by the incumbent.

1st degree (5 points)	Does not supervise.
2nd degree (10 points)	Supervises 1 person.
3rd degree (20 points)	Supervises 2 to 5 persons.
4th degree (40 points)	Supervises 6 to 10 persons.

5th degree   Supervises 11 to 24 persons.
(80 points)
6th degree   Supervises 25 or more persons.
(120 points)

3. *Knowledge* (Maximum 110 points)

This factor measures the depth of knowledge (as acquired through formal schooling or other means) required to perform effectively in the position.

1st degree (10 points)	Knowledge of arithmetic, English grammar, etc. Equivalent to 1 to 2 years of high school education.
2nd degree (20 points)	Knowledge of bookkeeping, variety of office routines, and simple accounting procedures. Operation of office equipment. Equivalent to 3 to 4 years of high school education.
3rd degree (40 points)	Specific skills training. Equivalent to high school or trade school.
4th degree (50 points)	Elaborate specific skills training in a specialized field. Equivalent to 1 to 2 years of college training.
5th degree (70 points)	Broad knowledge of a general or technical field such as accounting, advertising, business administration, engineering, public administration, sociology, etc. Equivalent to attaining a university or college degree.
6th degree (90 points)	Specific knowledge of a general or technical field. Equivalent to a master's degree.
7th degree (110 points)	Expert knowledge of a specific nature in a technical field. Equivalent to a doctoral degree.

4. *Decision Making* (Maximum 100 points)

This factor measures the nature and complexity of decisions made in performing assigned duties.

1st degree (10 points)	Usually the ways of completing the task are prescribed by my supervisor or agency manual. My job is rather structured; I operate within prescribed boundaries.
2nd degree (30 points)	Although there are prescribed ways of performing the tasks, I have to choose from among several alternatives. My job is structured, but I often have to choose from many alternatives within the established boundaries.
3rd degree (50 points)	There are *few* prescribed ways of performing the tasks. My job is loosely structured.
4th degree (70 points)	There are *very few* prescribed ways of performing the tasks. I have to study the conditions and often innovate methods of dealing with the situations.
5th degree (100 points)	There are *no* prescribed ways of performing tasks. Information to make decisions is incomplete, and

heavy reliance on judgment is necessary. My job is
not structured. Each situation is unique.

5. *Impact of Decisions and Job Performance* (Maximum 100 points)
This factor measures the impact of the decision and job performance
on clients and the operating effectiveness of the agency.

1st degree (5 points)	Incorrect decision or faulty performance has little impact on the clients and/or the operating efficiency of my unit.
2nd degree (10 points)	Incorrect decision or faulty performance will cause client dissatisfaction and/or will have small effect on the operating efficiency of my unit.
3rd degree (25 points)	Incorrect decision or faulty performance will cause client dissatisfaction and/or will have small effect on the operating efficiency of my department (program) beyond the scope of a specific unit.
4th degree (40 points)	Incorrect decision or faulty performance results in adverse effect on the client and/or will cause major problems in the operation of my unit.
5th degree (60 points)	Incorrect decision or faulty performance results in adverse effect on the client and/or will cause major problems in the operation of my department (program) beyond the scope of a specific unit.
6th degree (80 points)	Incorrect decision or faulty performance results in adverse effect on the client and/or will cause major problems in the operation of the entire agency.
7th degree (100 points)	Incorrect decision or faulty performance will cause significant adverse effects on the client and will also result in failure of the agency to meet its objectives.

6. *Supervision Received* (Maximum 80 points)
This factor measures the degree to which the employee's work is
checked by others and the degree to which the immediate supervisor
outlines the methods to be followed or the results to be attained on
the job and follows the progress of work.

1st degree (10 points)	Progress of work is checked by others most of the time and/or receives instructions 60% to 90% of the time in performing regular duties.
2nd degree (20 points)	Progress of work is often checked by others and/or receives instructions 40% to 60% of the time in performing regular duties.
3rd degree (40 points)	Progress of work is checked by others some of the time and/or receives instructions 25% to 40% of the time in performing regular duties.
4th degree (60 points)	Progress of work is seldom checked by others and/or receives occasional instruction (less than 25% of the time).
5th degree (80 points)	Progress of work is not checked by others and/or receives no instructions.

7. *Stress* (Maximum 80 points)

This factor measures pressure, strain, or tension imposed on the position in terms of meeting deadlines, exposure to unpleasant situations, heavy workload, and/or variety of tasks performed.

1st degree (10 points)	Normal stress found in most jobs.
2nd degree (20 points)	Deadlines, heavy workloads, or unpleasant situations occur 3 to 4 times a month, but they are predictable.
3rd degree (30 points)	Deadlines, heavy workloads, or unpleasant situations occur routinely, but they are predictable.
4th degree (50 points)	Deadlines, heavy workloads, or unpleasant situations occur 3 to 4 times a month on an unpredictable basis.
5th degree (80 points)	Deadlines, heavy workloads, or unpleasant situations occur continuously on an unpredictable basis.*

8. *Contact with Public and/or Clients* (Maximum 50 points)

This factor measures the responsibility that goes with the job, for meeting, dealing with, or influencing the public and/or the clients of the agency.

1st degree (0 points)	No contact with the public and/or clients.
2nd degree (15 points)	Little contact with the public and/or clients.
3rd degree (35 points)	Some contact with the public and/or clients.
4th degree (50 points)	Substantial contact with the public and/or clients.

9. *Intra-Agency Relationships* (Maximum 50 points)

This factor measures the scope and nature of the relationship with others in the agency.

1st degree (0 points)	No contact with others in performing assigned tasks.
2nd degree (20 points)	Little contact with others. Relationships involve providing and/or receiving information or documents.
3rd degree (30 points)	Some contact with others. Relationships often require explanation or interpretation of information, agency policies/procedures, programs, and services.
4th degree (40 points)	Substantial contact with others. Relationships usually involve negotiation or recommendations on issues regarding policies, programs, etc. Impact is

*This is found in only a very few positions.

considerable but is limited primarily to individual departments or regions (programs).

5th degree (50 points) — Substantial contact with others. Relationships usually include broad decisions involving key personnel and requiring negotiation on agency issues. Impact is considerable and may affect several areas within the agency.

10. *Confidential Data* (Maximum 40 points)

This factor measures the extent of work with information requiring discretion and confidentiality in areas such as personnel, finance, grants, and clients' records.

1st degree (0 points) — None.

2nd degree (10 points) — One type of information (1 area).

3rd degree (20 points) — Two types of information (2 areas).

4th degree (30 points) — Three types of information (3 areas).

5th degree (40 points) — Four types of information (4 areas).

11. *Responsibility for Equipment* (Maximum 30 points)

This factor measures the extent of the employee's direct responsibility to maintain and/or safeguard equipment used at work.

1st degree (5 points) — Very little responsibility for equipment.

2nd degree (15 points) — Responsibility for small equipment (such as typewriter, adding machine, hand tools, movie projectors).

3rd degree (30 points) — Responsibility for large equipment (such as vans, buses).

12. *Responsibility for Files and Records* (Maximum 30 points)

This factor measures the extent of responsibility to maintain and/or safeguard agency records and files.

1st degree (5 points) — Very little responsibility.

2nd degree (10 points) — Some responsibility.

3rd degree (20 points) — Moderate responsibility.

4th degree (30 points) — Major responsibility.

13. *Working Conditions* (Maximum 30 points)

This factor measures the physical condition and surroundings under which the job is normally done.

1st degree (5 points)	Good working conditions, absence of disagreeable elements such as noise, heat, cold, chemicals, fumes, crowding. Most office situations.
2nd degree (10 points)	Good working conditions, exposed to elements, but not to the extent of being disagreeable.
3rd degree (15 points)	Somewhat disagreeable working conditions, with one element being disagreeable.
4th degree (20 points)	Disagreeable working conditions, with more than one element being disagreeable, such as noise, cold, chemicals, fumes, crowding.
5th degree (30 points)	Very disagreeable working conditions, with several elements being very disagreeable, such as noise, cold, chemicals, fumes. (Exceptional cases only.)

14. *Physical, Mental and Visual Demands* (Maximum 30 points)

This factor measures the physical effort required to perform the job. It includes periods of travel, mental and visual concentration, standing, lifting, etc.

1st degree (5 points)	No unusual physical, mental, and visual demands.
2nd degree (15 points)	The task requires short periods of travel, mental or visual concentration, standing, or lifting objects, to the point of being very taxing to the individual.

References

Chapter 1

1. Guvenc G. Alpander, "Human Resource Planning," *California Management Review*, Vol. 22, No. 3 (1980), pp. 24–33.
2. I. Gascoigne, "Manpower Forecasting at the Enterprise Level," *British Journal of Industrial Relations*, Vol. 6 (1968), pp. 94–106.
3. K. F. Lane and J. E. Andrew, "A Method of Labour Turnover Analysis," *Royal Statistical Society Journal Series A*, Vol. 118 (1955), pp. 296–323.
4. Elmer H. Burak and James W. Walker, eds., *Manpower Planning and Programming* (Boston: Allyn & Bacon, 1972).
5. Andrew F. Sikula, *Personnel Administration and Human Resources Management* (New York: Wiley, 1976), p. 32.
6. James W. Walker, "Human Resource Planning: Managerial Concerns and Practices," *Business Horizons*, Vol. 19, No. 3 (June 1976), pp. 55–56.
7. Eric W. Vetter, *Manpower Planning for High Talent Personnel* (Ann Arbor: University of Michigan Press, 1967), p. 17.
8. Gordon McBeath, *Manpower Planning and Control* (London: Business Books, 1978), p. 1.
9. Lawrence A. Wangler, "The Intensification of the Personal Role," *Personnel Journal*, Vol. 58, No. 2 (1979), p. 16.
10. George S. Odiorne, "Personnel Management for the '80's," *Personnel Administrator*, Vol. 22, No. 6 (1977), p. 20.

Chapter 2

1. Donald G. Revelle, "Human Resource Planning: Who Is in Charge?" *Human Resource Planning*, Vol. 2, No. 3 (1979), p. 119.

Chapter 3

1. A. H. Maslow, *Motivation and Personality* (New York: Harper & Row, 1954).
2. J. W. Atkinson, "Some General Implications of Conceptual Development in the Study of Achievement Oriented Behavior," in M. R. Jones,

ed., *Human Motivation: A Symposium* (Lincoln: University of Nebraska Press, 1965).

3. F. Herzberg, "The Motivation-Hygiene Concept and Problems of Manpower," *Personnel Administration*, Vol. 27 (1967), pp. 3–7.

4. R. T. Mowday, "Equity Theory Predictions of Behavior in Organizations," in Richard M. Steers and Lyman W. Porter, eds., *Motivation and Work Behavior* (New York: McGraw-Hill, 1979), pp. 125–146.

5. D. A. Nadler and E. E. Lawler III, "Motivation: A Diagnostic Approach," in Steers and Porter, *op. cit.*, pp. 216–246.

6. R. L. Opsahl and M. D. Dunnette, "The Role of Financial Compensation in Industrial Motivation," *Psychological Bulletin*, Vol. 66, No. 2 (1966), pp. 94–97.

7. Guvenc G. Alpander, "Closing the Supervisor-Superior Gap," *California Management Review*, Vol. 13, No. 1 (1970), pp. 84–89.

8. J. M. Ivancevich and J. H. Donnelly, Jr., "A Study of Role Clarity and Need for Clarity for Three Occupational Groups," *Academy of Management Journal*, Vol. 17, No. 1 (March 1974), pp. 28–36.

9. Rensis Likert, *The Human Organization* (New York: McGraw-Hill, 1967), pp. 96–105.

Chapter 4

1. William Glueck, *Personnel: A Diagnostic Approach*, 2nd ed. (Dallas: Business Publications, Inc., 1978), p. 169.

2. Leonard R. Sayles and George Strauss, *Managing Human Resources* (Englewood Cliffs, N.J.: Prentice-Hall, Inc., 1977), pp. 205–209.

3. *Ibid.*, p. 129.

4. Jacob K. Javits, "The Scandal of Our Pension Plans: What's Wrong and What We Can Do About It," *Family Weekly*, November 11, 1973.

5. Charles J. Coleman, *Personnel: An Open System Approach* (Cambridge, Mass.: Winthrop Publishers, Inc., 1979), p. 441.

Chapter 5

1. Guvenc G. Alpander, "Human Resource Planning in U.S. Corporations," *California Management Review*, Vol. 22, No. 2 (Spring 1980), pp. 24–31.

2. Joseph Famularo, ed., *Handbook of Modern Personnel Administration* (New York: McGraw-Hill, 1972), pp. 111–119.

3. Elmer Burack, *Strategies for Manpower Planning and Programming* (Morristown, N.J.: General Learning Press, 1972).

4. David W. Belcher, *Compensation Administration* (Englewood Cliffs, N.J.: Prentice-Hall, 1974).

5. Allen N. Nash and Stephen J. Carrol, Jr., *The Management of Compensation* (Monterey, Calif.: Brooks/Cole, 1975).

6. Thomas E. Milne, *Business Forecasting: A Managerial Approach* (London: Longman, London Business School Series, 1975), pp. 45–53.

Chapter 6

1. J. M. Shafritz, W. L. Balk, A. C. Hyde, and D. H. Rosenbloom, *Personnel Management in Government* (New York: Marcel Dekker, 1978), p. 86.

Chapter 7

1. A. K. Rice, J. M. M. Hill, and E. L. Trist, "The Representation of Labor Turnover as a Social Process," *Human Relations*, Vol. 3 (1950), pp. 349–370.
2. James L. Price, *The Study of Turnover* (Ames: Iowa State University Press, 1977); Lyman Porter and Richard Steers, "Organizational Work and Personal Factors in Employee Turnover and Absenteeism," *Psychological Bulletin*, Vol. 73 (April 1973), pp. 151–176.
3. René V. Davis, George W. England, and Lloyd H. Hofquist, *A Theory of Work Adjustment* (Minneapolis: Industrial Relations Center, University of Minnesota, 1964); A. P. Brief and J. Aldag, "Employee Reactions to Job Characteristics: A Constructive Replication," *Journal of Applied Psychology*, Vol. 60 (1975), pp. 182–186; J. R. Hackman and G. R. Oldham, "Motivation Through the Design of Work: Test of a Theory," *Organizational Behavior and Human Performance*, Vol. 16 (1976), pp. 250–279.
4. Magnus Hedberg, *The Process of Labor Turnover* (Stockholm, Sweden: The Swedish Council for Personnel Administration, 1967).
5. F. J. Gaudet, "The Literature of Labor Turnover," *Industrial Relations News Letter* (1960).
6. H. Silcock, "The Phenomenon of Labor Turnover," *Royal Statistical Society*, Journal Series A, 117 (1954).
7. *Employee Absenteeism and Turnover*, PPF Survey No. 6 (Washington, D.C.: The Bureau of National Affairs, May 1974).

Chapter 10

1. Discussion of the three-dimensional evaluation of change is adapted from Guvenc G. Alpander and W. R. Fannin, "Assessing Decision Anchors and Method of Innovation Introduction as Determinates of Organizational Resistance," a proposal submitted to National Science Foundation, December 24, 1980.

Chapter 11

1. P. G. Gyllenhammer, *People at Work* (Reading, Mass.: Addison-Wesley, 1977); C. H. Gibson, "Volvo Increases Productivity Through Job Enrichment," *California Management Review*, Vol. 15, No. 4 (1973), pp. 64–66; *Wall Street Journal*, "Auto Plant in Sweden Scores Some Success with Work Teams," Vol. 189, No. 41 (March 1, 1977).

Chapter 12

1. Greater Philadelphia Chamber of Commerce, *Personnel Practices Survey* (1976), p. 13.
2. Donald B. Miller, "Career Planning and Management in Organizations," *S.A.M. Advanced Management Journal* (Spring 1978).
3. *Ibid.*
4. *Ibid.*

Chapter 14

1. Guvenc G. Alpander, "Personnel Executives Rank Relative Importance of Job Factors for Managerial Positions," *Working Paper No. 14*, College of Business Administration, University of Maine at Orono, 1980.
2. Guvenc G. Alpander and J. Kobritz, "Prepaid Legal Services: An Emerging Benefit," *Industrial and Labor Relations Review*, Vol. 31. No. 2 (1978). pp. 172–181.
3. Andrew Sikula, *Personnel Administration and Human Resources Management* (New York: Wiley, 1976), p. 332.

Bibliography

Alpander, Guvenc G. "Closing the Supervisor-Superior Gap." *California Management Review*, Vol. 13, No. 1, 1970.

Ansoff, H. Igor. *Corporate Strategy*. New York: McGraw-Hill, 1965.

Argyris, Chris. "Personality and Organization Theory Revisited." *Administrative Science Quarterly*, Vol. 18, 1973.

Atkinson, J. W. "Some General Implications of Conceptual Development in the Study of Achievement Oriented Behavior." In M. R. Jones, ed., *Human Motivation: A Symposium*. Lincoln: University of Nebraska Press, 1965.

Belcher, David W. *Compensation Administration*. Englewood Cliffs, N.J.: Prentice-Hall, 1974.

Burack, Elmer H. "Why All the Confusion About Career Planning?" *Human Resource Management*, Summer 1977.

———. *Strategies for Manpower Planning and Programming*. Morristown, N.J.: General Learning Press, 1972.

———. and James W. Walker, eds. *Manpower Planning and Programming*. Boston: Allyn and Bacon, 1972.

Carroll, S. J., Jr., and H. L. Tosi, Jr. *Management by Objectives*. New York: Macmillan, 1973.

Cascio, Wayne. *Applied Psychology in Personnel Management*. Reston, Va.: Reston, 1978.

Chruden, Herbert J., and Arthur W. Sherman, Jr. *Personnel Management*. Cincinnati: South-Western, 1976.

Coleman, Charles J. *Personnel: An Open System Approach*. Cambridge, Mass.: Winthrop, 1979.

Davis, Keith, *Human Behavior at Work: Organizational Behavior*. New York: McGraw-Hill, 1977.

Famularo, Joseph, ed. *Handbook of Modern Personnel Administration*. New York: McGraw-Hill, 1972.

Fleishman, E. and J. Hunt, eds. *Current Development in the Study of Leadership*. Carbondale, Ill.: Southern Illinois University Press, 1973.

Glueck, William. *Personnel: A Diagnostic Approach*, 2nd ed. Dallas: Business Publications, 1978.

Greater Philadelphia Chamber of Commerce. *Personnel Practices Survey*, 1976.

Greenan, Russell L., and Eric J. Schmertz. *Personnel Administration and the Law*. Washington, D.C.: Bureau of National Affairs, 1972.

Haire, Mason. *Psychology in Management*. New York: McGraw-Hill, 1964.

Hedberg, Magnus. *The Process of Labor Turnover*. Stockholm, Sweden: The Swedish Council for Personnel Administration, 1967.

Huse, Edgar F. *Organization Development and Change*. New York: West Publishing, 1975.

Hussey, D. E. *Corporate Planning Theory and Practice*. Oxford: Pergamon Press, 1976.

Jakubauskas, Edward B., and Neil A. Palomba. *Manpower Economics*. Reading, Mass.: Addison-Wesley, 1972.

Jelinek, Mariann. *Career Management for the Individual and the Organization*. Chicago: St. Clair Press, 1979.

Likert, Rensis. *The Human Organization*. New York: McGraw-Hill, 1967.

Lorange, Peter, and Richard F. Vancil. *Strategic Planning Systems*. Englewood Cliffs, N.J.: Prentice-Hall, 1977.

March, J. G., and H. A. Simon. *Organizations*. New York: Wiley, 1958.

Maslow, A. H. *Motivation and Personality*. New York: Harper & Row, 1954.

McBeath, Gordon. *Manpower Planning and Control*. London: Business Books, 1978.

Milne, Thomas E. *Business Forecasting: A Managerial Approach*. London: Longman, London Business School Series, 1975.

Mitchell, Terence R. *People in Organizations: Understanding Their Behavior*. New York: McGraw-Hill, 1978.

Nash, Allan N., and Stephen J. Carrol, Jr. *The Management of Compensation*. Monterey, Calif.: Brooks Cole, 1975.

Porter, Lyman, and Richard Steers. "Organizational Work and Personal Factors in Employee Turnover and Absenteeism." *Psychological Bulletin*, Vol. 73, April 1973.

Price, James L. *The Study of Turnover*. Ames: Iowa State University Press, 1977.

Robinson, John P., Robert Athanasiou, and Kendra B. Head. *Measures of Occupational Attitudes and Occupational Characteristics*. Ann Arbor: Survey Research Center, University of Michigan, 1969.

Sayles, Leonard R., and George Strauss. *Managing Human Resources*. Englewood Cliffs, N.J.: Prentice-Hall, 1977.

Shafritz, J. M., W. L. Balk, A. C. Hyde, and D. H. Rosenbloom. *Personnel Management in Government*. New York: Marcel Dekker, 1978.

Sikula, Andrew F. *Personnel Administration and Human Resources Management*. New York: Wiley, 1976.

Smith, Howard P., and Paul J. Brouwer. *Performance Appraisal and Human Development*. Reading, Mass.: Addison-Wesley, 1977.

Steers, Richard M., and Lyman W. Porter, eds. *Motivation and Work Behavior*. New York: McGraw-Hill, 1979. See especially R. T. Mowday, "Equity Theory Predictions of Behavior in Organizations;" and D. A. Nadler and E. E. Lawler III, "Motivation: A Diagnostic Approach."

Stewart, Valerie, and Andrew Stewart. *Practical Performance Appraisal: Designing, Installing and Maintaining Performance Appraisal Systems.* Westmead, England: Gower Press, Teakfield Ltd., 1977.

Timperly, Stuart R. *Manpower Planning and Occupational Choice.* London: George Allen and Unwin, 1974.

Vetter, Eric W. *Manpower Planning for High Talent Personnel.* Ann Arbor: University of Michigan Press, 1967.

Index